The CIVIL WAR on the WEB

The CIVIL WAR on the WEB

A Guide to the Very Best Sites

William G. Thomas ★ Alice E. Carter

Foreword by Gary W. Gallagher

SR BOOKS

A Scholarly Resources Inc. Imprint
Wilmington, Delaware

© 2001 by Scholarly Resources Inc.

All rights reserved

First published 2001

Printed and bound in the United States of America

Scholarly Resources Inc.

104 Greenhill Avenue

Wilmington, DE 19805-1897

www.scholarly.com

Library of Congress Cataloging-in-Publication Data

Thomas, William G., 1964–

The Civil War on the Web: a guide to the very best sites / William G. Thomas and Alice E. Carter; Foreword by Gary W. Gallagher.

p. cm.

Includes bibliographical references.

ISBN: 0-8420-2848-X (cloth : alk. paper) — ISBN: 0-8420-2849-8 (paper : alk. paper)

1. United States—History—Civil War, 1861–1865—Computer network resources—Directories. 2. Web sites—Directories. I. Carter, Alice E., 1964– II. Title.

E468.9.T46 2000

025.06'9737—dc21

00-044002

♾ The paper used in this publication meets the minimum requirements of the American National Standard for permanence of paper for printed library materials, Z39.48, 1984.

CONTENTS

Foreword by Gary W. Gallagher xi
Introduction by William G. Thomas xiii
User's Guide by Alice E. Carter xxv

PART I

THE VERY BEST CIVIL WAR WEB SITES—
REVIEWS AND RATINGS

PART II

SITES WORTH A VISIT—A TOPICAL INDEX

FOREWORD

Gary W. Gallagher

Future generations might know the official statements of generals and the outlines of major battles, observed Walt Whitman, but they would "never know the seething hell and black infernal background of countless minor scenes and interiors ... of the Secession War." Contemporary Civil War scholarship promises to deliver all that Whitman envisioned and much that he did not. Long considered primarily the province of military historians, the field embraces an increasingly spacious definition of the conflict, extending from superlative work on campaigns and generals to treatments of subjects well beyond the battlefield. The daily lives and concerns of common soldiers stand out in sharper relief than before. Studies relating to emancipation, civilian morale, and gender complement books on military and political history. Authors increasingly attempt to show the reciprocal influence of home front and battlefield, a sign that long-standing barriers between scholars of military and nonmilitary bents may be eroding. In short, it is a very productive time for anyone interested in the nation's greatest crisis, and all signs point to continued expansion of the field.

Some of the most striking evidence of that expansion lies in the profusion of Civil War–related sites on the World Wide Web. The online offerings appeal to scholars who write about the war as well as to lay readers who seek to understand it better. A number of sites include documents and images of potential benefit to serious researchers, and literally thousands of others beckon nonprofessional readers who already confront a surfeit of published materials. Many sites are amateurish, clearly reflecting the zealous interests of single individuals. Others contain a mass of information but are so poorly constructed as to defy easy use. Any online search for "Civil War" reveals the intimidating scale and chaotic nature of the offerings—and highlights the need for assistance in separating the meat of the grain from the chaff.

As one who cannot devote a great deal of time to trying to differentiate among the many web sites, I was delighted when I learned about *The Civil War on the Web: A Guide to the Very Best Sites*. My enthusiasm grew on reading an advance version of the manuscript. The authors had saved me countless hours of frustrating work by examining thousands of sites, then selecting ninety-five they considered particularly valuable and placing them in eight broad categories. They also adopted a sensible and effective format. As well as analyzing contents, the entry for each site rates aesthetics and ease of navigation. Excellent introductory essays open each chapter, and brief bibliographies point toward some of the best published material. In terms of organization, clarity, and utility, the *Guide* stands as a model. It is limited in the sense that the web does not include sites relating to all facets of the war. But its ninety-five entries address enormously important dimensions of the war and should afford welcome guidance to most people, whether they are interested in generals and military campaigns or events behind the lines.

Beyond its value as a superior reference tool, the *Guide* provides an excellent overview of the current state of Civil War scholarship. The introduction and opening sections of the chapters lay out basic issues in the field, address some of the tensions between popular and academic approaches to the conflict, and offer insights into why web sites do not engage the full spectrum of current work on the Civil War era. In this way, the *Guide* highlights the rich and often contentious nature of the field.

The World Wide Web will occupy an increasingly important place in the field of Civil War studies. The Lincoln and Soldiers Institute at Gettysburg College recently announced a new "eLincoln Prize" that will award $50,000 annually to the best web site, CD-ROM, or other scholarly high-technology contribution to exploring the Civil War era. This inducement should promote the creation of more impressive sites that will yield benefits to scholars and lay students alike. For now, anyone hoping to gain some mastery over current sites should consult the *Guide*. It deserves a place on any short shelf of basic reference books on the Civil War.

INTRODUCTION

William G. Thomas

The Civil War has done well on the World Wide Web. Since the web's first appearance in 1993, sites devoted to the subject have sprouted up for nearly every aspect of the history of the war—weaponry, medical treatment, soldiering, camp life, generalship, and on and on. There are sites dedicated to uniforms and flags, spies and engineers, railroads, and muskets. Entering "Civil War" in a popular search engine, such as Google, returns 220,000 sites. Some estimates put the number of Civil War sites at more than 600,000. A recent search on Northern Light's search engine for the term "Robert E. Lee" turned up 596,215 site matches. The leading journal of academic libraries reviewed Civil War sites in 1998 and concluded, "Some days, it appears that the Internet consists of equal parts *Star Trek,* stock market reports, soft-core pornography—and Civil War sites." History, as a subject, rarely finds itself so cozy with mass media, so adjacent to popular culture, so faddish and hip as to be in the same sentence as *Star Trek.*[1]

That the Civil War is popular on the Internet is no accident and might seem to be no surprise. The World Wide Web appears on close inspection to be exactly the sort of medium in which history might thrive. It can deliver large volumes of data quickly and accurately. It can handle images, video, audio, and text with equal facility. It can offer its patrons a sense of shared interests and community through discussion lists, video conferencing, chat rooms, and web rings. It can provide an environment for animated sequencing of images, maps, and hypertext narratives. Finally, the web is an open marketplace of ideas and thoughts where print space is relatively cheap. Into this open domain all sorts of individuals, companies, educational institutions, nonprofits, and government agencies have rushed to stake out claims, run wiring, set up homesteads, and plant the seeds of tomorrow's knowledge crop. They all expect high yields, and Internet traffic suggests they will achieve them.

The Civil War's popularity on the web did not appear out of thin ether, however. Its story is just as twisted and unexpected as that of the World Wide Web itself. It is a story that reveals the connections between various media—print, television, digital, and even face-to-face meeting. It is also a story that brought together previously distant and unconnected audiences, including researchers, scholars, high school students, parents, history buffs, genealogists, librarians, and pop culture fans. While the web matured in the mid-1990s, its boosters grabbed ideas, plans, and strategies from traditional media, melding them for the new online environment. Traces of older analog media cropped up online, and the Civil War as a subject provided an avenue for transference from old media to new. Like its counterparts, *Star Trek*, soft-core pornography, and stock market reports, the Civil War made the leap from old media to new seem effortless, sensible, and positively like something out of a ballet performance. To the eyes of those observing, even the most exteme balletomanes of the web, it was a stunning achievement, largely because it seemed to be directed by no single investor, director, or choreographer.

How did the Civil War move with such speed and apparent ease onto the World Wide Web? In large part the online popularity of the Civil War comes from several connected sources that have inspired Civil War traffic. Coinciding with the rise of the web, these bursts of interest in the Civil War emerged first in traditional media. The 1990 PBS airing of Ken Burns's nine-part series, *The Civil War*, attracted an audience of forty million viewers, turning the Civil War into a media event on the order of *Roots*. The show is credited with spurring millions of Americans to investigate their family history, visit battlefields, read new books on battles and campaigns, listen to period music, and dress up as reenactors in mock Civil War battles. Burns's work, though, followed closely the example set by *The Killer Angels*, a Pulitzer Prize–winning historical novel by Michael Shaara about the battle of Gettysburg. The book sold more than six million copies, pushed up visitations to the battlefield at Gettysburg, almost single-handedly rehabilitated the reputation of Confederate general James Longstreet, and spawned equally successful prequel and sequel volumes by Shaara's son twenty years after its initial publication. *The Killer Angels* led also to the film *Gettysburg* by Turner Broadcasting Corporation, the screenplay of which was based directly on the novel. It only increased the visibility of and interest in the Civil War for Americans. Even Ken Burns attributed his interest in the Civil War to Shaara's book, stating on the dust jacket of a recent edition, "A book that changed my life. . . . I had never visited Gettysburg, knew almost nothing about the battle before I read the book, but here it all came alive." Burns is not alone in his praise and admiration for *The Killer Angels*. One reader's review on amazon.com gushed, "There is nothing bad I can say about this extraordinary piece of work. . . . A history buff would be ADDICTED to it!"[2]

Academic historians have watched the rising tide of interest in the Civil War with amazement. Only James M. McPherson, who published the best-selling history

Battle Cry of Freedom in 1988, has been able to float up with the tide, publishing popular books and articles on nearly every aspect of the war. McPherson, among academic historians, stands out for his ability to connect with the general public's interest in the Civil War. *Battle Cry of Freedom,* first published in 1988, sold nearly 600,000 copies in six years. McPherson points out that the large interest in the Civil War is based on the fact that "momentous issues were at stake: slavery and freedom; racism and equality; sectionalism and nationalism; self-government and democracy; life and death." But McPherson also argues that academic historians have failed to connect with the large, growing Civil War audience. He blames the profession and its inability to produce compelling narratives. Into this void, he suggests, Burns and others have moved, producing popular accounts that tell a good story and tap into Americans' longing for resolution on the Civil War.[3]

McPherson's views on Burns's and Shaara's works offer a stark contrast to those of many academics historians. Criticism of Burns by professional historians was severe. In 1996 several historians wrote essays in *Ken Burns's The Civil War: Historians Respond.* They criticized Burns for failing to account fully for the institution of slavery, the sectional crisis, the role of women and African Americans in the war, and the Reconstruction experience, as well as faulting him for ending his story with the reunions of blue and gray late in the nineteenth century. Social historians wondered how Burns could tell such a moving, appealing, and long story, yet miss scholarship that they spent the previous thirty years writing. Military historians wondered how Burns and his team of advisors could make so many small errors of fact. Generally, academic historians have praised Burns for his amazing ability as a storyteller but have dismissed him as "not a great historian."[4]

Throughout the twentieth century, Civil War writing has received infusions of talent from nonacademics who were terrific storytellers. Most of the popular writers about the Civil War came out of journalism, including Bruce Catton, Shelby Foote, Douglas Southall Freeman, and Allan Nevins. Academic historians tended to disdain this literature, refusing to write for popular audiences and shunning those nonacademics who did write with a more popular audience in mind. Allan Nevins, who moved from journalism into academe at Columbia University, lashed out at academic historians in 1939. "The pedant," he accused with a bitter tone, "is chiefly responsible for the present crippled gait of history in America."[5]

Nevins served in 1959 as president of the American Historical Association and delivered his keynote address on the growing division between academic historians and other writers and producers of history. Nevins argued that historians seemed to have abandoned any effort to reach the general reader, the informed and well-read citizen, the voter and democratic participant. "The central explanation of the change," he suggested, "is connected with the sweeping transfer of history into scientific channels. . . . In proportion as history took a scientific coloration, employed mechanistic or evolutionary terms, and abandoned its old preoccupation with individual act and motive, . . . its significance to the ordinary citizen paled." Nevins also understood the effect that new media could have on the profession of history: "The new mass media have heightened the spirit of apprehensive caution within our guild [history] by increasing the danger that careless popularizations of history will mean their vulgarization."[6]

Nevins pointed out a crucial difference between popular and academic history. He suggested that four characteristics describe the work of historians: full and complete research of the subject, avoidance of factual errors, judgment and insight into the past, and use of the imagination. The main criticism of the popular writers against academic historians, he noted, is that they emphasize the first two—research and avoidance of factual errors—and ignore the latter two—insight and imagination about the past. The main criticism of the academic historians of the popular writers is that they overvalue the latter two. The criticism of Ken Burns's *The Civil War* follows this pattern exactly. No one would deny that Burns displayed insight and imagination in his rendering of the past, in his ability to evoke the feel, concerns, and emotions of the era.[7]

As historians survey the new media of the Internet and the World Wide Web, they do so with Nevins's words of caution ringing in their ears. On the web there is little to differentiate validated, professionally produced material from the multitude of opinion pieces by individuals on personal home pages. Search engines make little effort to distinguish these materials; their robots and searching mechanisms apply blunt instruments to the task. An online search for historical information can return a third-grader's report side by side with a dissertation chapter. The sheer proximity of these returns concerns academic historians. The web's openness, its democratic nature, troubles many that expect more careful prioritization.

What is the state of Civil War history on the World Wide Web? In one respect, it is healthy and in another anemic. The web hosts hundreds of thousands of sites on the Civil War. On the surface it appears a vibrant, expectant place, full of promise and growth. Some of the very best web sites are built around Civil War history, such as the University of Virginia's Valley of the Shadow and sections of the Library of Congress's American Memory. Both of these sites comprise thousands of original documents, including letters, diaries, photographs, maps, and images. Teams of researchers, scholars, librarians, computer programmers, and digital media specialists built these sites. The large institutions behind them have poured resources into their development. The results of this intense effort are beautifully developed, carefully constructed, pedagogically sound sites that attract thousands of visitors each day. They receive traffic from every part of the world, including Asia, Africa, South America, and Australia. They have become part of the curriculum at K–12 schools, universities, and colleges across the United States.[8]

The Valley of the Shadow and American Memory differ in several important respects. The Valley of the Shadow is, according to its creators, an "intentional archive." An intentional archive is defined as a set of documents and materials that are assembled by a scholar for the purposes of advancing a particular direction of inquiry into the past. A lead scholar sets the direction of the research and creates a set of materials from a wide array of institutions, intentionally including some and excluding others. At some point the archive is available for the scholar to use to seek avenues of inquiry. The Valley of the Shadow pioneered the concept of the intentional archive on the web. It invites its visitors to explore the archive and use it to pursue their own inquiries into the past. It challenges its visitors to construct their own narratives out of the materials assembled into the archive. Edward L. Ayers is the lead scholar and director of The Valley of the Shadow project. Ayers plans to write a narrative of the Civil War from the project's archives and welcomes others to have access to the research and compile their own narratives from it as well.[9]

The Library of Congress's American Memory site represents another approach to the Civil War on the World Wide Web. It is a digital library of materials, not at all intentional in its direction of inquiry and led by no single scholar. The collection includes items in the Library of Congress's archives and is a systematic effort to put all of the library's materials online. American Memory holds two large sets of documents important to the study of the Civil War as well as materials from other subjects in American history. The library has initiated a massive digitization effort to put several million of its holdings online. To accomplish this feat, it has recruited digital library specialists and has developed an infrastructure of hardware and software to handle one of the largest online collections in the world. The success of the American Memory project comes from its depth of coverage and quality of materials. Other libraries approach the Civil War in similar fashion. The Electronic Text Center at the University of Virginia's Alderman Library holds one of the largest online collections of mid-nineteenth–century American literature, including hundreds of Civil War materials. These works are part of a larger collection of Early American materials that comprises first editions, rare books, and letters and accounts. Documenting the American South at the University of North Carolina at Chapel Hill and Digital Scriptorium at Duke University represent other notable digital library initiatives. Even smaller institutions' libraries, such as the Virginia Military Institute and Virginia Polytechnic Institute, have developed digital library efforts around their Civil War holdings.[10]

Most Civil War web sites are not the product of universities or libraries, however. They are the work of dedicated individuals without financial reward or scholarly credit. Despite the limitations of little or no financial support for their work, these enthusiasts have produced a wide array of successful sites. Two examples come immediately to mind. Thomas Fasulo, an entomologist at the University of Florida, has created a vast archive on the Battle of Olustee. Visitors to his site can read Official Records, letters from participants, and histories of the Confederate and Union regiments that fought in the battle, including two African American regiments. A second excellent site, United States Sanitary Commission, is the work of Civil War reenactor Jan P. Romanovich. This site contains digitized documents ranging from diagrams of horse-drawn ambulances to appeals for support of the commission's work printed in national newspapers.[11]

The National Park Service (NPS) has assembled one of the largest sets of Civil War sites on the web. The NPS showed remarkable agility as the web developed in the 1990s and moved aggressively to build sites on each Civil War battlefield that it oversees. Although some of these sites contain little more than directions to the battlefield, many show every aspect of the battle from social dimensions of the communities nearby to the political importance of the battle. Some NPS sites, such as Second Manassas, offer online visitors Geographic Information Systems maps, letters from the battle, official accounts of the fighting, and overviews of the tactics and strategy of the commanders. Other NPS sites provide scholars and researchers with packaged information on the battlefield. The NPS maintains more than a hundred web sites on the Civil War, which are accessed thousands of times daily. It quickly adapted its mission of education, outreach, and preservation to the new media, and NPS sites account for the largest set of web-based materials on the Civil War directed by one agency or institution. While the NPS moved online successfully, it allowed a remarkable degree of latitude to its sites. The result is uniformity of coverage—every battlefield has a web site—but sporadic evidence of depth. Not all NPS web sites are the same. Each site bears the imprimatur of the NPS but is largely the creation of the historians, interpreters, and superintendents of the battlefield site.[12]

Coverage of the Civil War on the web might seem sadly anemic in some respects, despite the impressive work of the Library of Congress, the NPS, universities, museums, and dedicated Civil War enthusiasts. Few sites advance new ideas about the history of the period. While recent scholarship has turned to questions of social history, most Civil War web sites focus on a general, a battle, or a regiment. Whereas Ken Burns wove the daily life of soldiers into his grand narrative, many sites simply provide more minibiographies of the most famous Civil War generals. The graphic elements, navigational design, and narrative structure of most web sites are pitifully poor, especially in comparison with professionally produced sites. Too many sites recycle the standard images of Robert E. Lee and Abraham Lincoln, of Ulysses S. Grant and William T. Sherman. Flags are also popular.

A few notable exceptions stand apart from the usual uninspired presentation of text and images. One, Chattanooga: A Road Trip Through Time, is a beautiful evocation of the battle of Chattanooga through a pictorial road trip. Its design, layout, and narrative create a sense of investigation into the past and of the events of November 1863. The spirit of the venture is neatly encapsulated in the site's opening sentences: "November 25th, 1997, marked the 134th anniversary of the battles for Chattanooga. On that day, Dave Buckhout and T. C. Moore retraced the route along which these battles flowed, from Lookout Mountain, through the city, and onto its finale atop Missionary Ridge. They had cameras, a road map, and an '86 Buick." Another well-designed site is Camp Life, created by the NPS's Division of Cultural Resources using artifacts on display at Gettysburg National Military Park. Beautiful digital photographs of soldiers' common possessions, which range from prayer books to playing cards, effectively evoke a sense of the Civil War soldier's daily life.[13]

Unfortunately, many web sites broadcast old prejudices, ancient theories, and long-disproved arguments about the Civil War. One of the most persistent myths concerns its origins. The idea that the Civil War was fought not over slavery but over economic differences having to do with the tariff has long since been disproved, yet it maintains a fierce grip on the minds of many Americans. One privately maintained web site, for example, featuring North Georgia travel and history, puts tariffs and constitutional questions at the heart of the struggle. The designer of the site sneers, "Some say simplistically that the Civil War was fought over slavery," and even downplays the brutality of slavery, instead emphasizing the paternalistic nature of the institution: "Slaves often spoke of 'our cotton' or 'our cattle.' The only item they would concede was the master's carriage. Trusted slaves were permitted to go to town unescorted. Others suffered horribly. Conditions in northern factories were as bad or worse than those for a majority of the slaves, but it would be 40 years after the war when they were properly addressed."[14]

Historians have put slavery at the center of the struggle between the North and South, and their work during the past thirty years has made a significant difference in the treatment of the war's causes on the web. Academic historians in the 1960s, 1970s, and 1980s ignored the war itself, preferring to address questions of race, class, and gender, seeing more promising fields of inquiry in the antebellum era and Reconstruction. Perhaps they were put off by the Centennial celebration of the war, with its reenactments, publications, and heightened general interest. Perhaps the brutality and frustration of the Vietnam War led many historians to look to subjects other than war itself. Perhaps, too, they were dissuaded from studying the war by such critics as Edmund Wilson and Robert Penn Warren. Wilson's influential book *Patriotic Gore* dismissed Lincoln as a grasping autocrat, no different from other nineteenth-century proponents of the centralized state, Bismarck and Lenin. Wilson considered the war emblematic of man's brutality and not at all an uplifting, progressive part of American history; he emphasized further that an event that killed so many Americans should be considered a failure not a triumph. Warren shared Wilson's detachment about the war's positive outcomes.

He wrote in *The Legacy of the Civil War* that Americans had developed convenient but problematic approaches to the war. Northerners used the war, Warren wrote, as a "Treasury of Virtue," a limitless piggy bank of goodness to draw on in the future. Southerners, he suggested, used the war as "The Great Alibi," a tireless excuse for all that is wrong in the region. Warren worried the war had become "part of our divinely instituted success story, and to think, in some shadowy corner of the mind, of the dead at Gettysburg as a small price to pay for the development of a really satisfactory and cheap compact car with decent pick-up and road-holding capability."[15] Wilson and Warren were skeptical about the value of typical Civil War histories, and so were many scholars who saw them as excessively popular, not at all concerned with the common person, and feeding into a distorted view of American history.

In the 1980s and 1990s, scholars discovered the importance of constructing a social history of the war itself. They turned their attention particularly to the reasons for Southern defeat. In the wake of the Vietnam War, many scholars wondered about the South's strategy and its loss despite significant resources, territory, and military leadership. Some historians argued that the white South lost the war because it lost the popular will to fight it. They pointed to a variety of explanations for the loss of the will necessary for victory: a growing disquiet with the moral rightness of slavery, fears that God favored the North, an emerging class conflict within the Confederacy, and the defection of women, who grew ambivalent about the war's objectives and skeptical of its effects on Southern gender roles. Other historians, notably Gary Gallagher, dispute the idea that the South lost because of a loss of popular will, whether a product of unease over slavery, class conflict, or gender roles. "Preoccupation with fissures within the wartime South," Gallagher wrote in *The Confederate War,* "arises from an understandable tendency to work backward from the war's outcome.... Historians begin with the fact that the North triumphed."[16]

While many academic historians argued about the reasons for the South's loss, others worked on the experience of the home front in the war. Studies of the Southern home front emphasized division among citizens over the Confederacy, but they also made clear the experience of people usually left out of the more popular literature, including African Americans, women, children, and even conscientious objectors. Drew Gilpin Faust wrote about elite Southern women on the home front: "The harsh realities of military conflict and social upheaval pushed women toward new understandings of themselves and toward reconstructions of the meanings of southern womanhood that would last well beyond the Confederacy's demise." Important conflicts and far-reaching changes were under way at home during the war, and nearly every man, woman, and child could feel them. These community histories reveal different views of the war experiences, perspectives that show the roles of churches, hospitals, schools, and neighborhoods in the conflict. Northern community studies, while fewer in number, also demonstrate the ways Northern life changed when the soldier left home.[17]

The vibrant renewed interest in the Civil War among academic historians has coincided with the rise of both new Internet technology and interest in the Civil War generally. The Civil War's legacies remain a point of heated conflict in American life. South Carolina's debate over the flying of the Confederate flag at the statehouse marks one example; the effort to tear down Civil War monuments across the country marks another. Controversy swirled in Richmond in the summer of 1999 as the city openly debated the public display of a mural of Confederate general Robert E. Lee on the Richmond Canal Walk. Lee was displayed initially in full military uniform, alongside other Virginia figures in history, most notably Nat Turner. Lee's image became a point of conflict over the shape of racial politics in present-day Richmond. Hundreds of people attended Richmond city council hearings on the subject. Tempers flared and long-held opinions flooded the newspapers. Even David Duke, the former head of the Ku Klux Klan, came to Richmond to stage a race-baiting rally in favor of keeping Lee's image up on the Canal Walk.[18]

Ironically, the World Wide Web is full of Confederate flags, photos of Civil War monuments, and mural-sized images of General Robert E. Lee in military dress uniform, yet no protests over their public display has emerged. In many cases the images are simply part of an enthusiasm about the study of the Civil War that permeates many amateur sites. Still, the explanation lies in the both the web's capacity and its nature as a domain that does not privilege one space over another. On the web, in other words, there is no discernable proximity or distance from central points. A monument in one place on the web does not displace another, as it might in limited city physical landscapes. A banner in one place on the web does not privilege one leader over another when the space to post banners is limitless. For this reason the openness of the Internet allows a new landscape for history, one in which there can be unprivileged and unlimited public space. The result is an exhibition environment like no other in American life and culture. It allows for the creation of sites such as Civil War Women, The Harvard Regiment, and the 5th Regiment Cavalry U.S. Colored Troops. In the Jews in the Civil War site, the American flag flies next to documents about Jews in the Union, while the Confederate stars and bars waves next to documentation from the South.[19]

The open space of the web has prompted academic historians and librarians, reenactors, Civil War enthusiasts, publishers, educators, schoolchildren, graduate students, undergraduates, and opinionated Americans to stake out their ideas and evidence. The result is a vast landscape of Civil War sites. We have examined thousands of these sites and written reviews of the very best. In our work at the Center for Digital History at the University of Virginia, we were engaged in the production of a major Civil War web site, The Valley of the Shadow, and had close experience with the subject and the medium. In 1998–99 we developed a series of training seminars for the NPS on the state of the Civil War on the web and worked with more than forty NPS historians, interpreters, and rangers. Our experience led us to produce a guide for the Civil War on the World Wide Web, one that both seasoned Civil War researchers and those just beginning to explore the history would find useful, comprehensive, and readable.

NOTES

1. *Choice: Current Reviews for Academic Libraries* 35, no. 8 (April 1998). See www.google.com and www.northernlight.com for search engines to explore Civil War sites. The World Wide Web network was first created in 1989 by CERN, the European Particle Physics Lab in Geneva and made available on the Internet in August 1991. The appearance in 1993 of software (Mosaic) that displayed the web in a format that used text and graphics marks the beginning of the web as the kind of communications environment it is today. Netscape released its browser software Navigator in 1994. In 1993 there were 26,000 registered domain names on the Web. In 1999 there were more than 1.3 million.

2. *The Civil War,* a film by Ken Burns, aired as a ten-part series on PBS in 1990. Estimates of the audience size vary: James McPherson states 40 million viewers, whereas Gary Gallagher quotes a *Newsweek* article that "fourteen million Americans, more than the entire population of the Confederacy, gave themselves over to 'The Civil War' last week." On audience size, see James M. McPherson, *Drawn with the Sword: Reflections on the American Civil War* (New York: Oxford University Press, 1996), 238, and Gary Gallagher, *Lee and His Generals in War and Memory* (Baton Rouge: Louisiana State University Press, 1998), 246. Michael Shaara, *The Killer Angels* (New York: Ballantine Books, 1993 [38th printing]). *The Killer Angels* was originally published in 1974. See also Jeff Shaara, *Gods and Generals* (New York: Ballantine Books, 1998) and *The Last Full Measure* (New York: Ballantine Books, 1998). See www.amazon.com for reader comments on these books.

3. McPherson, *Drawn with the Sword,* viii. See especially Chapter 5 for McPherson's views on the popular interest in the Civil War and the reasons academic historians have failed to connect with this audience.

4. Robert Brent Toplin, ed., *Ken Burns's The Civil War: Historians Respond* (New York: Oxford University Press, 1996). See also Gallagher, *Lee and His Generals in War and Memory*. For a military history review, see A. Cash Koeniger, "Ken Burns' 'The Civil War': Triumph or Travesty?" *Journal of Military History* 55 (April 1991): 225–33; Robert Brent Toplin, "Editors Report: History and the Media," *Journal of American History* 80 (December 1993): 1175–79.

5. Quoted in McPherson, *Drawn with the Sword,* 232. See Alan Nevins, "What's the Matter with History?" *Saturday Review of Literature* 19 (February 4, 1939): 4.

6. Allan Nevins, "Not Capulets, Not Montagues," *The American Historical Review* (January 1960): 253–70.

7. Ibid., 262–63.

8. See http://valley.vcdh.virginia.edu for The Valley of the Shadow: Two Communities in the American Civil War and http://www.loc.gov/ammem for the American Memory Project. On traffic to the Valley Project, see William G. Thomas, " 'Fax Me Everything You Have on the Civil War!': A Look at Web Audiences," *AHA Perspectives* (February 1998). On pedagogy and the use of the Valley Project in university curriculum, see Michael J. Galgano, " 'The Best of Times': Teaching Undergraduate Research Methods Using the Great American History Machine and the Valley of the Shadow," *History Computer Review* (Spring 1999): 13–28; Andrew McMichael, "The Historian, the Internet, and the Web: A Reassessment," *AHA Perspectives* (February 1998): 29–32; and Michael O'Malley and Roy Rosenzweig, "Brave New World or Blind Alley? American History on the World Wide Web," *Journal of American History* (June 1997): 132–55.

9. The Valley of the Shadow will be released in CD-ROM format by W. W. Norton & Co. in 2000. For information on the CD-ROM, see http://www.wwnorton.com/vos.

10. For Etext's collection, see http://etext.lib.virgniia.edu, and for Virginia Military Institute and Augustana College, see http://www.vmi.edu/~archtml/cwsource.html and http://sparc5.augustana.edu/library/civil.html.

11. For the Battle of Olustee, see http://extlab1.entnem.ufl.edu/olustee, and for the United States Sanitary Commission, see http://www.netwalk.com/~jpr/index.htm.

12. See http://www.nps.gov for the complete listing of the NPS's web resources.

13. See http://mediaalchemy.com/civilwar and http://www.cr.nps.gov/csd/gettex.

14. See http://www.ngeorgia.com.

15. Robert Penn Warren, *The Legacy of the Civil War: Meditations on the Centennial* (New York: Random House, 1961), 49–50; Edmund Wilson, *Patriotic Gore: Studies in the Literature of the American Civil War* (New York: Oxford University Press, 1962).

16. On the efforts of social historians of the Civil War, see Maris A. Vinovskis, *Toward a Social History of the American Civil War: Exploratory Essays* (Cambridge: Cambridge University Press, 1990). For interpretations of the loss of popular will in the South, see Gary Gallagher, *The Confederate War* (Cambridge: Harvard University Press, 1997); E. Merton Coulter, *The Confederate States of America 1861–1865* (Baton Rouge: Louisiana State University Press 1950); Richard E. Beringer, Herman Hattaway, Archer Jones, and William N. Still, Jr., *Why the South Lost the Civil War* (Athens: University of Georgia Press, 1986); Drew Gilpin Faust, *Mothers of Invention: Women of the Slaveholding South in the American Civil War* (Chapel Hill: University of North Carolina Press, 1996); William Blair, *Virginia's Private War: Feeding Body and Soul in the Confederacy, 1861–1865* (New York: Oxford University Press, 1998); and Paul D. Escott, *After Secession: Jefferson Davis and the Failure of Confederate Nationalism* (Baton Rouge: Louisiana State University Press, 1978).

17. For examples of community studies, see also Stephen Elliott Tripp, *Yankee Town, Southern City: Race and Class Relations in Lynchburg* (The American Social Experience Series, New York: New York University Press, 1997); Reid Mitchell, *The Vacant Chair: The Northern Soldier Leaves Home* (New York: Oxford University Press, 1993); LeeAnn Whites, *The Civil War as a Crisis in Gender: Augusta, Georgia, 1860–1890* (Athens: University of Georgia Press, 1995); Daniel E. Sutherland, *Seasons of War: The Ordeal of a Confederate Community, 1861–1865* (New York:

The Free Press, 1995); and Iver Bernstein, *The New York City Draft Riots: Their Significance in American Society and Politics in the Age of the Civil War* (New York: Oxford University Press, 1990).

18. On the flag controversy in South Carolina, see *Charleston Daily News,* February 23, 2000. On the monument issue, see *Charlottesville Daily Progress,* February 20, 2000. On the Richmond Canal Walk controversy, see the compendium of articles online from the *Richmond Times-Dispatch* at http://www.gatewayva.com/rtd/special/canal/.

19. For Jews in the Civil War, see http://www.jewish-history.com/civilwar.htm.

USER'S GUIDE

Alice E. Carter

The World Wide Web contains many sites rich with content about the Civil War. Researchers can go on line to read soldiers' letters and diaries, examine diagrams of cannons and gunboats, and study Official Reports of major battles and minor skirmishes. But this valuable material can be difficult to find. Entering "Civil War" into a typical search engine will produce a list of hundreds of thousands of sites, most of which are of little value to serious researchers. Many are nothing more than pages of links. Others provide only the hours of operation of a historic site or museum in a distant state. Researchers relying on search engines can find themselves sifting through site after site looking for high-quality material. Searching for sites about certain aspects of the Civil War, such as emancipation, soldiers' lives, or a particular battle, can be even more frustrating. The designers of the best Civil War web sites tend to be educators, government employees, and lay researchers. They generally are inexperienced with "metatags" and costly promotion schemes designed to ensure that the sites will be found by commercial search engines.

Sites such as The United States Civil War Center (http://www.cwc.lsu.edu) and The American Civil War Homepage (http://sunsite.utk.edu/civil-war) begin to meet the needs of serious researchers, but they too are of limited usefulness. The hundreds of thematically categorized links on these sites take visitors to material that varies widely in quality. Some of the linked sites consist only of short excerpts of out-of-print books. Others contain a few paragraphs of poorly researched secondary material. The true gems linked from most links pages are outnumbered by sites that are quite mediocre.

Unlike search engines and links pages, this book identifies only those sites that are of value to serious researchers. A guide rather than series of lists, this book provides ninety-five in-depth reviews of the best Civil War sites on the World Wide Web. Each review gives a detailed description of the site's subject matter. For example, the book's discussion of Civil War Women, part of Duke University's Digital Scriptorium, explains that the site features the personal papers (http://scriptorium.lib.duke.edu/collections/civil-war-wmen.html) of three women: Rose O'Neal Greenhow, famous Confederate spy and diplomat; Alice Williamson, a young Tennessee woman coping with life under Union occupation; and Sarah Thompson, a pro-Unionist who aided federal efforts against Confederate guerrilla activity around her Tennessee home. The reviews also describe the type of content on the site. Civil War material on the web ranges from excerpts of previously published but important historical accounts, to collections of documents with explanatory intro-ductions, to original hypertext essays. Digital library sites that consist exclusively of searchable, exquisitely digitized rare primary texts represent another extreme.

The detailed reviews found here are designed to help students, educators, geneal-ogists, academic scholars, and lay historians find web sites that match their inter-ests and needs. In reviewing only ninety-five sites, this book emphasizes quality over quantity. Taken together, however, these sites offer endless opportunities for exploration and research.

Some of the sites reviewed were created and maintained by enthusiastic individu-als on their own time, with the navigation and page design that one would expect from amateur designers. Others represent years of work by professional historians and archivists, graphic designers, and programmers. The common element in all the sites reviewed is high-quality content. To be selected for a review, a site needed to meet several criteria. First, it had to have material that would help researchers learn about the American Civil War. The content had to be extensive, accurate, and well documented. Second, the site had to make effective use of the medium of the World Wide Web. The information superhighway has the potential to give anyone with a computer and a phone line access to otherwise unavailable material. A site with con-tent that could be found in most bookstores or public libraries did not qualify for a review. The best sites reviewed here feature innovative navigation and searching techniques possible only on the Internet. A selection was never made solely on the basis of aesthetics and technical sophistication, but sites hampered by poor appear-ance or navigational problems were generally disqualified.

The reviews are divided into eight chapters: Battles and Campaigns, Political and Military Leaders, Life of the Soldier, Naval Operations, The Experience of the U.S. Colored Troops, Slavery and Emancipation, Women in the Civil War, and Civil War Regiments. These subjects are certainly not the only important areas of Civil War study, but they reflect the current focus of Civil War resources on the web. With the exception of Civil War Era Editorials (http://history.furman.edu/~benson/docs) and Part I of The Valley of the Shadow (http://valley.vdch.virginia.edu), there are no significant sites on the coming of the Civil War. The home front experience has also been large-ly neglected by web site designers.

Each chapter opens with an introduction that provides a historic overview of the subject and that serves as a jumping off point to the reviews themselves. The reviews describe the contents and structure of the site and provide some navigational hints. They close with ratings on the site's content, aesthetics, and navigation with five stars indicating "excellent," four stars indicating "good," and three stars indicating "average." A list of books at the end of each chapter invites the reader to explore the topic in greater detail.

The sites given a rating of five stars for content generally center on an important problem in Civil War history and feature extensive collections of primary documents placed in an explanatory context. Although almost all of the reviewed sites receive four or five stars in the content category, the ratings for aesthetics and navigation are not as consistently high. The bulk of the sites reviewed here were not made by professional web designers but by librarians and archivists, reenactors and preservationists, students and educators—people more interested in the Civil War than in slick appearance or sophisticated menus. The few sites that earned ratings of "excellent" in the navigation category are those that cleanly separate historic content from other information, give visitors a clear sense of what lies behind each link, allow easy movement from section to section, and invite visitors to chart their own paths through the material. Of the three categories, aesthetics generally show the lowest ratings, with quite a few sites earning only three stars. The pages in these sites are generally well laid out but make clumsy use of background images, colors, headings, or icons. Sites earning four stars in aesthetics have clean design and effective graphics, and the few sites with five stars for this category are of extraordinary quality, constructed with a level of professionalism that warranted special mention.

The topical index at the end of the book provides the names, addresses, and short descriptions of more than four hundred Civil War web sites. Most of them were not deemed Best of the Web and so are not reviewed in the main chapters. Although the sites in this category provide valuable historic content, they generally do not have the level of scholarly engagement, depth of analysis, or breadth of coverage exhibited by the reviewed sites. Many of the sites listed in the index but not deemed Best of the Web have less effective page layout and navigation.

These sites are still worth a visit. Some are extremely interesting but not sufficiently engaged with central issues of the Civil War study to warrant a full review. For example, The Trial of Captain Henry Wirz (http://www.law.umkc.edu/faculty/projects/ftrials/wirz/wirz.htm), a site made by a team of law students at University of Missouri–Kansas City, offers a fascinating look into the trial and execution of the captain of the notorious Andersonville Prison. Another example is Civil War Richmond (http://www.mdgorman.com), which contains an impressive collection of documents about businesses, hospitals, and prisons in the Confederate capital city.

This site would be of use to people interested in Richmond during the war, although researchers seeking an in-depth study of issues such as the home front, medical care, and prisons will not be satisfied here.

Creating print guides to web sites is always risky undertaking. Most web sites, including many of the ones reviewed and listed here, are works in progress, and the layout, navigation, and content can be altered fundamentally without notice. Readers of this book may find that some of the sites reviewed here have transformed considerably since the time the review was written. Happily, we have found that these changes are generally for the better, with new material, better appearance, and improved overall design. Sadly, some sites may simply disappear or fall into disrepair. Many of the sites reviewed and listed here are constructed and financed by private individuals or nonprofit organizations. Changes in interests, priorities, and resources may result in the site's decay or ultimate demise. With luck, this problem will not occur with more than a few of the sites reviewed or listed here.

In an era in which the World Wide Web is dominated by e-commerce, it is important to recognize the sites that provide a genuine public service. For the most part, the men and women who made these web sites—those reviewed and those not reviewed—did so with little or no remuneration. They were motivated not by profit but by a desire to share their knowledge, their family papers, or their library's or archive's resources with the general public. Thanks to the designers of these fine sites, history has a secure a place in this new powerful new medium.

PART I

THE VERY BEST
CIVIL WAR
WEB SITES

REVIEWS

AND

RATINGS

CHAPTER 1

BATTLES AND CAMPAIGNS

Anyone who has browsed the U.S. history sections of bookstores can attest to the enduring fascination that Civil War battles and campaigns hold for scholars and readers. The vast quantity of published works about the Battle of Gettysburg alone could easily fill a small library. The attention is not misplaced, because generals and armies determined the outcome of the conflict.

Military histories of battles and campaigns in the Civil War abound. During the past decade these books have become progressively more detailed and microscopic in their approach. A 600-page volume published in 1987, for example, is devoted to a single day of the battle of Gettysburg. Every year, publishers release new books on major battles and even on secondary engagements, such as Port Republic and Kernstown. These books tend to concentrate on the movements of troops and the orders and counterorders at the regimental level.

Despite the excruciating detail of current battle histories, their coverage confirms the widely held notion that battles and campaigns determined the political outcome of the war. While some historians have looked to the home front to explain Confederate defeat and Northern victory—focusing on such aspects as loss of popular will, uneasiness about slavery, and dissent within the civilian population—battles and campaigns played an obvious role in the outcome, so obvious that they are often overlooked or taken for granted.

The public and the politicians in both North and South measured victories and defeats in the calculus of political, economic, and diplomatic

3

outcomes. Early conquests in the Mississippi Valley provided the North with control over important western transportation networks, and the Union's success at Antietam and Gettysburg halted large-scale Confederate incursions into Northern territory. These and other timely victories on the battlefield bolstered Northern public support for the war effort and headed off British assistance to the Confederacy. The Northern victory at Atlanta in September 1864 virtually ensured reelection for President Abraham Lincoln and the continuation of the war.

The South shared in the experience of timely victory and costly defeat. The Confederacy's Army of Northern Virginia handed defeat after defeat to the Union's Army of the Potomac in 1862–63, or so it seemed to many observers. As the conflict dragged on through these years and casualties mounted, Northern public support for the war diminished while Southern hopes for independence brightened. Even a battle such as Antietam, widely viewed as a marginal Northern victory, gave the Northern public serious cause for concern, as the losses there amounted to the single bloodiest battle in American history. The number of American casualties on this hot day in September in Maryland was four times the number of Americans killed or wounded on D-Day in World War II. In the shadow of Antietam, many Northerners in 1862 wondered about the human costs of fighting the war. Congressional elections in the North in 1862 showed weakening support for the war, as Republicans lost ground to Democrats and Lincoln's ability to prosecute the war without opposition eroded. For the South, though, the loss at Atlanta in 1864 ended any hope of altering the Northern political landscape.

Victory and defeat on the battlefield helped reshape the war's goals in unforeseen ways. Union failures, by lengthening the war far beyond what most Americans had expected, served to alter the war's aims. After the battle of Antietam, President Abraham Lincoln drafted the Emancipation Proclamation. When the proclamation was enacted on January 1, 1863, the war became a war to end slavery, not just a war to save the Union. In the South also the war's aims shifted with the armies' fortunes on the battlefields. Offensive campaigns into Northern states followed military success for the Confederacy in 1862 and 1863, and the influence of these campaigns on Northern and foreign public opinion was never far from the minds of Confederate strategists.

Civil War campaigns and battles are popular for reasons other than their strategic significance alone. The development and use of technology over the course of the war is still of interest to scholars of the military, and strategies and tactics employed by generals on both sides of the war are hotly debated by Civil War roundtables, online discussion groups, and academic historians. Perhaps the factor most responsible for the enduring fascination with the war is the role of the common soldier in the conflict. In no other war did so many American men fight. The Confederacy mobilized between 750,000 and 850,000 men in all, almost 75 to 85 percent of its draft-age white male population. The North mustered in 2.2 million soldiers, about 50 percent of its draft-age population. By the end of the war, more than 600,000 men had died of wounds or disease, and hundreds of thousands more were permanently disabled. The number of casualties in the Civil War surpasses American casualties in World War I, World War II, the Korean War, and the Vietnam War combined.

Every year, millions of Americans make pilgrimages to archives and battlefields in search of a connection with these figures from the past. Americans are still struggling with the meaning of the Civil War. Many are seeking answers by studying battles and campaigns, and by building web sites to share their knowledge with the public. Civil War battle and campaign web sites have also been made by custodians of the battlefields, such as the National Park Service and other government organizations. As a result, the online researcher will be rewarded with a wealth of excellent material.

WEB SITE REVIEWS

GENERAL SITES

The Civil War Artillery Page
http://www.cwartillery.org

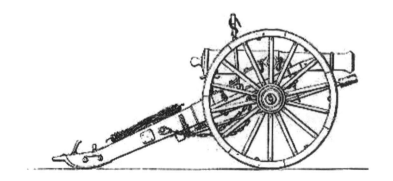

FIGURE 1.1
A number one carriage, carrying a 6-pounder

As the authors of the Civil War Artillery Page point out, artillery played a crucial role in many battles, even though only 6 percent of Civil War soldiers served in artillery units. This site contains practically everything a person would want to know about this important component of the war. Informative essays and excellent illustrations make the Civil War Artillery Page one of the best Civil War sites on the World Wide Web.

Sections include Organization and Drill, which explains how artillery (both heavy and light) fit into the general organization of the Union and Confederate armies and displays the flags and insignia of different units and ranks. The Weapons section explains in simple terms how different types of artillery guns worked and how the design of cannons changed over the course of the war. Black and white drawings are used to illustrate the text. The Ammunition section explains the difference between shells, case shot, grape shot, solid shot, and canisters. The section also contains excellent photographs and diagrams of ten types of projectiles, from the Schenkl shell used by the Union army to the Confederate army's Read bolt. A page titled The Effects of Artillery Fire contains firsthand accounts of the horrible carnage inflicted by these weapons.

The section Famous Weapons describes the history and current condition of important Civil War artillery pieces, such as the Widow Blakely, which fired on federal boats attacking Vicksburg, and the 17,000-pound gun called the Dictator that pounded Confederate forces during the Siege of Petersburg. Quoting Napoleon's belief that the best generals have served in the artillery, a page titled Famous Artillerists summarizes the contributions made by men such as John Pelham, a captain in Stuart's Horse Artillery, and Robert Parker Parrott, whose innovations in cannon production proved essential to the Union's war effort.

The Civil War Artillery Page is exhaustive but never tedious. All of the information is presented in a lively fashion, and visitors will find themselves fascinated as they explore this excellent site.

CONTENT   ★ ★ ★ ★
AESTHETICS   ★ ★ ★
NAVIGATION   ★ ★ ★

Civil War Sites Advisory Commission Battle Summaries
http://www2.cr.nps.gov/abpp/battles/tvii.htm

Created by the American Battlefield Protection Program of the National Park Service, this site contains brief summaries of both major and minor Civil War battles. The descriptions can be accessed from two menus, one listing the battles by theater and campaign, and the other by state. The site provides the following information for each battle: all names that the battle has been known by, location (county and state), campaign, date(s), principal commanders, forces engaged, estimated casualties, description, and result(s).

The descriptions are minimal, with none of the details necessary to create a sense of the battle experience or of its larger significance, and there no maps.

With information on more battles than any other single Civil War web site, however, this site is an excellent source for basic information.

CONTENT   ★ ★ ★ ★
AESTHETICS   ★ ★ ★
NAVIGATION   ★ ★ ★ ★

Selected Civil War Photographs in the American Memory Collection

http://memory.loc.gov/ammem/cwphome.html

FIGURE 1.2

Chevaux-de-frise **on Marietta Street, Atlanta, Georgia—photographic wagons and darkroom beyond**

Shortly after the beginning of the Civil War, Washington portrait photographer Matthew Brady organized a corps of photographers to document the historic events taking place. These men traveled to major battlefields and supplied Brady with more than a thousand negatives. The Library of Congress bought these negatives from collectors in 1943, and now excellent digital versions can be seen as part of the Library of Congress American Memory Collection.

Although the most famous Brady photographs are of fallen men on the battlefield, most of the images on the site are of men in camp, battlefield landscapes, and fortifications and buildings. Photography at the time was in its infancy, and the technology did not permit moving objects to be captured. The tradition of the combat photographer had not taken hold, and photographers remained safely behind lines until the fighting was over.

A visitor to the site can access the photographs in three ways. First, one can search by the name of a battle (or other term). The second option, browsing by subject, takes the visitor to a table of terms arranged alphabetically, which one would click to get actual subject headings. Browsing by subject would be very difficult for anyone not highly familiar with Library of Congress subject terms. The third way to access the photographs is through a timeline, which is by far the most useful option. Each year of the war has its own page containing brief summaries of that year's major battles and campaigns, as well as links that automatically execute searches for relevant images.

Any search, whether launched from the search page, a subject term, or the timeline, generates a new page with a list of items that match the search criteria.

The items on the list can be clicked to access a thumbnail version of the image and corresponding catalog information. Clicking on the thumbnail accesses a large version of the same image, as well as a link to download a high-quality tiff file.

By far the most extensive collection of Civil War photographs available on the web, this Library of Congress site should not be missed.

CONTENT   ★ ★ ★ ★ ★
AESTHETICS   ★ ★ ★ ★
NAVIGATION   ★ ★ ★ ★

Shotgun's Home of the American Civil War
www.civilwarhome.com

The work of one extremely enthusiastic individual, Shotgun's Home of the American Civil War shares many of the characteristics of privately made sites: incomplete citations, grammatical and spelling errors, and an admitted pro-South bias.

But it is the most comprehensive single source on the web for orders of battle, official records, and other first-hand accounts of practically every major Civil War battle. As with the CWSAC Battle Summaries site, Shotgun's Home of the American Civil War does not provide enough details or the context necessary to gain a good understanding of Civil War battles and campaigns. But with primary sources on more battles than any other single site on the web, this is a valuable source for researchers.

CONTENT   ★ ★ ★
AESTHETICS   ★ ★
NAVIGATION   ★ ★ ★

The Valley of the Shadow: Two Communities in the American Civil War, The War Years

http://jefferson.village.virginia.edu/cwhome.html

By focusing on two communities, Franklin County, Pennsylvania, and Augusta County, Virginia, the Valley of the Shadow site creates a sense of the Civil War as it was experienced by the people who lived it.

Interesting material on battles can be found in site's Images, Newspapers, and Letters and Diaries sections, but the best material for the study of battles and campaigns is found in its collection of interactive theater maps. These maps, which require a free plug-in to view, show troop movements of three Augusta County and three Franklin County regiments as they participated in the major battles and campaigns of the Eastern theater.

The base map shows topography and rivers, and the user can click on and off additional features, such as modern and historic roads, major cities and towns, and railroads. Clicking the play button starts a movie, and clicking on a battle location opens a summary page with basic facts on that unit's experience there, including the weather and the number of casualties. The summary page also contains links to soldiers' letters, official reports, and individual dossiers for the men of that unit who were killed and wounded in the battle. These maps can take up to five minutes to load over a modem connection during heavy Internet traffic, but they are worth the wait.

CONTENT ★ ★ ★ ★ ★
AESTHETICS ★ ★ ★ ★
NAVIGATION ★ ★ ★ ★

ANTIETAM/SHARPSBURG

Antietam National Battlefield

http://www.nps.gov/anti/home.htm

This site is only a sample of the many excellent Civil War sites made by the National Park Service (NPS). Entrusted with the care of dozens of Civil War battlefields and with educating the public about these places, the NPS has become the most prolific producer of online material on the Civil War. A visitor to the Antietam National Battlefield web site will find excellent content on this crucial battle. The site's opening page contains a brief description of the battle, and clicking Battlefield Information takes the visitor to a more detailed history with links to eyewitness accounts, casualty figures, biographical sketches, and photographs. Separate sections include portraits of six generals killed in the battle, photographs of the battlefield by Alexander Gardner, and several paintings made after the battle by eyewitnesses. A page dedicated to the use of artillery shows Union superiority in firepower at Antietam. Other highlights include an explanation of events leading to the battle titled Why Lee Invaded Maryland, an analysis of the role that the battle played in Lincoln's Emancipation Proclamation, and a description of the Dunker Church, which stood at the center of the battlefield. This site also contains information for visitors interested in more general aspects of the Civil War. The frequently asked questions answered in the Special Subjects section include "What were the tactics of battle in those days?" and "Who exactly were the Zouaves?"

The only primary documents consist of six eyewitness accounts (for which no citations are provided) and the Gardner photographs. This Park Service web site provides visitors with a basic understanding of the Battle of Antietam, but those seeking a more in-depth analysis of the battle will probably be better served at other sites.

CONTENT   ★ ★ ★ ★
AESTHETICS   ★ ★ ★
NAVIGATION   ★ ★ ★

Brian Downey's Antietam on the Web

http://www.geocities.com/Athens/Olympus/1845

Brian Downey's Antietam on the web is one of the best privately made Civil War battlefield web sites. A visitor can read a brief overview of the entire battle as well as a more detailed description of its three major stages. Some of these descriptions are accompanied by excellent maps made by the author. The site also contains biographical sketches of Union and Confederate generals who fought at Antietam. The Exhibits section features dozens of memoirs, letters, and official reports from battle participants, with helpful explanatory text accompanying every document. Included among these are Robert E. Lee's letter to Confederate president Jefferson Davis in which he makes the case for taking Southern troops into Maryland and official reports filed by key individuals after the battle. Throughout the site, Downey carefully documents and credits his sources.

The design of this site creates a pleasant visiting experience. Downey makes good use of navigational frames and attractive menu icons, and he does not clutter his pages with extraneous images and links. Pop-up windows in Exhibits and other sections lead to problems, however. These windows do not have any back buttons, and the only way to return to an earlier page is to close the pop-up window and start the exhibit again. Nevertheless, this site is a required stop for anyone interested in the Battle of Antietam, as well as for anyone looking for a good model of a privately made history web site.

CONTENT   ★ ★ ★ ★ ★
AESTHETICS   ★ ★ ★ ★
NAVIGATION   ★ ★ ★

APPOMATTOX

See Richmond

CHANCELLORSVILLE

See Fredericksburg

CHICKAMAUGA AND CHATTANOOGA

The Battle of Chickamauga: An Alabama Infantry Regiment's Perspective

http://www.19thalabama.org/battles/chickamauga/index.html

This site, created by a reenactment organization, provides a good overview of the Battle of Chickamauga. The opening page contains a summary of the major events of the battle, and subsequent pages take the visitors through a virtual tour of the experience of the 19th Alabama Infantry during this two-day battle. The tour consists of small color photographs, maps, and explanatory text. Visitors will learn that on the first day of the battle, the 19th Alabama participated in an unsuccessful attempt to trap the Union army on the east side of Lookout Mountain. On the second day, the 19th took part in the Confederate advances made at the Tan Yard field and at Horseshoe Ridge. The Battle Summary page contains several paragraphs on the casualties of the battle and the change in Union command that followed, as well as several public domain primary documents. The site also provides a list of print sources on the Battle of Chickamauga.

CONTENT   ★ ★ ★
AESTHETICS   ★ ★ ★
NAVIGATION   ★ ★ ★ ★

Chattanooga: A Road Trip Through Time
http://www.mediaalchemy.com/civilwar/

FIGURE 1.3
Cannons atop Lookout Mountain

This well-designed site chronicles the journey of its two designers to the major land-marks of the Battle of Chattanooga. As they go from place to place, they tell the story of the battle that put an end to the Confederate siege of Union-held Chattanooga and that set the stage for Sherman's March to the Sea. The history, while not terribly detailed or analytical, is beautifully written. The authors describe the balance of troops at the start of the battle, the successful Union attacks on Lookout Mountain and Orchard Knob, the foiled attack on Tunnel Hill, and the final victorious advance up Missionary Ridge. On the spot where General Philip Sheridan supposedly raised a glass of whiskey to Confederate officers atop the ridge, the authors paused to toast and drink in Sheridan's honor.

One of the few Civil War sites created by a professional design firm, this site features many artistic photographs taken on their trip, as well as a series of original maps depicting the military balance before the battle and the events on Lookout Mountain, Tunnel Hill, and Missionary Ridge. A final map of the authors' journey contains links to discussions of various locations important during the battle.

CONTENT   ★ ★ ★
AESTHETICS   ★ ★ ★ ★
NAVIGATION   ★ ★ ★ ★

COLD HARBOR

See Richmond

CORINTH

See Western Theater

FLORIDA

Battle of Olustee

http://extlab1.entnem.ufl.edu/olustee

The Battle of Olustee, Florida's largest Civil War battle, took place in February 1864, when federal troops ventured from Jacksonville into central Florida seeking to cut off supply routes and recruit black soldiers. Confederate forces under Brigadier General Joseph Finegan stopped the Union advance near the town of Olustee. Northern troops suffered heavy casualties and retreated back to Jacksonville, never to attempt another large-scale movement into the Florida interior.

A labor of love on the part of one passionate individual, this site contains photographs of battle reenactments, a large collection of public domain primary documents, invitations to join a battlefield preservation group, and a poem penned in 1989 ("The mist hung low o'er Ocean Pond / That frosty winter's morn; / Many hopeful hearts at dawnings light, / By night would be forlorn").

The site provides an informative account of a little-studied Civil War battle, with a capsule history of the battle as well as a more detailed account titled Ambush at St. Mary's River. Primary documents include official reports filed after the battle and numerous letters and newspaper articles written by participants. A section on the U.S. Colored Troops in the battle includes a detailed description and many additional primary documents.

CONTENT	★ ★ ★ ★
AESTHETICS	★ ★ ★
NAVIGATION	★ ★ ★

FREDERICKSBURG

Battle of Fredericksburg

http://members.aol.com/lmjarl/civwar/frdrksburg.html

AoP CORPS LOSSES

	KILLED	WOUNDED	* MISSING	TOTAL
Sumner's Grand Division				
Couch's 2nd Corps	412	3207	488	4107
Wilcox's 9th Corps	111	1067	152	1300
Hooker's Grand Division				
Stoneman's 3rd Corps	145	834	200	1179
Butterfeild's 5th Corps	307	1669	300	2276
Franklin's Grand Division				
Reynold's 1st Corps	345	2391	581	3317
Smith's 6th Corps	14	322	64	430

ANV CORPS LOSSES

	KILLED	WOUNDED	*MISSING	TOTAL
Jackson's Corp	395	2517	430	3342
Longstreet's Corps	261	1530	162	1953

FIGURE 1.4

Casualties at the Battle of Fredericksburg

This site, created by a private individual, features a detailed account of the battle and excellent maps. Full-scale treatment of topics such as Burnside Takes Over, Day of Battle, Union Order of Battle, and Casualties makes for an extremely informative visit. The illustrated narratives portray the squabbles that took place between Union commanders during the battle and convey a sense of the courage and suffering of the Union soldiers who made the doomed assaults on Confederate positions. The site also contains a lengthy bibliography and credits page.

CONTENT   ★ ★ ★ ★
AESTHETICS   ★ ★ ★
NAVIGATION   ★ ★ ★ ★

Fredericksburg and Spotsylvania National Military Park Visitor Center

http://www.nps.gov/frsp/vc.htm

The Fredericksburg and Spotsylvania National Military Park Visitor Center web site is a useful starting point for studying the battles of Fredericksburg, Chancellorsville, the Wilderness, and Spotsylvania. It contains detailed descriptions of the battles, an explanation of why the area was the scene of so much fighting, and a small collection of documents about the experience of civilians during the battles. All of this material can be found by clicking Civil War History on the home page.

The description of the Battle of Fredericksburg opens with General George B. McClellan handing over his command to Ambrose Burnside and concludes with Burnside's withdrawal of his men from Fredericksburg after suffering more than 12,500 casualties. The description is not overly detailed, but it provides enough texture to create a sense of drama.

The essay on Chancellorsville credits the Confederate victory to bold leadership, particularly that of Stonewall Jackson, who led more than thirty thousand troops on a twelve-mile trek to attack unprepared Union forces. The essay concludes that the Confederate victory there was a hollow one: Jackson's death cost the South one of its most important heroes, and overconfidence inspired by his success at Chancellorsville caused Lee to launch his ill-fated invasion of Pennsylvania.

The site contains two essays on the battles of Wilderness and Spotsylvania Courthouse. One, a general summary of the battles, provides an overview of the main events. The account opens with a description of the 1864 change in the command of the Union army. Impressed by General Ulysses S. Grant's stunning victories in the Western theater, Lincoln appointed him to the position of supreme commander of the Union army. The essay describes the battle in straight chronological order and concludes with a discussion of the heavy cost that the South paid for its tactical victory there. The second essay covers the events at Todd's Tavern, where Confederate soldiers harassed the Union army as it marched toward Spotsylvania Courthouse.

Although extremely informative, the site has several faults. First, it contains no primary documents. Transcriptions of letters and contemporary newspaper articles would have helped create a more textured sense of the battles and their aftermath. Countless links to private, non–National Park Service web sites take visitors to sites of extremely uneven quality.

CONTENT   ★ ★ ★ ★
AESTHETICS   ★ ★ ★
NAVIGATION   ★ ★ ★

GETTYSBURG

Carl Reed's Gettysburg Revisited

http://home.sprynet.com/~carlreed/

Novices and experts alike will find Carl Reed's Gettysburg Revisited well worth their time. The Analysis section contains essays by Reed about issues that have long preoccupied Civil War scholars, such as whether General James Longstreet should have attacked earlier on the second day and whether J. E. B. Stuart was truly AWOL at the beginning of the battle. Although rather inelegantly written, Reed's essays are well documented and balanced. Simple but effective computer-generated maps accompany many of them. The section titled Resources contains the standard fare of official reports and orders of battle, as well as excerpts of previously published firsthand accounts such as Robert Johnson and Clarence Buel's edited four-volume series titled *Battles and Leaders of the Civil War* and William F. Fox's *New York at Gettysburg*. Not a professional historian, Reed does not provide full citations for these materials, but he clearly took pains to document his work.

Each page of Gettysburg Revisited is clean and attractive. Reed makes skillful use of background images and arranges his text carefully. His menu items are intuitive, and, just in case one needs a little help, a site map lists all the contents on one page.

```
CONTENT        ★  ★  ★
AESTHETICS     ★  ★  ★  ★
NAVIGATION     ★  ★  ★  ★
```

Gettysburg Discussion Group

http://www.gdg.org

The stated mission of the Gettysburg Discussion Group is to digitize and preserve documents related to the battle. Their effort in this area has been focused on the papers of Union Brigadier General Henry Hunt, a Library of Congress collection that has been partially transcribed by group members and made available on the site. The papers include Hunt's correspondence with other Union officers about their units' actions during the battle and letters to Hunt from William Tecumseh Sherman referring to a dispute over the proper organization of the peacetime army. Since the site provides no information about Hunt or his role in the Battle of Gettysburg, the nonexpert may find this section's contents confusing.

The bulk of the material on the Gettysburg Discussion Group site is secondary accounts of different aspects of the battle, most of which were submitted by group members. Topics in this category include Devil's Den: A History and a Guide, and Who Saved Little Round Top? A small collection of essays by

National Park Service senior historian Kathleen Georg Harrison covers the formation and early planning of the Gettysburg National Cemetery and Park. The third source of secondary accounts is *Gettysburg Magazine*, which allows the site to post one article from every issue.

The volume of content on this site is overwhelming. Attempting to impose some order on this abundance of material, the site designers have created several entry points. One of these is a lovely scanned print of the battlefield apparently made by the Pennsylvania Railroad in the late nineteenth century. A visitor can click many of the locations of interest and be taken to a page with additional links to pertinent articles. For the most part, the site is of value primarily to members of the organization and other knowledgeable Gettysburg scholars. Nonexperts will find it difficult to judge the quality of the pieces submitted by members of the group and would be better served by other sites.

CONTENT   ★ ★ ★ ★
AESTHETICS   ★ ★ ★
NAVIGATION   ★ ★ ★

Gettysburg National Military Park

http://www.nps.gov/gett/home.htm

This web site contains a vast amount of material for people interested in the Battle of Gettysburg as well as in the Civil War in general.

The virtual tour takes the visitor through the battle day by day, with lengthy explanations of the main events. Links to pages covering locations of interest, such as McPherson's Farm and Oak Hill, contain photographs and detailed accounts of what took place there. Several animated maps that show the general movements of troops for each day and an extensive collection of first-hand accounts round out the virtual tour. Taken in its entirety, this is probably the single most informative web site about the Battle of Gettysburg.

The Gettysburg National Military Park web site also contains exhibits on topics not strictly about Gettysburg but about the Civil War in general. Informative essays in Soldier Life list the contents of a typical soldier's pack, explain how soldiers passed the time in camp, and describe their tents, food, and arms. Separate discussions of cavalry and artillery describe how these divisions were organized and the role that they played in the war. A beautiful exhibit of objects from the Gettysburg Museum, including prayer books, letters, and musical instruments carried by soldiers, can be accessed in Camp Life.

Most of the material on the site is well suited for secondary school students, and several sections are designed strictly with children in mind. Be a Junior Historian presents in simple terms topics such as causes of the war (What were they fightin' about?), food and medical care for soldiers, and backgrounds of the war's major leaders. The Teacher's Features section in the Teacher's Guide offers a comprehensive lesson plan (that unfortunately shows the Battle of Shiloh occurring in 1861 rather than 1862), essay topics about the battle, and bulletin board ideas.

CONTENT   ★ ★ ★ ★
AESTHETICS ★ ★ ★
NAVIGATION ★ ★ ★

Military History Online—Battle of Gettysburg
http://www.militaryhistoryonline.com/gettysburg

FIGURE 1.5
Cannons at the Gettysburg Battlefield

Military History Online is a high-quality commercial site with valuable Civil War material. Its section on the Battle of Gettysburg contains analysis, documents, and highly detailed descriptions of the battle. The descriptions vary from overviews of the events of each day to more focused pieces such as The Peach Orchard and Pickett's Charge. The Articles section contains pieces contributed by various writers, including "First Night, First Mistake: Lee and Ewell" and "A Matter of Numbers and Good Timing." The articles vary in quality of analysis and writing, and all suffer from a lack of citations. The primary documents (accessed by clicking the Reference link in the menu) consist of orders of battle. The site also features a large collection of beautiful photographs of the present-day battlefield.

Every inch of practically every page is filled with text and images, but restrained use of colors and tables prevents the site from seeming cluttered, and it has a very professional overall appearance.

CONTENT ★ ★ ★
AESTHETICS ★ ★ ★
NAVIGATION ★ ★ ★ ★

MANASSAS/BULL RUN

Manassas National Battlefield Park
http://www.nps.gov/mana/home.htm

This National Park Service site is designed primarily for secondary school students, but it will be of value to anyone interested in Civil War battles and campaigns.

The site's brief history of the First Battle of Manassas provides an account of the early federal success on Henry Hill and of the Confederate reinforcements that forced Northern troops to retreat toward Washington. Thumbnail portraits of key figures such as General Irvin McDowell and General Joseph E. Johnston are linked to larger images and biographical information. The battle account describes the overconfidence felt by both North and South as they headed toward this first significant encounter with the enemy. This naïveté can be seen in one of the six documents in the Letters from the Civil War section. "I am very much afraid your boys are not to have a serious brush with the rebels," wrote a friend to an officer of a New York Zouave regiment. "It will be like running the machine to a fire and finding the fire out. I hope, for their own sakes, they will have a chance to do a big thing with those infernal traitors before they get home."

The Park Museum focuses on the First Battle of Manassas. One of the more interesting exhibits illustrates how similarities between Union and Confederate uniforms at this early stage of the war created costly confusion on the battlefield. Another exhibit, Women of the Civil War, describes the death of eighty-year-old Judith Henry, killed in her bed when Union forces opened fire on Confederate sharpshooters in her home.

The narrative on the Second Battle of Manassas describes how General John Pope, commanding the Union Army of Virginia, ordered an attack on General Stonewall Jackson's units, unaware that Jackson would soon be reinforced by men under General James Longstreet. After suffering heavy losses, the Union army retreated, just as it had a year earlier in the same place. The one primary document about the Second Battle of Manassas is the report filed by Lieutenant Colonel C. B. Brockaway of the First Pennsylvania Artillery. Finding his men without infantry support, he surrendered to Confederate soldiers and was marched to Libby Prison in Richmond.

Material designed specifically for teachers round out the offerings on the Manassas Park web site. Educational material includes classroom activities designed to prepare students for a class trip to the park as well as a vocabulary lesson plan in which students learn terms such as *recruitment, bounty jumper,* and *regimental colors.*

The most comprehensive single source of online material on the First and Second Battles of Manassas, the Manassas National Battlefield Park Online Visitor Center provides online researchers with an excellent overview of these two battles.

CONTENT   ★ ★ ★ ★
AESTHETICS   ★ ★ ★ ★
NAVIGATION   ★ ★ ★

MISSOURI

See Western Theater

NEW MARKET

The Battle of New Market, Virginia, May 15, 1864
http://www.vmi.edu/~archtml/cwnm.html

FIGURE 1.6
New Market veterans

The Virginia Military Institute (VMI) is closely intertwined with the history of the Civil War. According to historian James M. McPherson, in 1861, 1,781 of the 1,902 current and former students of VMI joined the Confederate armed services, and its alumni led one-third of Virginia's regiments. In 1864, as Union forces were advancing up the Shenandoah Valley, VMI's superintendent sent students from their classrooms to join Confederate forces in a successful attempt to halt the Union advance. These young men had their first encounter with the enemy at the Battle of New Market. Ten cadets died on the battlefield or afterward from wounds inflicted there, and forty-five others were wounded.

The VMI New Market exhibit consists of a brief background essay, the names and portraits (if available) of the entire corps that fought, and biographical sketches of the men who were killed during or after the battle. Transcriptions of the superintendent's records are also available, including two letters to the families of young men who died. The superintendent assured the brother of Henry Jenner Jones that "[p]rovidence has so ordained it that these young men should be sent off in early youth—they fell nobly fighting in a just cause, in which all Southern youths are willing to pour out [their] heart's blood."

In addition to the material on New Market, VMI's archives contain an extensive collection of online Civil War manuscripts. Clicking Civil War Resources at the bottom of the main New Market page takes the visitor to the home page of the archives' Civil War Resources section. Clicking the Unit and Battle Resources Guide, about halfway down the opening page, and then clicking Civil War Battles takes the visitor to a list of manuscripts organized by battle. All combined, there are twelve online collections of letters and diaries that cover sixteen Eastern theater battles and campaigns and made available online.

Few sources can match the power of letters and diaries to convey the experience of the Civil War battle. Clayton G. Coleman, a lieutenant colonel in the 23rd Virginia Infantry, wrote to a friend after the Battle of Antietam, "Our brigade lost eight out of ten in the last fight, and my company lost 22 out of 23 men. . . . Every one of your acquaintances in the 4th Alabama and 11th Mississippi were either killed or wounded and indeed I reckon it is almost the case in every Regiment." A member of the 33rd Virginia Infantry, Derastus E. W. Myers, wrote about Chancellorsville, "I was in a thicket and there was not a twig as thick as a man's finger that was not struck with a ball."

This site also contains a letter from Sidney Marlin, who served in one of the Pennsylvania regiments that burned VMI buildings to the ground in June 1864. Marlin wrote his wife, "This is a nice place. There is about 6 thousand inhabitants and the buildings are good. There was a military school here but we have burnt all the buildings. It was a pitty to do it but I suppose it could not be helpt."

VMI's close connection with the Civil War and its extensive archival material have allowed it to make a significant contribution to the World Wide Web.

CONTENT   ★ ★ ★ ★
AESTHETICS   ★ ★ ★
NAVIGATION   ★ ★ ★ ★

NORTH CAROLINA

Bentonville Battleground

http://www.ah.dcr.state.nc.us/sections/hs/bentonvi/bentonvi.htm

Created by the North Carolina Division of Archives and History, this site provides a highly informative account of the last major Confederate offensive. As the Battle Synopsis section explains, the battle occurred after Confederate General Joseph E. Johnston quickly assembled units from scattered Confederate armies in an attempt to halt the advance of General Sherman's Union army through North Carolina. After several minor engagements, the mass of the Confederate and Union troops met near the town of Bentonville on March 19, 1865. Rebel troops retreated after three days of fighting, and Johnston accepted Sherman's surrender terms less than four weeks later. The site's excellent account of this little-studied battle is accompanied by maps, orders of battle, and lists of units engaged on both sides.

The navigation and appearance of this site are generally strong. The links found under The Battle in the left frame provide the best way to move about. (The JavaScript tour suggested for first-time visitors is confusing and should be ignored.) Although most of the illustrations are good, the maps have not been scanned at a resolution high enough to make them entirely readable.

CONTENT	★ ★ ★ ★
AESTHETICS	★ ★ ★
NAVIGATION	★ ★ ★

PENINSULAR CAMPAIGN

See Richmond

PETERSBURG

Petersburg National Battlefield

http://www.nps.gov/pete/mahan/PNBhome.html

This National Park Service site rewards patient visitors with a wealth of material about the crucial events that took place around Petersburg, Virginia, during the Civil War. Designed primarily with the needs of teachers and students in mind, the site is also extremely valuable to lifelong learners of all ages.

Most of the valuable content lies behind the "Education" link on the site's home page. Visitors can read biographical sketches of dozens of historic figures including Ambrose Burnside, Clara Barton, and Richard Eppes. Eppes, a physician and planter who owned over a hundred slaves at the outset of the war, saw all but twelve of them leave for Union lines in 1862. Two years later, his City Point home was turned into General Ulysses S. Grant's headquarters.

Clicking "History" from the main education page invites the visitor to explore subjects ranging from African Americans to Battles to the U.S. Military Railroad. The discussion of African Americans contains a lengthy description of the role played by U.S. Colored Troops regiments in the siege and discusses how members of Petersburg's free black community worked as laborers for the Confederate Army. The Battles section take the visitor through a chronological narrative of the major events of 1864 and 1865. The narrative is illustrated by excellent computer-generated maps.

Entire sections devoted to teachers and students support the Park Service's educational mission. Teachers can choose from pre- and post-visit lessons about slavery, prisoners of war, and military strategy. The kids' pages include an illustrated dictionary of terms such as *carbine*, *hardtack*, and *primer*. This section also invites students to complete a series of activities that will allow them to qualify as a "junior ranger." In one, students are instructed to outfit a soldier for service using the items described in the illustrated dictionary.

Civil War enthusiasts of all ages will enjoy the Siege Challenge. Visitors are encouraged to test their "Siege IQ" by taking a series of tests. The "Cavalry" level questions, such as "How many patients could the Depot Field Hospital hold?" can be answered using material found on the Petersburg National Battlefield web site. Answering the "Artillery" questions requires exploring additional National Park Service web sites. Finally, the "Infantry" level involves writing a one- to two-page essay on topics such as "Did the Siege of Petersburg insure the demise of Gen. Lee's army or did it keep the army alive longer than it could have hoped for otherwise? Or both?"

Although the site suffers somewhat in its navigation and appearance, the sheer wealth of excellent content and its integration of social and military history make it an outstanding example of a battlefield site and serves as a testament to the creativity, hard work, and enthusiasm of Park Service historians and interpreters.

CONTENT	★ ★ ★ ★
AESTHETICS	★ ★ ★
NAVIGATION	★ ★ ★

The Siege of Petersburg
http://members.aol.com/siege1864/

FIGURE 1.7
The crater

This site, produced by Jim Epperson, the organizer of Civil War newsgroups and web rings, will be appreciated by users seeking a greater level of detail about the Siege of Petersburg than that provided on the Park Service site.

One of the most valuable sections can be accessed by clicking Chronology of the Siege on the opening page. It presents day-by-day details of the entire ten-month campaign, beginning with the arrival of ten thousand Union men under General W. F. "Baldy" Smith to the Petersburg fortifications on June 15, 1864, and ending on April 2, 1865, the day that Union forces penetrated three separate Confederate lines guarding the city, forcing General Lee to order the evacuation of both Petersburg and Richmond. Another section, Brief Accounts of Each Action in the Siege, contains illustrated descriptions of specific events, such as the fighting around the crater, First and Second Hatcher's Run, and the Beefsteak Raid. The site includes maps of the Petersburg and the Deep Bottom areas, which Epperson has traced from various authoritative sources.

The design of this site is very simple, and the navigation is straightforward, with menu items clearly indicating the nature of the linked material. The Siege of Petersburg is a valuable site for researchers seeking details about the military aspects of these crucial events in the Civil War.

CONTENT   ★ ★ ★ ★
AESTHETICS   ★ ★ ★ ★
NAVIGATION   ★ ★ ★ ★ ★

RICHMOND

Appomattox Courthouse National Historic Park
http://www.nps.gov/apco/

This National Park Service site provides basic information on Lee's surrender to Grant and on the events leading up to it. The Appomattox Campaign section contains a description of the Confederate army's retreat from Petersburg and Richmond in search of rations, supplies, and reinforcements. Northern forces confounded Lee's plans, first by cutting off his initial route at the Battle of Sailors Creek and then by beating the Confederate troops to the town of Appomattox. On April 9, 1865, Lee accepted Grant's surrender terms, disbanding the Army of Northern Virginia. The site provides a description of Lee and Grant's meeting in the McLean house as well as an interesting explanation of how the more than twenty-eight thousand parole forms were printed, signed, and distributed to the defeated Confederate army. For the most part, the historic material on this site consists of secondary accounts, with few documents. This site provides a good introduction to the important events at that took place at Appomattox.

CONTENT   ★ ★ ★ ★
AESTHETICS ★ ★ ★
NAVIGATION ★ ★ ★

Richmond National Battlefield Park Homepage
http://www.nps.gov/rich/home.htm

The Richmond National Battlefield home page focuses on military events around Richmond, Virginia, during the Civil War. Only sixty miles from Washington, Richmond seemed to be an easily attainable goal for the Union army, but successive campaigns against it failed. In the spring of 1862, General George B. McClellan launched the ill-fated Peninsular campaign to take Richmond, only to be stopped seven miles outside of the city. It took more than two years of bloody fighting for Union troops to make significant advances toward the city, which was evacuated in 1865 after a ten-month siege of Petersburg left Richmond defenseless.

This site discusses the Peninsular campaign in two sections. Embattled Capital provides an overview of Richmond during the entire Civil War and briefly sketches the main facts of the campaign. A separate page on Drewry's Bluff explains how Confederate gunfire stopped the Union naval advance up the James River just miles from Richmond.

Most of the material on the site covers battles around Richmond that took place in 1864 and 1865. A day-by-day account of the Battle of Cold Harbor includes a description of Union forces pinned down by Confederate gunfire on the fourth day of fighting who desperately dug protective trenches with bayonets, cups, and plates. The costly Union defeat at Cold Harbor led Grant to abandon attempts to attack Richmond directly and to opt for taking Petersburg instead. The site also discusses the Battle of Chaffin's Farm, or New Market Heights, and has a large, separate section on the role of the U.S. Colored Troops there. This section has a completely different design from the rest of the Richmond National Battlefield site and is the only part that contains any primary documents.

The site was not designed with the needs of researchers in mind. Rather, its purpose is to inform visitors about historically significant locations in the Richmond area. As a result, the historic content is not highlighted and can be difficult to find. Researchers seeking a basic understanding of some of the events around Richmond during the Civil War will nevertheless be rewarded by the good material here.

CONTENT ★ ★ ★ ★
AESTHETICS ★ ★ ★
NAVIGATION ★ ★ ★

SPOTSYLVANIA

See Fredericksburg

VICKSBURG

See Western Theater

WESTERN THEATER

Corinth: Crossroads of the Confederacy

http://www.corinth.org/

The Siege and Battle of Corinth Commission developed this site to educate the public and to encourage tourism in the Corinth, Mississippi, area. The best content can be found in the section titled Background, which is a series of pages that summarize the events leading up to the Union occupation of Corinth in April 1862 and describe the battle that took place when Rebel forces attacked that fall. The narration includes an explanation of the strategic importance of

Corinth and of Union General Henry Halleck's leadership. It also does a nice job of placing the battle in the context of events taking place in other theaters of the war. The walking and driving tours described on the site contain photographs of locations that were significant in the siege and battle.

Navigation within the Background section takes place through a series of forward buttons at the top and bottom of each page. Although there is a site map, it is generated by a Java applet that can take up to thirty seconds to be executed on a home computer. The slide show also relies on Java and is cumbersome to view on anything less than a very high-end computer. Nevertheless, the Corinth web site makes an important contribution to the online study of the Civil War. There are few sites devoted to the Western theater, and the material found here helps the researcher begin to gain an understanding of events in this important region.

CONTENT   ★ ★ ★ ★
AESTHETICS   ★ ★ ★ ★
NAVIGATION   ★ ★ ★

Vicksburg National Military Park

http://www.nps.gov/vick/home.htm

This is among the best of the National Park Service Civil War web sites. Clicking the Battle for Vicksburg hypertext link on the home page accesses a timeline of the entire campaign with links to informative, illustrated descriptions of the events and their significance. Links at the bottom of each description reveal large color maps showing the location of the events described.

Genealogists and other researchers will particularly appreciate the database of thousands of parole records given by the Union army to captured Confederate soldiers after the Vicksburg surrender. To search for a particular individual, a visitor can click the first letter of the soldier's last name to be taken to a file containing all the records for that letter in alphabetical order. Each record gives the full name, rank, and unit of the individual. (Visitors should avoid searching the database using the Park Service search engine because doing so will search not only the Vicksburg parole records but also every web page on the entire National Park Service server.)

The site also includes an interesting presentation about the USS *Cairo*, an ironclad warship sunk by a Confederate mine during the siege and restored a hundred years later. Finally, tailor-made educational packets on the siege are provided for different school subjects and subject levels. This is an outstanding example of a battlefield web site. The navigation is straightforward, the pages well designed, and the content extensive.

CONTENT ★ ★ ★ ★ ★
AESTHETICS ★ ★ ★ ★
NAVIGATION ★ ★ ★ ★

Wilson's Creek National Battlefield

http://www.nps.gov/wicr

This National Park Service site provides a description of the Battle of Wilson's Creek as well an interesting account of Missouri during the Civil War. After Missouri's governor and state legislators expressed their secessionist leanings in the spring of 1861, Captain Nathaniel Lyon, the commander of the U.S. arsenal in St. Louis, secretly moved the weapons stored there to a secret location, raised a pro-Union regiment, and took control of the state capital. The Battle of Wilson's Creek, fought on August 1, 1861, was a clash between Lyon's regiment and units raised by Missouri's exiled pro-Confederate governor. Lyon was killed while leading a charge during this five-hour battle, and federal forces eventually retreated. Although the battle was a Southern victory, Missouri remained in the Union and largely under federal control, despite the fierce guerrilla warfare waged by groups on both sides.

The Wilson's Creek National Battlefield web site contains only one page with historic content, with the rest of the site providing information for people planning physical trips to the battlefield. Despite its limitations, this site provides a good starting point for researchers unfamiliar with this battle or with Missouri during the Civil War.

CONTENT ★ ★ ★
AESTHETICS ★ ★ ★ ★
NAVIGATION ★ ★ ★ ★

WILDERNESS

See also Fredericksburg

The Battle of the Wilderness: A Virtual Tour

http://home.att.net/~hallowed-ground/wilderness_tour.html

Site designers and Civil War enthusiasts Jim Schmidt and Curtis Fears tell the story of the Battle of the Wilderness by way of a virtual tour. The tour begins with photographs of modern-day Germanna and Ely's Fords. Accompanying text explains how units under Generals Ulysees S. Grant and Winfield Hancock crossed the Rapidan River at these places in May 4, 1864. The tour continues with Saunders' Field, Widow Tapp Farm, the Brock Road–Orange Plank Road

Intersection, Ellwood/Grant's Knoll, and the Massaponax Church. Each stop on the tour contains at least several paragraphs of explanatory text and a small collection of photographs.

This site is recommended for researchers seeking a sense of the landscape in which the Battle of the Wilderness was fought. It would aid in preparation for a physical visit to the area. For an explanation of the main events of the battle, the best place would be the Fredericksburg and Spotsylvania National Military Park Visitors Center site reviewed above.

CONTENT   ★ ★ ★
AESTHETICS ★ ★ ★ ★
NAVIGATION ★ ★ ★ ★ ★

SUGGESTED READINGS

Catton, Bruce. *The Centennial History of the Civil War.* 3 vols. Garden City, NY, 1961–65.

———. *The Army of the Potomac.* 3 vols. New York, 1951–53.

Coddington, Edwin B. *The Gettysburg Campaign: A Study in Command.* New York, 1984.

Cozzens, Peter. *The Shipwreck of Their Hopes: The Battles for Chattanooga.* Urbana, IL, 1994.

Davis, William C. *The Imperiled Union: 1861–1865.* 2 vols. Garden City, NY, 1982–83.

Foote, Shelby. *The Civil War: A Narrative.* 3 vols. New York, 1958–74.

Gallagher, Gary. *The Fredericksburg Campaign: Decision on the Rappahannock.* Chapel Hill, NC, 1995.

———. *The Confederate War: How Popular Will, Nationalism, and Military Strategy Could Not Stave Off Defeat.* Cambridge, MA, 1997.

———. *The Wilderness Campaign.* Chapel Hill, NC, 1997.

Gallagher, Gary, ed. *The Third Day at Gettysburg and Beyond.* Chapel Hill, NC, 1994.

———. *Chancellorsville: The Battle and Its Aftermath.* Chapel Hill, NC, 1996.

———. *The Spotsylvania Campaign.* Chapel Hill, NC, 1998.

———. *The Antietam Campaign.* Chapel Hill, NC, 1999.

Hennessy, John. *Return to Bull Run: The Campaign and Battle of Second Manassas.* New York, 1993.

Josephy, Alvin M., Jr. *The Civil War in the American West.* New York, 1991.

McPherson, James M. *Battle Cry of Freedom: The Civil War Era.* New York, 1988.

Rhea, Gordon H. *The Battle of the Wilderness, May 5–6, 1864.* Baton Rouge, LA, 1994.

CHAPTER 2

POLITICAL AND MILITARY LEADERS

It might surprise even Civil War readers to know that generals suffered the highest combat casualties. They were 50 percent more likely to be killed in action than privates were. The list of fallen generals in the Civil War is long: Garnett, Armistead, Stuart, Jackson, Reynolds, and Kearny, to name a few. Historians, artists, and writers have glorified these leaders, casting images of their deeds across generations. Among the engravings of Civil War action in *Frank Leslie's Illustrated* is that of Lewis A. Armistead leading the assault on the stone wall at Gettysburg with his hat held high on his sword. One of the most recognizable and reprinted paintings concerning the Civil War is E. B. D. Julio's *The Last Meeting of Lee and Jackson*. Both generals are on horseback at the edge of a wood, and Lee is gesturing to his right, presumably indicating his approval of Jackson's plan to attack the far right flank of the Union army at Chancellorsville. More recently, artists such as Mort Kunstler have continued to make the heroics of generals a main part of their work. Civil War history enthusiasts today can buy chess sets with Lee and Jackson as the Confederate king and bishop, respectively.

Historians agree that leadership—both political and military—played a decisive role in the outcome of the war. Many note the advantage that the Confederacy seemed to maintain in officer-level leadership, especially in the beginning of the war. The presence in the South of seven of the eight military colleges in the United States helps to explain the initial disparity. Just as important, the regular U.S. Army officers and their units were kept intact rather than interspersed with the new volunteers; Union forces, therefore, failed to benefit from their highly trained leadership.

Both North and South witnessed the appointment of "political generals." In the North the term became synonymous with incompetence and failure. Governors of the states, as well as Lincoln and Davis, were under considerable pressure to satisfy political debts and obligations. Lincoln wanted to ameliorate the Democrats and so assigned generalship to Benjamin F. Butler, Daniel E. Sickles, and John A. Logan, prominent Democrats all. He also appointed ethnic leaders, such as Carl Schurz, Franz Sigel, and Thomas Meagher. Davis also named "political generals" to gain the support of various state leaders.

Despite the appointment of political generals, graduates of West Point held the vast majority of high-level appointments, so much so that one historian has labeled the war "preeminently a West Pointers' fight." In perhaps one of the most widely read essays on Civil War leaders, historian T. Harry Williams argues in *Why the North Won the Civil War* that "it is the general who is the decisive factor in battle." He pointed out that in the sixty biggest battles in the war West Pointers commanded the armies of both sides in fifty-five of them. He also argued that the dominance of Jominian strategy of warfare, which is divorced from political considerations, hindered the growth of both Union and Confederate generals. In another essay in that slim but important book, historian David Potter suggests that "there is a great deal of evidence to justify placing a considerable share of the responsibility for the Confederacy's misfortunes directly at the door of Jefferson Davis."

Leadership questions litter Civil War histories. They are at the center of many interpretations of strategic battles and turning points. Was Union general George McClellan afraid to commit his troops to battle and too slow to move, hence losing an opportunity in the Seven Days battles to win the war by capturing Richmond? Did Confederate Corps commander James Longstreet delay on the second day of Gettysburg and thereby lose the battle for the Confederates? What explains General Thomas J. "Stonewall" Jackson's slowness at the Seven Days battles? Was Union general Joseph Hooker drunk at Chancellorsville or hit in the head with a shell? Did Union general Gouverneur K. Warren act in an unprofessional manner at Five Forks?

Many military leaders of the Civil War would probably find the cutthroat criticisms of their decisions by today's scholars and enthusiasts disturbingly familiar. Even at the time, they were at the center of political recriminations, courts-martial, and public scrutiny from the newspapers. McClellan's officer corps, for example, was entrenched in political considerations, so much so that when General Ambrose Burnside succeeded McClellan a half dozen generals schemed to limit his influence in command. Internal dissension over the leadership of Confederate general Braxton Bragg nearly led to a formal duel between him and another general in the Confederate army of Tennessee after the battle of Stones River. Bragg court-martialed one of his generals for insubordination and threatened to do the same to the others.

Court-martial brought down more than a few Civil War generals. Defendants' peers reviewed their decisions and conduct in battle, either absolving or condemning them. General Stonewall Jackson had one of his division commanders, General A. P. Hill, arrested for failing to follow orders that gave the start time for his division to march on the morning of September 4, 1862. Hill fought the Maryland campaign at the head of his division under a cloud of potential court-martial and formally under arrest. Lee patiently resolved the conflict between the two generals. Union general Gouverneur K. Warren was not so fortunate. A hero at Gettysburg, he was court-martialed by General Philip Sheridan for failure to move on orders at the battle of Five Forks. Warren maintained that he had followed orders, that his maps were wrong, and that his corps behaved honorably. He was found guilty as charged and his reputation ruined. Finally, in 1885 Warren succeeded in having the verdict overturned by a court of inquiry.

Congressional committees and newspaper editors also took shots at military leaders, evaluating their performance not on the basis of military justice but instead on the basis of public opinion. The Joint Committee on the Conduct of the War investigated Union generals' losses and inefficiency and corruption in the army. Although no counterpart for the Joint Committee developed in the Confederate Congress, various members of the Confederate Congress led an opposition effort against Jefferson Davis, often conducting their investigations through the newspapers. Newspaper editors lambasted generals for any perceived incompetence. Few generals received such bad press as did Robert E. Lee when he took command of the Army of Northern Virginia. The Richmond *Examiner* derided him as "Evacuating Lee" for his poor performance in western Virginia in 1861.

The intense partisanship, courts-martial, infighting, and recriminations all reveal the complexities of an internecine war. It is no wonder then that business leaders today seek lessons from the leadership of Civil War generals and politicians, buying books about Lincoln and Lee with subtitles such as "Executive Strategies for Tough Times" and "Battlefield to Boardroom."

The World Wide Web offers sites on Civil War leaders that will please both business leaders looking for clues to successful strategies of management and serious scholars searching for the sequence of key decisions by Civil War generals. Some of the most comprehensive come from university libraries that hold the papers of these leaders, but others are freewheeling forums on the command decisions of the war.

W EB SITE REVIEWS

GENERAL SITES

Shotgun's Home of the American Civil War

http://www.civilwarhome.com

Evidently the work of one energetic individual, Shotgun's Home of the American
Civil War is the largest single source of Civil War biographical material on the
web. The Civil War Biographies section contains biographical sketches of more
than seventy military and political leaders, from U.S. Major Robert Anderson
to C.S.A. Brigadier General Felix Kirk Zollicoffer. Most of the biographies
consist of summaries of secondary accounts, and some contain portraits and full-
text excerpts of public domain sources. The site features little historical analysis, few images, and almost no primary source documents. But it is an excellent
starting point for the study of Civil War leaders.

CONTENT   ★ ★ ★ ★
AESTHETICS   ★ ★ ★
NAVIGATION   ★ ★ ★ ★

The *War Times Journal* Civil War Series: Longstreet, Sherman, Hood, and Gordon

http://www.wtj.com/wars/civilwar/

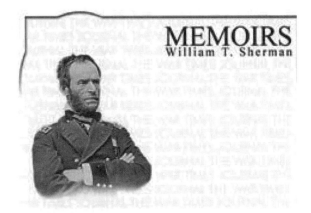

FIGURE 2.1

Cover image from the *War Times Journal* Civil War series

The *War Times Journal* Civil War Series contains lengthy excerpts from the public domain memoirs of four important Civil War generals: James Longstreet, William Tecumseh Sherman, John B. Hood, and John B. Gordon. The *War Times Journal* is a professionally made, commercial site about military history and science.

The selections from Confederate general James Longstreet's 1912 memoirs *From Manassas to Appomattox* cover Longstreet's Civil War and post–Civil War career. In the three chapters devoted to the Battle of Gettysburg, Longstreet presents a highly detailed defense of his actions there in an attempt to silence postwar critics who blamed him for the Confederate defeat. The final chapter chronicles Longstreet's postwar career as the Republican-appointed surveyor of customs in New Orleans and describes the opprobrium brought down on him for suggesting that white Southerners cooperate with the federal government during Reconstruction.

The excerpts from General William Tecumseh Sherman's *Memoirs* cover the events of the spring and summer of 1862—the Battle of Shiloh and the Union capture of Memphis. The site also contains two chapters from Confederate lieutenant general John B. Hood's *Advance and Retreat*, published in 1880. The excerpts discuss Hood's experience at Gainesville, Antietam, Fredericksburg, Gettysburg, and Chickamauga. Included in the selections from Confederate general John B. Gordon's *Reminisces of the Civil War: From Manassas to Gettysburg* is Gordon's version of the Battle of Gettysburg, which differs sharply from Longstreet's.

The memoirs may prove daunting to a researcher unfamiliar with the battles discussed and with the careers of the four generals. But they are essential for anyone seeking a full understanding of the careers of Longstreet, Sherman, Hood, and Gordon. This is a simple site in that the transcripts cannot be searched and there are few images, but the layout is clean and the navigation intuitive.

CONTENT   ★ ★ ★
AESTHETICS ★ ★ ★ ★
NAVIGATION ★ ★ ★ ★

DAVIS, JEFFERSON

The Papers of Jefferson Davis
http://www.ruf.rice.edu/~pjdavis/jdp.htm

This site offers selections from the multivolume series of Jefferson Davis's collected papers edited at Rice University. The documents cover the period from 1834 to 1863 and include Davis's speeches and letters as well as letters to Davis from the Civil War home front and battlefield.

The documents provide a vivid sense of the many pressures facing Davis as president of the Confederacy. In 1862, a woman wrote to him and demanded that her husband be released from military service. The forty slaves on the plantation she was left to manage alone could not be controlled with her husband gone: "Your Excellency is doubtless in constant attention to the ponderous business of the Government . . . yet I hope your Excellency will find time enough amidst all this, to give me a hearing and grant me the relief sought for." Davis was powerless to protect his own family's plantations as Union forces took command of the Mississippi River. He advised his brother to flee with his slaves and cotton before federal forces descended on the area. The papers also include Davis's addresses to the Confederate Congress, letters to his wife Varina, and a dispatch to Davis from General Robert E. Lee. The documents have been transcribed in full, and, although they cannot be searched, they are accompanied by helpful explanatory notes and listed in chronological order.

Other sections on the site discuss Davis's life before, during, and after the Civil War. The Jefferson Davis Chronology page provides a detailed timeline of his life, with important names and terms linked to other web pages. Because some of the linked pages are from outside sites of inconsistent quality and relevance, this feature is ultimately confusing. The FAQ page discusses the confusion over Davis's year of birth, his middle name, and the charges of treason brought against him after the war. The pages are illustrated by portraits of Davis in various stages in his life.

CONTENT   ★ ★ ★ ★ ★
AESTHETICS   ★ ★ ★
NAVIGATION   ★ ★ ★

GRANT,   ULYSSES   S.

The Ulysses S. Grant Association
http://www.lib.siu.edu/projects/usgrant

The Ulysses S. Grant Association has assembled Grant's correspondence, military papers, and government documents and published them in the multivolume series *The Papers of Ulysses S. Grant*. The association's web site contains a small selection of these documents as well as additional historic material about Grant's life.

The section titled Historical Information on U. S. Grant features a link to Grant's memoirs. The memoirs are not searchable, but a helpful table of contents helps visitors find where they need to go. They open with a discussion of Grant's ancestry and conclude with a description of the grand review of the victorious Union armies in Washington in May 1865. Written in Grant's distinctive, unadorned prose, the memoirs are a compelling summary of many of the important events of the Civil War. The Historical Information section also contains the reminiscences of James Crane, a military chaplain who became close to the general during the war. Crane depicted his friend as intensely religious and took pains to refute charges that Grant was a heavy drinker.

Other material includes a lengthy chronology of the general's life, a short essay on Grant by Civil War historian Bruce Catton, the poem written by Walt Whitman about Grant's death, and Julia Grant's description of their courtship, which was originally published in an 1890 *Ladies Home Journal*.

CONTENT ★ ★ ★ ★ ★
NAVIGATION ★ ★ ★
APPEARANCE: ★ ★ ★

JACKSON, THOMAS J. "STONEWALL"

Stonewall Jackson Resources at the Virginia Military Institute Archives

http://www.vmi.edu/~archtml/jackson.html

FIGURE 2.2

Cadets at Stonewall Jackson's grave, c. 1868

With extensive selections of documents about the life of Thomas "Stonewall" Jackson from the Virginia Military Institute (VMI) Archives, this site is an excellent resource for researchers at all levels.

Web visitors unfamiliar with Jackson's life may want to start by clicking Biographical Information. This link accesses a detailed timeline that starts with his birth in Clarksburg, West Virginia, and ends with his death from wounds sustained at the Battle of Chancellorsville. Certain events and individuals in the timeline are linked to pertinent document transcriptions. The Frequently Asked Questions page provides information as varied as how he got his nickname and where his amputated arm is buried. As with the timeline, certain names and events are hyperlinked to relevant documents elsewhere in the archives. The page titled Major Jackson, Professor at VMI, chronicles Jackson's controversial teaching career at the military institute. Jackson proved so unpopular with his students that in 1856 the Alumni Council petitioned for his dismissal.

The section called Stonewall Jackson Papers consists of transcriptions of several dozen letters Jackson wrote before and during the Civil War. Many were written to his sister while he was attending the U.S. Military Academy, fighting in the Mexican-American War, and beginning his teaching career at VMI. The Civil War era letters attest to Jackson's strong Christian faith. Jackson wrote to a friend who had earlier congratulated him on a recent victory, "Without God's blessing I look for no success, and for every success my prayer is that all the glory may be given unto Him to whom it is properly due."

This is an extremely rich site that merits lengthy exploration. The pages are simply designed, and the navigation is intuitive without being flashy.

CONTENT   ★ ★ ★ ★
AESTHETICS   ★ ★ ★
NAVIGATION   ★ ★ ★ ★

LEE, ROBERT E.

The Robert E. Lee Papers at Washington and Lee University

http://miley.uc.wlu.edu/LeePapers/

This site contains images of forty-six letters written by Robert E. Lee before, during, and after the Civil War. The documents include letters written to Jefferson Davis, George B. McClellan, Jubal Early, Ulysses S. Grant, and the

Washington College Board of Trustees, as well as General Orders No. 9, in which Lee said goodbye to his army at Appomattox: "After four years of arduous service marked by unsurpassed courage and fortitude, the Army of Northern Virginia has been compelled to yield to overwhelming numbers and resources."

As with a real archive, the documents have not been transcribed, there are no summaries of their contents, and there is no information to provide background or context. As a result, the site is not particularly easy to use. But as the largest online source of material penned by Lee, it will prove valuable to serious researchers.

CONTENT   ★ ★ ★ ★
AESTHETICS   ★ ★ ★ ★
NAVIGATION   ★ ★ ★ ★

LINCOLN, ABRAHAM

Abraham Lincoln Online

http://www.netins.net/showcase/creative/lincoln.html

This site contains a variety of material on the man who was president of the United States during the Civil War. The section called Lincoln This Week lists three or four events that occurred during particular weeks from various periods in Lincoln's life. Most of value to researchers is the section titled Speeches/Writings. Each of the several dozen documents in this section opens with an introduction that provides useful background information. The documents are generally well-known, such as the Gettysburg Address, Lincoln's First and Second Inaugural Addresses, and his letter to *New York Tribune* editor Horace Greeley about emancipation, wherein he wrote, "if I could save the Union without freeing any slave I would do it, and if I could save it by freeing all the slaves I would do it; and if I could save it by freeing some and leaving others alone I would also do that." Within months of this letter, of course, Lincoln issued the preliminary Emancipation Proclamation and fundamentally transformed the nature of the war.

A volunteer effort of a group of Lincoln enthusiasts, the site also contains an exhaustive bibliography, links to other sites, and the Lincoln Mailbag, to which visitors contribute their thoughts about Lincoln.

CONTENT   ★ ★ ★
AESTHETICS   ★ ★ ★
NAVIGATION   ★ ★ ★ ★

Abraham Lincoln Research Site

http://members.aol.com/RVSNorton/Lincoln2.html

FIGURE 2.3
Portrait of Abraham Lincoln

Created by a former teacher of U.S. history, the Abraham Lincoln Research Site is a rich source of interesting material. It is designed primarily for students, but it is of value to adult learners as well.

The Especially for Students page provides a thorough overview of Lincoln's life, with important names and terms linked to outside web sites such as Grolier's Encyclopedia. Photographs of Lincoln in various stages of his life accompany the text. Visitors seeking a more detailed account of Lincoln's life can visit the Chronology page, which is similarly illustrated and hyperlinked. The site also contains separate sections on Mary Todd Lincoln and Lincoln's assassination, both of which are complete enough to stand alone as their own sites. The section called The Lincoln Special provides a fascinating account of the journey of Lincoln's funeral train from Washington to Springfield, Illinois. On its fourteen-day route, the train stopped at ten cities where Lincoln's open coffin was placed for public viewing. Thousands of people lined the railroad tracks to watch the train pass while it traveled between cities.

The bulk the material concerns Lincoln's personal life. The site features a page about Ann Rutledge, who is billed as his first romance, a page about each of his sons, and a page about his wedding day. The site contains little about Lincoln's presidency or the Civil War.

CONTENT   ★ ★ ★
AESTHETICS   ★ ★
NAVIGATION   ★ ★ ★

Lincoln/Net: The Abraham Lincoln Digitization Project
http://lincoln.lib.niu.edu/

FIGURE 2.4
Lincoln, the rail splitter

Based at the University of Northern Illinois and directed by historian Drew Van-deCreek, the Abraham Lincoln Digitization Project makes transcribed, searchable documents related to Lincoln's life in Illinois available to the public on the World Wide Web. When completed, Lincoln/Net will be the most complete source of online archival material about Abraham Lincoln.

Currently, the site consists of a collection of sixty-nine campaign songs from Lincoln's 1860 and 1864 presidential campaigns. The collection can be searched by a variety of variables, such as title, lyricist, composer, arranger, or a word or phrase in the lyrics. Searching for "rail splitter" in the lyrics yielded three matches, including one titled "Western Star": "Mechanics and farmers / Hail the glad day, / When Free Labor gives them / Good price and pay. / Brightly the Western Star / O'er us appears— / LINCOLN, the 'Rail-Splitter!' / Give him three cheers."

The songs can also be accessed through a browsable list. A transcription of the lyrics and a scan of the page from the original sheet music are available for each song. Seven of the songs can be heard with a free plug-in.

Lincoln/Net provides visitors with a excellent sense of Lincoln's Illinois background as well as the political culture of the mid-nineteenth century.

CONTENT   ★ ★ ★ ★ ★
AESTHETICS   ★ ★ ★ ★ ★
NAVIGATION   ★ ★ ★ ★

LONGSTREET, JAMES

The Longstreet Chronicles
http://tennessee-scv.org/longstreet/

After the Civil War, General James Longstreet, who fought beside Lee throughout the Civil War, fell out of favor with many of his former fellow officers. These men, whose accounts formed the basis of early interpretations of the Civil War, blamed Longstreet for the Confederate defeat at Gettysburg. The Longstreet Chronicles site represents an attempt to rehabilitate Longstreet's reputation.

The section titled The Controversy contains essays by Brian Hampton, the site's author, that attribute the accusations against Longstreet to the need for a scapegoat to blame for the South's defeat. Longstreet, who became a Republican after the war and who urged his fellow Southerners to accept negro suffrage as the law of the land, was an easy target. Longstreet's public criticism of Lee's tactics at certain battles further fanned the flames of the anti-Longstreet clique. Hampton's essay also describes the formation and influence of the "Lee cult," which elevated Robert E. Lee to godlike status and cast Longstreet as the villain.

The Life and Career section contains a mixture of more than a hundred public domain primary and secondary accounts of various aspects of Longstreet's military record. Taken together, these accounts provide a rigorous defense of his career. The site also features an annotated bibliography of eleven books that address Longstreet's record.

CONTENT   ★ ★ ★ ★
AESTHETIC   ★ ★ ★
NAVIGATION   ★ ★ ★ ★

MCCLELLAN, GEORGE B.

The McClellan Society's MG George B. McClellan Pages
http://www.civilwarreader.com/McClellan/index.html

The work of avid McClellan partisans, this site seeks to rehabilitate the reputation of this controversial general. The list of McClellan "firsts" credits the general with creating the first wartime U.S. intelligence bureau and with leading the largest seaborne movement of troops prior to World War II. Instead of a Frequently Asked Questions page, the site features Frequently Asserted Claims in a section called Controversy, which offers rebuttals to much of the conventional wisdom about McClellan. Refuting the claim that McClellan failed to capitalize on the discovery of Lee's Special Order No. 191, for example, the site provides evidence that McClellan ordered the movement of federal troops toward Lee's destination within hours of receiving Lee's lost orders.

The site also contains numerous reviews of books about McClellan and an interesting interview with McClellan scholar Thomas J. Rowland. Rowland attributes the near-universal negative assessment of McClellan to the need for an explanation for why the Union, with its superior resources, failed to achieve a quick victory over the Confederacy. This is an interesting, if narrow, site.

CONTENT   ★ ★ ★ ★
AESTHETICS   ★ ★ ★
NAVIGATION   ★ ★ ★ ★

MEADE, GEORGE GORDON

The Meade Archive

http://adams.patriot.net/~jcampi/welcome.htm

FIGURE 2.5

Meade at Gettysburg, painted by Daniel R. Knight

The reputation of Union general George Gordon Meade suffered permanent damage as a result of criticism of his inaction after the Union victory at Gettysburg. The Meade Society created the Meade Archive to defend him against these charges. The archive consists of essays and public domain primary documents.

The site presents the charges against Meade in the His Critics section, which includes anonymous critical letters published in the *New York Herald* and *New York Times* and the testimony of Major General Daniel Sickles to Congress's Joint Committee on the Conduct of the War:

QUESTION. In your opinion, as a military man, what do you think of the propriety of again encountering the enemy at the river before he recrossed [after the Battle the Gettysburg]?
ANSWER. He should have been followed up closely, and vigorously attacked before he had an opportunity to recross the river.
QUESTION. Under the circumstances, as you understand them, could there have been any great hazard to our army in venturing an engagement there?
ANSWER. No, sir. If we could whip them at Gettysburg, as we did, we could much more easily whip a running and demoralized army, seeking a retreat which was cut off by a swollen river; and if they could march after being whipped, we certainly could march after winning a battle.

The defense of Meade is set forth in excerpts from a complimentary previously published biography, numerous contemporary and firsthand accounts of Meade's career, and his own letters and addresses. In his testimony to the Joint Committee on the Conduct of the War, Meade maintained that the Confederate army was not as weakened as Sickles had claimed:

QUESTION. Did you discover, after the battle of Gettysburg, any symptoms of demoralization in Lee's army, such as excessive straggling, or anything of the kind?
ANSWER. No, sir; I saw nothing of that kind. . . .

The site is illustrated with portraits of Meade and his critics as well as photographs of the Gettysburg Battlefield.

CONTENT   ★ ★ ★
APPEARANCE   ★ ★ ★ ★
NAVIGATION   ★ ★ ★

SUGGESTED READINGS

Catton, Bruce. *Grant Moves South*. Boston, 1960.

———. *Grant Takes Command*. Boston, 1969.

Connelly, Thomas L. *The Marble Man: Robert E. Lee and His Image in American Society*. New York, 1977.

Connelly, Thomas L., and Archer Jones. *The Politics of Command: Factions and Ideas in Confederate Strategy*. Baton Rouge, LA, 1973.

Donald, David Herbert. *Lincoln*. London, 1995.

Freeman, Douglas Southall. *R. E. Lee: A Biography*. 4 vols. New York, 1934–35.

———. *Lee's Lieutenants: A Study in Command*. 3 vols. New York, 1942–44.

Jones, Archer. *The Politics of Command: A Military Study of the Civil War*. 5 vols. New York, 1949–59.

Marszalek, John F. *Sherman: A Soldier's Passion for Order*. New York, 1993.

Nolan, Alan. *Lee Considered: General Robert E. Lee and Civil War History*. Chapel Hill, NC, 1991.

Pitson, William G. *Lee's Tarnished Lieutenant: James Longstreet and His Place in Southern History*, Athens, GA, 1987.

Simpson, Brooks D. *Let Us Have Peace: Ulysses S. Grant and the Politics of War and Reconstruction*. Chapel Hill, NC, 1991.

Warner, Ezra J. *Generals in Gray*. Baton Rouge, LA, 1959.

Williams, Kenneth P. *Lincoln Finds a General: A Military Study of the Civil War*. 5 vols. New York, 1949–59.

Williams, T. Harry. *Lincoln and His Generals*. New York, 1952.

Woodworth, Steven. *Jefferson Davis and His Generals*. Lawrence, KS, 1990.

CHAPTER 3

LIFE OF THE SOLDIER

In the 1940s and 1950s, Bell Irvin Wiley pioneered the history of the common soldier with his books *The Life of Johnny Reb* and *The Life of Billy Yank*. He contended that if you threw the letters of the common soldiers from both sides in the air, you would not be able to tell the difference enough to separate them between North and South. His books examined camp life, training, music, punishment, hospital treatment, prison life, religion, homesickness, food, weapons, and other daily experiences of the soldiers.

Historians and others interested in the Civil War continue to find the world of the common soldier fascinating. Thousands of Americans participate in Civil War reenactments, painstakingly recreating the minutiae of the soldier's daily life. Some take the living history to extremes by using only authentic materials in camp, speaking in supposedly authentic tones and dialects, and mimicking the movements of their historical counterparts in every respect. The urge among Civil War enthusiasts to live the life of the common soldier seems almost as pervasive as the urge to second-guess the leading commanders.

The average Civil War soldier was twenty-five years old and volunteered for duty. He was most likely single, although 30 percent of his fellow soldiers were married. Approximately 78 percent of the men in the army served in the infantry, with 15 percent in the cavalry and 7 percent in the artillery. About 5 percent of the Union forces fought in the navy. On the Union side, 9 percent of the soldiers were African American, and about

33 percent of the Confederate soldiers' families owned slaves. Because so many sons of slave owners fought for the Confederacy, the war can hardly be labeled "a rich man's war and a poor man's fight." That saying was nevertheless commonplace at the time in both the North and South and suggests the internal divisions within both societies.

Disease presented a graver danger to common soldiers than did enemy bullets. Nearly two Civil War soldiers died of disease—most often diarrhea or dysentery, typhoid fever, pneumonia, or even malaria—for every one killed in action. For all the deaths by disease, Civil War soldiers were better off than their counterparts in earlier wars. This was hardly comforting news to soldiers who faced time in a Civil War hospital, however. Most believed that these institutions were places of failure from which few returned. Drunken doctors, dirty conditions, and rampant disease threatened to make a soldier's hospital stay short and terminal.

Common soldiers were imprisoned if captured and had to wait a long time in desperate conditions for possible exchange. Early in the war, field commanders sometimes agreed to an informal exchange or mutual parole of prisoners. Parole simply meant that the prisoner swore not to take up fighting again until he had been formally exchanged with a counterpart on the other side. The Confederacy's resources were strained, and it could barely feed its growing prisoner of war population. In 1862 both sides agreed to an exchange cartel in which most prisoners were exchanged smoothly. The practice was halted in 1863 because Northerners objected to Confederate threats to reenslave or execute black prisoners of war and because the Confederacy began treating parolees as if they had been fully exchanged. Andersonville Prison in Georgia became the North's symbol of the mistreatment of prisoners of war in the Confederacy. The prison was severely overcrowded, and more than a hundred men died there each day in 1864. Elmira Prison in New York was generally considered the worst Union prisoner of war camp, but its conditions did not compare in severity to Andersonville.

Soldiers who managed to avoid both disease and enemy capture faced the hardships of marching and battle. Casualties in the war were extremely high, especially for the Confederacy. In his book *The Confederate War*, historian Gary Gallagher shows that the Confederacy sustained a casualty rate of 37 to 38 percent of its men under arms, whereas the North's casualties amounted to 17 percent. Gallagher compares this rate with other American wars, such as World War II, where American forces experienced a lower casualty rate of 5.8 percent.

Many soldiers wrote letters or kept diaries. Their stories tell the full range of human emotion in war. One Union soldier's August 1862 letter from his post in Port Royal, South Carolina, to his relatives in Pennsylvania suggests the complexity of these documents:

We have only about six thousand men here, but I wish they would bring forty thousand and try to lick us. . . . You may do as you think proper with the money put in the bank or keep it yourself, change is getting scarce here too. At first you could see nothing but gold, now you get all one dollar bills. We get paid in United States Bank Notes. That was a fine turtle you was writing about, but it was not as large as the one the boys brought in about two weeks ago. It came out on land to lay—they were out on picket and five of them run their bayonets in to it and could hardly master it. It weighed two hundred and thirty five pounds. . . . Leave me know how recruiting takes in York. If they would know what I know, it would be a hard time to raise a company in York. I'm afraid the nigger question will raise a rumpus in the army yet. If I ever get back I'll shoot all the niggers I come across. Give my respects to all of my enquiring friends. No more at present. The boys are catching plenty of fish about here. We are making a large seine to drag. Write Soon.

This document and many others from the period raise difficult questions that can apply to both sides in the war. What were soldiers fighting for? How did soldiers view African Americans and Emancipation? What did soldiers think of these distant places they visited and how did they report these impressions to their family and friends at home? What effect did their letters have on recruiting and the morale of the home front? How did soldiers spend their time? How did national issues, such as fiscal and currency policies, filter down to the common soldier? Did these national policies affect the morale of the troops and the home front?

Web sites about the common soldier address many of these questions through the use of effective primary sources such as letters, diaries, and items of material culture. Researchers can find a wealth of firsthand accounts from the Civil War on the World Wide Web. Both universities and government agencies have led the way in the digital publication of soldiers' letters and diaries, but individuals and other nonprofit organizations have contributed sites examining camp life, hospitals, prisons, and other aspects of daily life in the army.

WEB SITE REVIEWS

CAMP LIFE

Camp Life: Civil War Collections from Gettysburg National Military Park

http://www.cr.nps.gov/csd/gettex/

FIGURE 3.1

Soldier's prayer book of Sylvester Carr, 143rd New York Volunteer Infantry

As the authors of this National Park Service site point out, a typical soldier's day was passed neither in battle nor on the march but in camps where troops lived for months at a time. Using artifacts on display at the Gettysburg National Battlefield Park, this site conveys a vivid sense of soldiers' day-to-day camp life.

The exhibit makes it apparent that men tried to make themselves as comfortable as possible under difficult conditions. Although officers had trunks to carry their possessions, enlisted men were limited to what they could carry on their backs. Their tents consisted of little more than tarps draped over poles. Men mended their own clothes using sewing kits known as "housewives" and attacked head lice with special combs.

The exhibit also features cards, dice, and dominoes that soldiers used to battle boredom. Wood and bone carvings, musical instruments, and sheet music are examples of more creative means of passing the time. Soldiers also spent hours reading and writing letters, several of which are on display here. Prayer books and bibles indicate that troops attended to their spiritual needs as well.

Although the site is beautifully designed, it is cumbersome to view on an 800 × 600-pixel or smaller monitor. Nonetheless, the beautiful digital images of soldiers' common possessions and the helpful explanatory text create a powerful sense of life in a Civil War camp.

CONTENT   ★ ★ ★ ★
AESTHETICS   ★ ★ ★
NAVIGATION   ★ ★ ★

ETHNIC GROUPS

Jews in the Civil War
http://www.jewish-history.com/civilwar.htm

This section of a large Jewish history and genealogy site contains interesting documents about the experience of Jewish soldiers in the American Civil War. Many of them are transcriptions of postwar articles contributed by Union veterans to *The Jewish Messenger*. In the 1867 article "Passover—A Reminiscence of the War," a former member of the 23rd Ohio Regiment recalled celebrating Passover while stationed in West Virginia. The Jewish sutler of his unit purchased matzo and prayer books from stores in Cincinnati. Cider, lamb, chickens, and eggs were obtained from the countryside, and in lieu of horseradish the men ate a bitter-tasting weed found in the woods. As the author recalled, the weed proved to be troublesome: "The herb was very bitter and very fiery like Cayenne pepper, and excited our thirst to such a degree, that we forgot the law authorizing us to drink only four cups, and the consequence was we drank up all the cider. Those that drank the more freely became excited, and one thought he was Moses, another Aaron, and one had the audacity to call himself Pharaoh." Despite the disruption, the ceremony proceeded according to custom. "There, in the wild woods of West Virginia, away from home and friends, we consecrated and offered up to the ever-loving G-d of Israel our prayers and sacrifice."

The site also contains an interesting collection of correspondence from official records on the campaign to allow rabbis to serve as Union military chaplains as well as material related to General Grant's order to expel all Jews from the Department of the Tennessee. Grant's order stated that "Jews, as a class violating every regulation of trade established by the Treasury Department and also department orders, are hereby expelled from the department within twenty-four hours from the receipt of this order." Protested vehemently by Jewish soldiers and civilians, the order was revoked by General Halleck within weeks.

Documents about Jews in the Confederacy include a prayer for victory written by a Richmond rabbi and distributed to Jewish troops, biographical sketches of prominent Jewish Civil War veterans, and previously published letters, memoirs, and diaries of Jewish soldiers, such as Louis Leon, of the 53rd North Carolina Infantry, who wrote of his participation in the Battle of Gettysburg. The Confederate collection also contains General Robert E. Lee's letter denying Richmond Rabbi M. J. Michelbacher's request that Jewish Confederate soldiers be granted furloughs for the holy days: "It would give me great pleasure to comply with a requests so earnestly urged by you, & which I know would be so highly appreciated by that class of our soldiers. But the necessities of war admit of no relaxation of the efforts requisite for its success, nor can it be known on what day the presence of every man may be required. I feel assured that neither you or any member of the Jewish congregation would wish to jeopardize a cause you have so much at heart by the withdrawal even for a season of a portion of its defenders."

One of the most impressive features of this site is the Jewish Civil War veterans database. A search using the name "Schwartz" led to the records for fourteen men from five different states. Four of these men were wounded in battle, and one died. All but one, who enlisted in the 17th Virginia Infantry, fought for the Union.

This rich collection of documents and searchable individual-level data sheds light not only on the experience of Jews in the American Civil War but on the life of Civil War soldiers in general. Interesting documentary content, intuitive navigation, and uncluttered (if utilitarian) design make this site valuable to a variety of researchers.

CONTENT   ★ ★ ★ ★
AESTHETICS   ★ ★ ★
NAVIGATION   ★ ★ ★ ★

HOSPITALS AND MEDICINE

Whitman's *Drum Taps* and Washington's Civil War Hospitals

http://xroads.virginia.edu/~CAP/hospital/whitman.htm

Several years after caring for wounded Civil War soldiers in Washington, DC, the poet Walt Whitman published a collection of poems titled *Drum Taps*. To explore the impact of Whitman's Civil War experience on his work, a student at the University of Virginia has created an interesting online account of Washington's Civil War hospitals.

Soldiers hospitalized in the first months of the war found themselves in makeshift structures set up by their regiments that consisted of little more than tents with bare floors. These impromptu arrangements soon proved inadequate, and the military converted sections of the Patent Office, the Capitol, and other buildings into hospitals for wounded soldiers. New hospital buildings were constructed as well, under the direction of the U.S. Sanitary Commission.

As the site explains, poor security, sanitation, and nutrition rendered a soldier's hospital stay harrowing. Little could be done to prevent the theft of soldiers' possessions. Surgeons, unaware of the dangers of microbes, wet suture thread with saliva and sharpened instruments on the soles of their boots. Unsafe drinking water carried more hazards. Fresh fruit and vegetables were rarely part of a patient's diet, so scurvy and other types of malnutrition were common.

For wounded soldiers, the transport from the battlefield to the hospitals may have proved to be more terrifying than a hospital stay. Ambulance drivers, according to a surgeon quoted on the site, were "the most vulgar, ignorant, and profane men I ever came in contact with . . . such as would disgrace . . . any menials ever sent out to the aid of the sick and wounded."

Although centered on the effect of Civil War hospitals on Whitman's poetry, the well-researched narrative and Civil War era photographs will be of interest to anyone seeking a basic understanding of Civil War hospitals.

CONTENT   ★ ★ ★ ★
AESTHETICS   ★ ★ ★ ★
NAVIGATION   ★ ★ ★ ★

LETTERS AND DIARIES

American Civil War Resources in the Special Collections Department, University Libraries, Virginia Tech
http://spec.lib.vt.edu/civwar/cwhp.htm

The Virginia Polytechnical Institute Library has made much of its impressive Civil War manuscript collection available to researchers over the World Wide Web. The memoirs, diaries, and letters found here allow visitors to read about the experience of Civil War soldiers in their own words and in the words of their loved ones at home.

The documents capture the pain that soldiers suffered by being separated from their families. Lorenzo Dow Hylton, away from his home in Rockbridge County, Virginia, missed the birth of his daughter. One month after he enlisted in the 54th Virginia Infantry, his wife sent him the news. "I can inform you that I have another Daughter, it was born April 17th. . . . [S]end the name that you choose that it should be called. Your Father and Brothers will do all they can to get our corn in. . . . I want you to come home about harvest if you can." Far from their families, soldiers not only missed significant events such as the birth of a child, they were also unable to help with household production. Hylton never returned to the comforts of home. The final letter in the collection was written to his wife by a fellow soldier who informed her that Hylton had died in a Georgia hospital.

Similar anguish was felt on the Union side. William Latham Candler, a captain in General Hooker's staff, wrote about his fear of leaving his new wife a widow: "I have but one life and could not render that in a better cause. But I cannot bear to think about Fannie, should anything happen to me."

After years of fighting, soldiers fervently hoped for an end to the war, but only on terms favorable to their sides. In his third year as an assistant surgeon in three different Virginia regiments, Isaac White wrote to his wife, "The Lord [I] think is on our side + I hope he will soon put a stop to the diffusion of blood; for I + all of us are tired of it + desire peace (honorable)."

Helpful introductions accompany each group of documents, and for at least one of the sets of letters, key terms are linked to explanatory information. There are, however, two drawbacks to this rich site. First, the contents page does not indicate whether the collections referred to have been transcribed, whether they have been photographed, or whether only descriptions have been provided. Second, some of the collections are hampered by confusing navigation and distracting colors. On the whole, however, this is a significant contribution that should prove invaluable to online researchers.

CONTENT   ★ ★ ★ ★ ★
AESTHETICS   ★ ★ ★
NAVIGATION   ★ ★ ★

The Calvin Shedd Papers

http://www.library.miami.edu/archives/shedd/index.htm

No well-known Civil War battles were fought in Florida, and troops stationed there experienced all of the drudgery of war but little of the terror and excitement of battle. Although grateful for their safety, these soldiers occasionally felt deprived of the glory associated with war. The University of Miami Archives has made a web site about one such soldier—Calvin Shedd of the 7th New Hampshire Volunteers. Shedd's letters, fully transcribed and nicely indexed, capture the experience of Civil War soldiers serving in remote areas.

Shedd's correspondence with his wife was filled with news of illness, bad food, and boredom. He vented his frustration at being so far from the main action of the war, while still acknowledging his relative comfort. In one letter, he wrote, "LATER I should like to see active service somewhere I dont care much where it is for we dont seem to be doing the Country much service, but I suppose it is just as neccessary to keep this Fort well defended as any other, but I want to see a rebel before I am discharged." More serious than boredom was the threat of smallpox. In one letter, Shedd reported that a man a day was dying of the fatal disease. Almost as bad, according to Shedd's letters, were meals which typically featured worm-infested food: "We had boiled Mutton & Broth with Hard-Bread for dinner the best dinner we have had for 2 weeks notwithstanding worms & inch long that came out of the Bread were crawling on the table yesterday there was one full an inch long on my plate I poked him off, and continued my dinner; nothing is supposed to turn a Soldiers stomach." Chronic diarrhea, almost certainly due to ingestion of parasites, eventually rendered Shedd unable to work. Deemed unfit for duty, he was discharged from his unit in 1863.

The opening page of the Calvin Shedd Papers contains helpful summaries of each document, a biographical sketch of Shedd's life, and a capsule history of the 7th New Hampshire Infantry. In the transcriptions, key terms in the letters are linked to helpful definitions. The combination of interesting documents and explanatory narrative makes this site a good stop for any researcher interested in the experience of Civil War soldiers, especially those far removed from the main theaters of action.

CONTENTS   ★ ★ ★ ★ ★
AESTHETICS ★ ★ ★
NAVIGATION ★ ★ ★ ★ ★

Civil War Diaries

http://sparc5.augustana.edu/library/civil.html

The library at Augustana College in Rock Island, Illinois, has made two Civil War diaries available on its web site. For Gould D. Molineaux's diary, the site contains only scans of the original documents, which are difficult to read on a computer screen. Fortunately, the diary of Basil H. Messler has been painstakingly transcribed and annotated, and it provides a vivid sense of the experience of Union soldiers in the Western theater. Messler served in the Mississippi Marine Brigade, an amphibious unit that patrolled the Mississippi River and suppressed Confederate guerrilla activity in Union-held areas.

Messler's diary captures the drudgery of a soldier's daily life. Poor drinking water made Messler so ill that he was bedridden for days. When well, Messler apparently spent much of his time acquiring food from the countryside: "Saturday 28th (1864) went out again after cattle again and drove in some 20 and they were killed and divided among the 3 Boats John Raine Autocrat & Fairchilds went out Berry hunting and got all I could eat Brother John and T. D. Moran was with me after eating all we wished we picked a Gallon or more it was sprinkling all the afternoon Spent the evening in reading." Like many Civil War soldiers, Messler participated in no famous battles and rarely came under enemy fire.

A helpful opening page serves as a gateway to the Messler letters. Links found there jump to particular points in the diary, and each link is accompanied by a summary of that section's contents. The opening page also provides a brief sketch of Messler's Civil War service.

CONTENT   ★ ★ ★ ★
AESTHETICS   ★ ★ ★
NAVIGATION   ★ ★ ★ ★ ★

Electronic Text Center: Subject: American Civil War

http://etext.lib.virginia.edu/subjects/American-Civil-War.html

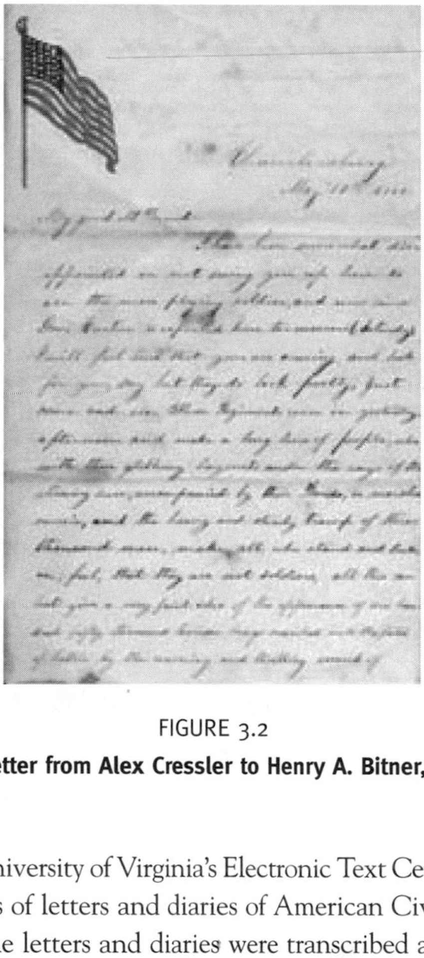

FIGURE 3.2

Page one of letter from Alex Cressler to Henry A. Bitner, May 17, 1861

This site, part of the University of Virginia's Electronic Text Center, is one of the largest online collections of letters and diaries of American Civil War soldiers. A sizeable portion of the letters and diaries were transcribed and indexed in collaboration with the Valley of the Shadow project. Since the Valley project follows the experience of Augusta County, Virginia, and Franklin County, Pennsylvania, over the course of the Civil War, most of the letters and diaries in this Electronic Text Center site are written by men and women from these two places.

The site allows researchers to examine countless issues affecting Civil War soldiers, such as the controversial practice of hiring substitutes. James Booker wrote to his cousin about substitutes in the summer of 1862: "[S]ome of our boys are getting very anxious to put in substitutes, John Milner . . . put in a substitute last week. . . . I dont blame no man to put in a substitute if he can, tho I think if it is kept up much longer it will ruin our army." James's brother John was less charitable about substitutions in a letter written a year later: "[N]early all the men say they will [desert] if they [don't] call out all the men that have put in substitute. . . . I am a posed to desertion as much as any boddy can bee but I say put every one on equal foottin for this is a rich mans war an a por mans fight, I be leave thare are some of the men that have but in substitute are dooen a great deal of good but the most of them are doo en more harm than good they are just speculaten on the poor people, an soldiers."

Many of the letters provide a vivid sense of a soldier's life on the march. Samuel M. Potter, an assistant surgeon in the 16th Pennsylvania Cavalry, gave a wry account of his diet and shelter in a letter to his wife. If his son wants to play soldier, Potter wrote, he should

> put his cup full of water on the fire. Let it boil. Put in a spoonful of coffee & let it burn his fingers when it boils over & he tries to take it off. Then take a piece of fat pork. Get a rod about 2 feet long. Sharpen one end & stick it in the pork. Then hold it over the fire. The grease dripping will make it blaze. Nicely roast his meat a little then put some water over it to wash off the salt which the fire draws out. Then hold it over the fire again & it is done & very good it will be to eat if he has not had anything to eat since yesterday morning. That is our style of cooking sometimes on the march. Then if he wants a bed let him go into a fence corner when it rains. Put a blanket on the ground, an over coat over him & an oil cloth over all & let it rain.

With much less humor than Potter, John Snider, of the 14th Virginia Cavalry, wrote to his sister about having to buy meat at inflation prices: "[I]t was for one week that we did not get no meet only what we bought. our mess bought one side of bacon and it cost us four dollars and thirty cts apiece. it was seventy five cts a pound. we have the half of it et and the side that Jacob Anderson brought with him. we are getting plenty of beef a gain it is dried beef."

The Electronic Text Center's Civil War collection is a true digital archive, with impeccable transcriptions, detailed scans, and refined searching. As with most digital archives, only minimal background material is provided to help visitors understand the context of the letters. But visitors with even the most basic knowledge of the Civil War will enjoy exploring this site for hours.

CONTENT   ★ ★ ★ ★
AESTHETICS ★ ★ ★
NAVIGATION ★ ★ ★

Letters from an Iowa Soldier in the Civil War
www.civilwarletters.com

Made by descendents of the letters' authors, this site features transcripts of more than a dozen letters written by Newton Robert Scott of the 36th Iowa Infantry to friends and family at home. Accompanied by a biographical sketch of Scott and other useful background information, the letters capture many aspects of the experience of the Civil War soldier.

Like most men who fought, Scott, who had never been far from his hometown before the war, was amazed by his new, unfamiliar surroundings. Traveling down the Mississippi River, Scott wrote in wonder that the "little towns on the Mo. Side of the River are Hard looking Places little Dirty cabins with nothing to Sell Hardly But whiskey & the People looks to Suit the Places." Scott traveled to strange lands as far off as Arkansas and Mississippi, where his unit participated in the Vicksburg and other campaigns.

As Scott's missives illustrate, letters provided a lifeline for soldiers far from home. In his correspondence, Scott reported on the health of hometown soldiers and was occasionally forced to give the tragic news of their deaths. In return, Scott received packages of berries and butter, as well as intelligence about hometown courtship and marriage. One letter carried the sad news that Scott's "sweetheart," Mattie, had married another man. Scott replied in dismay, "Well you Stated in your letter that Many changes had taken Place up in Monroe here of late and the most heart-breaking of all is my Darling has long ago Forsaken me and Married and left me to mourn my life away or in other words Do the best I can During my future life." Unlike many men in his company, Scott survived the war. He returned to Iowa in the summer of 1865 and married Hannah Cone, his most faithful correspondent.

Good design, intuitive navigation, and compelling documentary content make Letters from an Iowa Soldier in the Civil War an excellent starting point for studying the life of a Civil War soldier.

CONTENT   ★ ★ ★ ★
AESTHETICS   ★ ★ ★
NAVIGATION   ★ ★ ★ ★

PRISONS

Alton in the Civil War: Alton Prison

http://www.altonweb.com/history/civilwar/confed/index.html

The community web site for the city of Alton, Illinois, contains an interesting section on the prisoner of war camp that operated in the area from early 1862 until the end of the war. Confederate prisoners of war first arrived at Alton Federal Military Prison in February 1862, and by the time it closed, 11,764 prisoners had passed through its gates. As the site explains, harsh conditions in the form of overcrowding and extreme weather took a high toll on both inmates and Union guards.

The Alton Prison site contains a brief history of the prison as well as a database of approximately 1,300 men who died while imprisoned there. The records can be searched a variety of ways. A search using "Alabama" revealed that 126 soldiers from Alabama died at Alton Prison, including James Ashbill, a private in Company B, 4th Alabama Infantry. According to his records, Ashbill was captured on August 27, 1863, at Corinth, Mississippi. He died of smallpox on January 5, 1864, and was buried near the prison on Small Pox Island. Searching the database for the word "pneumonia" showed that 234 men died of this cause.

With interesting historical narrative as well as searchable individual-level records, the Alton Prison site is an outstanding example of a local history web initiative. By inviting visitors to comb through the fragmentary records about the men who lived and died in the prison, the site illuminates a central aspect of the Civil War soldier's experience. A small gem, this site should not be overlooked.

CONTENT   ★ ★ ★ ★
AESTHETICS   ★ ★ ★ ★ ★
NAVIGATION   ★ ★ ★ ★ ★

Archeology at Andersonville

http://www.cr.nps.gov/seac/andearch.htm

This small National Park Service site presents a brief history of the notorious Andersonville Prison, built for the Confederate Army in 1864 in Sumter County, Georgia. Originally designed to hold ten thousand men, the breakdown of prisoner exchanges between North and South increased the population to as high as thirty-two thousand. Strained food supplies, lack of shelter, and deadly sanitary conditions led to almost thirteen thousand prisoner deaths. Inmates were forced to find shelter under scraps of wood or in holes in the ground, and they subsisted on a pound of meat plus a pound and a quarter of cornmeal a day.

In addition to a brief history of the prison, the site contains a detailed description of three seasons of archeological work at the prison site. Excavations have allowed the Park Service to reconstruct the prison's walls exactly as they were originally built. In the course of their work, field researchers found what must have been a uncompleted escape tunnel. Wide enough for a man to squeeze through, the tunnel ends underground just a few yards past the prison walls.

Archeology at Andersonville provides a basic outline of the history of the notorious prison supplemented with photographs and diagrams. Visitors seeking a basic introduction to Civil War prisons will find this site useful.

CONTENT   ★ ★ ★
AESTHETICS   ★ ★ ★
NAVIGATION   ★ ★ ★

SUGGESTED READINGS

Gallagher, Gary. *The Confederate War: How Popular Will, Nationalism, and Military Strategy Could Not Stave Off Defeat*. Cambridge, MA, 1997.

Hess, Earl J. *The Union Soldier in Battle*. Lawrence, KS, 1997.

Linderman, Gerald F. *Embattled Courage: The Experience of Combat in the Civil War*. New York, 1987.

McPherson, James M. *For Cause and Comrades: Why Men Fought in the Civil War*. New York, 1997.

Mitchell, Reid. *Civil War Soldiers: Their Expectations and Their Experiences*. New York, 1988.

———. *The Vacant Chair: The Northern Soldier Leaves Home*. New York, 1993.

Paludan, Phillip Shaw. *A People's Contest: The Union and Civil War, 1861–1865*. Lawrence, KS, 1988.

Wiley, Bell I. *The Life of Johnny Reb*. 1943. Reprint. Baton Rouge, LA, 1979.

———. *The Life of Billy Yank*. 1952. Reprint. Baton Rouge, LA, 1952.

CHAPTER 4

NAVAL
OPERATIONS

From the first battle at Fort Sumter, naval operations played a crucial role in the American Civil War. The Union naval blockade of Confederate seaports limited the South's ability to acquire crucial war material and brought practically every Southern seaport under Union control. In the western rivers, the U.S. Army and Navy coordinated a series of successful attacks that ultimately gave the Union control of the entire Mississippi River and effectively split the South in half. The war ushered in a new era of naval technology, with the advent of the ironclad ram and combat submarine. Although the Union and Confederate navies tend to be overlooked in academic and popular accounts of the war, a number of interesting web sites are giving the Civil War navy its proper attention.

By the end of the second full month of the war, U.S. Navy Secretary Gideon Welles, assisted by the capable Gustavus V. Fox, deployed dozens of ships to the waters off Southern seaports, establishing the beginning of what would become a powerful naval blockade. The blockade represented a key component of General-in-Chief Winfield Scott's Anaconda Plan, which envisioned the slow strangulation of the South by Union forces deployed along the Atlantic and Gulf seacoasts as well as the Mississippi River. Although the Union eventually abandoned the Anaconda Plan, the blockade, which by the final year of the war was enforced by more than five hundred ships, remained essential to the Union war effort.

The blockade was far from complete. Southern merchants and their European trading partners shipped goods via specially designed blockade runners. These fast and shallow-drafted ships could outrun pursuing Union patrollers, and their gray exteriors, adjustable smokestacks, and sleek design enabled them to slip in and out of Southern ports undetected. Even as late as 1865, one of every two ships successfully eluded the blockade. Still, the Union blockade severely hampered Southern trade and limited the Confederacy's ability to equip its army. Historian James McPherson, using prewar trade volumes as a baseline, maintains that the blockade reduced the number and size of ships that merchants were willing to put to sea, creating trade levels that were a third of what they would have been without it.

The blockade and other naval operations extended the geographic scope of the Civil War and created diplomatic complications for the Union. Seeking to capitalize on British resentment at the disruption of their lucrative trade with the South, Confederate officials encouraged the British to take armed action against the blockade. The British did not comply, choosing instead to maintain official neutrality. Its government did, however, turn a blind eye to the decidedly unneutral activities of certain English shipbuilders, who constructed blockade runners and carried on a lively, if dangerous, trade with the South. At the urging of Confederate agent James D. Bullogh, one English shipbuilder built two commerce raiders for the Confederate navy. These English-built vessels, the CSS *Florida* and the CSS *Alabama,* cruised the high seas and destroyed more than a hundred American merchant ships before they were finally sunk by U.S. warships far from the American coast.

The damage inflicted by these commerce raiders stoked anti-British sentiment in the North, but the Lincoln administration, which was determined to keep the British out of the war, had few options. The Union had already angered the British with its heavy-handed enforcement of its blockade. American warships captured British vessels carrying goods destined for South and even went as far as to board a British steamer to arrest two Confederate foreign ministers. Resentment against this insult to British sovereignty was fanned in the popular presses, and tensions between the two nations increased to a dangerous level before the crisis was defused by the U.S. release of the two ministers.

With its naval strategy, the Union was able to bring about a significant reduction in Southern trade without jeopardizing British retaliation. An additional benefit of the blockade was the Union capture of major Confederate seaports. Blockading ships needed coaling stations. At the start of the war, the only Union-held coastal positions were Hampton Roads, Virginia, and Key West, Florida. Within a year, Union gunboats had captured every major port from Norfolk to New Orleans except Charleston and Wilmington, North Carolina. These toeholds provided a base for military operations into the interior.

Even before these seacoast toeholds were secured, federal navy forces operating in the Western theater had helped bring about some of the Union's first significant military victories. This "Brownwater Navy," led by Flag Officer Andrew H. Foote, steamed up the Tennessee and Cumberland Rivers as part of General Ulysses S. Grant's successful operations against Fort Henry and Fort Donelson. Control of these rivers provided a base for naval operations against Confederate positions in the upper Mississippi. These operations resulted in the capture of Ship Island and the important city of Memphis. Meanwhile, pressure on the lower Mississippi was applied by forces under Flag Officer David Glasgow Farragut, which captured New Orleans in April 1862 and went on to take Baton Rouge and Natchez. By June 1862, while the Army of the Potomac floundered through the Peninsula campaign, the U.S. Navy had helped the Union gain control over most of the Mississippi River. With the capture of Vicksburg a little over a year later, the control over major western river systems was complete.

The Civil War brought about important developments in naval technology. Confederate navy secretary Stephen R. Mallory initiated the naval arms race by covering the CSS *Virginia* (formerly the USS *Merrimack*) with layers of inch-thick iron plate and mounting it with ten guns. The Union responded by commissioning engineer John Ericcson to build the first Union ironclad, christened the USS *Monitor*. In March 1862, the CSS *Virginia* embarked on its first voyage against Union ships patrolling the mouth of the James River. Shots fired by these well-armed ships practically bounced off the surface of this odd-looking boat, which proceeded to ram and fire at the USS *Cumberland* and the USS *Congress* until they both sank When the *Virginia* went out the next day to continue on its deadly mission, it was met by the *Monitor*, which had steamed down the coast from New York. The world's first battle between ironclad ships lasted several hours before it ended in a draw. The *Monitor* sank off the coast of North Carolina before it saw action a second time, and the *Virginia* was exploded by rebel forces retreating from Norfolk.

With the construction of the world's first combat submarine, the South led naval innovations in another area as well. The *H. L. Hunley*, named after its inventor, was powered by men turning a giant crankshaft. It dove by means of fins and giant ballast tanks. "The Porpoise," as it was called, was to break the Union blockade by ramming ships with a torpedo that would be detonated by a rope connected to the submarine as it pulled away. After three trial runs that resulted in the deaths of the entire crew each time, the *Hunley* went out again and successfully destroyed a Union blockade patroller off the Charleston harbor. On its return to the harbor, the *Hunley* sank a fourth time, and its entire crew drowned. It remains today where it sank in 1864.

A number of individuals, organizations, and government agencies have created excellent web sites to educate the public about the Civil War navy. Online researchers can read Official Records of navy operations, examine diagrams of historic ships, and follow the progress of underwater excavations of the *Hunley*, the *Monitor*, and other famous vessels. With material suitable for both experts and novice researchers, these sites, taken together, provide an excellent sense of Civil War naval operations.

WEB SITE REVIEWS

Confederate Navy Collection Index at the Virginia State Library

http://image.vtls.com/collections/CN.html

In 1924, veteran Confederate captain W. MacElroy typed information on hundreds of Virginians who had served in the Confederate Navy during the Civil War. These cards were used to establish proof of military service for individuals applying for state pensions. The Virginia State Library has scanned these cards and made them available here. The cards provide name, rank, and information about service for several hundred individuals.

The records are not searchable, and they can be accessed only through a cumbersome alphabetical list. Finding the record for George W. Harrison, requires clicking Hage on the main menu, and then going through several other individual's cards before Harrison's is reached. The card reveals that Harrison was born in the West Indies and that he commanded various Confederate ships along the Virginia and North Carolina coast in the first year of the war, served in naval stations in Richmond and Charlotte in 1862, and commanded the CSS *Morgan* in Mobile Harbor in 1863 and 1864. For other individuals, the cards also list the names and place of residence of the their descendents.

As one of the only sites that provides detailed individual-level information on hundreds of men who served in the Confederate navy, the site is of great value to genealogists and other researchers seeking to learn about particular individuals.

CONTENT   ★ ★ ★ ★
AESTHETICS   ★ ★ ★
NAVIGATION   ★ ★ ★

CSS *Neuse* State Historic Site

http://www.ah.dcr.state.nc.us/sections/hs/neuse/neuse.htm

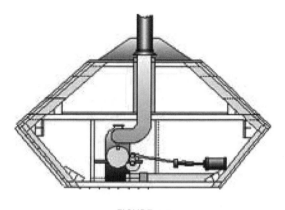

FIGURE 4.1
Cross-section of the CSS *Neuse*

Created by the North Carolina Department of Cultural Resources, this web site describes the CSS *Neuse*, a Confederate ironclad built in eastern North Carolina but destroyed before it could be put to use against the enemy. The remains of the ship are on display at the CSS *Neuse* State Historic Site in Kinston, North Carolina.

Menu items under the heading The Gunboat take the visitor to a host of interesting information about the *Neuse*. Background provides a concise essay about the Confederate ironclad program, which was enthusiastically endorsed by Confederate secretary of navy Stephen R. Mallory but hampered by insufficient rail transport for the necessary iron ore. A section called "The Ram is no Myth" tells of the many delays in the construction of the gunboat and its destruction by federal forces before it ever left the dock. In its report on the Union invasion that destroyed the gunboat, the New York *Herald* wrote, "The ram *Neuse* was destroyed by fire and sunk. Her smokestack can still be seen be when the river is shallow. She must have been a formidable craft." Clicking Historical Gallery takes the visitor to an illustrated summary of the construction of the Confederate gunboat and its ultimate fate.

The CSS *Neuse* web site, like all of the Civil War sites made by the North Carolina Department of Cultural Resources, is well designed and informative. Anyone seeking to explore the Confederate ironclad construction program would be well served by a visit.

CONTENT ★ ★ ★ ★
AESTHETICS ★ ★ ★ ★
NAVIGATION ★ ★ ★ ★

The *Denbigh* Project

http://nautarch.tamu.edu/projects/denbigh/index.htm

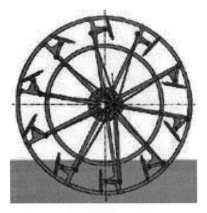

FIGURE 4.2

Feathering sidewheel of the Confederate blockade runner *Denbigh*

Originally used to carry goods between ports in Britain, the *Denbigh* began running the Union blockade of Mobile, Alabama, in 1863. Admiral Farragut, charged with enforcing the Union blockade, wrote in frustration after yet another failed attempt to capture this fast ship: "We came very near catching the *Denbigh* . . . but he was too smart for us and doubled us all and got in and now lies under the fort." After Mobile was taken by Union forces in 1864, the *Denbigh* began running to Galveston, Texas. After five successful trips, the ship came under heavy Union fire in 1865 and sank. The wreck is occasionally visible from the coast of Galveston during low tides.

The Institute of Nautical Archaeology at Texas A&M University is conducting an ongoing investigation of the wreckage and has created this interesting site. In addition to providing an excellent history of the *Denbigh*, it features a variety of primary documents such as newspapers articles and Official Reports. One letter from the quartermaster at Richmond gives a sense of the essential nature of the supplies brought in by blockade runners such as the *Denbigh*. Writing to a colleague who was attempting to build a shoe factory in Alabama, the quartermaster reported that the "steamer *Denbigh* has fortunately just arrived at Mobile with a large lot of shoemakers' tools and findings, and Major Barnewall, the depot officer at that point, has been instructed to send you all you may require."

The site also includes essays on the economics of blockade running. The page titled Investors describes the French, British, and Southern owners of the *Denbigh* and gives a good sense of the high risks and even higher profits associated with running the Union blockade. According to the essay, about one in four attempts to pass through the blockade resulted in destruction or capture of the ship and, subsequently, the loss of its cargo. The Erlanger Loan concerns the notes issued by the French co-owners that served as a de facto international currency for the Confederacy. With its excellent description of the ship and of blockade running in general, this site makes an important contribution to the World Wide Web.

CONTENT   ★ ★ ★ ★

AESTHETICS   ★ ★ ★

NAVIGATION   ★ ★ ★

Monitor: History and Legacy

http://www.mariner.org/monitor/

This site has been created by the Mariner's Museum in Newport News, Virginia. The National Oceanic and Atmospheric Administration, which has authority over the *Monitor* shipwreck, designated the Mariner's Museum to be the official museum of this famous craft. Drawing on its collection of photographs and documents, the museum has established an informative and interesting site.

The section titled Naval Strategy of the Civil War provides the strategic context of the building of the first Union ironclad. Included in the subsection titled The Revolutionary Union Ironclad *Monitor* is the report presented by a special committee to Secretary of the Navy Gideon Welles. In outlining the advantages and disadvantages of ironclad ships, the committee concluded that "armored ships or batteries may be employed advantageously to pass fortifications on land for ulterior objects of attack, or run a blockade, or to reduce temporary batteries on the shores of rivers and the approaches to our harbors." The committee also evaluated the proposals that had been submitted to build the ironclads. About John Ericsson's revolutionary design, the committee wrote, "This plan of a floating battery is novel, but seems to be based upon a plan which will render the battery shot and shell proof. We are somewhat apprehensive that her properties for sea are not such as a sea-going vessel should possess." Despite the committee's reservations, Welles commissioned Ericcson. The committee's concerns proved accurate. The *Monitor* survived the Battle of Hampton Roads only to sink in high seas off the North Carolina coast. This battle is discussed in the section titled The Battle of Hampton Roads: March 8 and 9, 1862, which includes eyewitness accounts that vividly render the historic clash.

Other firsthand accounts on the site include a letter from a crew member to his wife about life on the Union ironclad. He wrote the following description of a typical Sunday morning. "At 9 oclock the word is passed to get ready for muster. . . . [T]he Captain takes a look at each one as our names are called, and woe to the one who is found dirty, as he will be given over to the Master at Armes, whose business it is to take him on deck, strip him naked, and take a scrubbing brush and give him a cleaning. We have not had but one case occur; I think I had rather do my own washing."

Rounding out the offerings on this informative site are a biography of John Eric-sson, a detailed chronology that begins with Ericsson's proposal to build an iron-clad for Napoleon III in 1854 and ends with the sinking of the *Monitor* in December 1862, a description of recent explorations of the shipwreck, and extensive teaching materials designed for the fourth grade.

Confusing organization and vague menu items make navigating this site frustrating. No distinction is made in the menus between primary sources and secondary accounts, and moving from one section to another is difficult. Nonetheless, any-one seeking a good understanding of the historic USS *Monitor* would benefit great-ly from the excellent material on this site.

CONTENT   ★ ★ ★ ★
AESTHETICS   ★ ★ ★ ★
NAVIGATION   ★ ★ ★

The Official Site of the *H. L. Hunley*

http://www.hunley.org

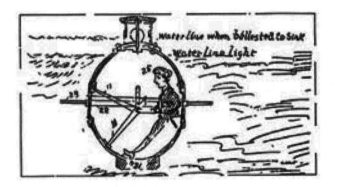

FIGURE 4.3
Diagram of the *H. L. Hunley*

This small, interesting site was built by the Friends of the *Hunley*, an organization established to raise money for the excavation of the world's first combat sub-marine from the bottom of the Charleston Harbor. It provides an excellent account of this historic Confederate vessel.

According to the accounts found here, New Orleans merchants built the sub-marine in hopes that it would break the Union blockade of key Southern ports. After it was successfully tested in Mobile Bay, military authorities moved the

Hunley to Charleston, South Carolina. Charleston residents cheered the arrival of the strange craft and nicknamed it "The Porpoise." A young Charleston woman wrote, "It is forty feet long and can contain eight or nine men. . . . It can go twenty feet under water. . . . It certainly is a wonderful thing, and we hope for its success. It was to go out Saturday to try and blow up the 'Ironsides,' but I have heard nothing since of it." Her hopes were dashed, however, and the documents and narrative on the remainder of the site chronicle the *Hunley*'s tragic end.

In addition to the historical information on the submarine, this site provides an interesting explanation about how the *Hunley* worked. With a propeller powered by men turning a crankshaft, the submarine could dive using fins and water ballast tanks. A torpedo affixed to its bow could be rammed into the sides of ships and detonated by a wire pulled as the submarine backed away.

Finally, the site describes the recent discovery of the *Hunley*'s remains by author Clive Cussler, and it encourages visitors to buy merchandise and donate funds to help with the excavation. With excellent narratives, illustrations, and primary sources, the Official Site of the *H. L. Hunley* succeeds admirably in its goal of generating interest in the Confederate submarine.

CONTENT   ★ ★ ★ ★
AESTHETICS   ★ ★ ★ ★ ★
NAVIGATION   ★ ★ ★ ★

Shotgun's Home of the American Civil War: Naval War
http://www.civilwarhome.com/navalwar.htm

With a large collection of excerpts from many out-of-print books and public domain primary sources on the role of the navy in the Civil War, Shotgun's Home of the American Civil War is a valuable site. The material ranges from general overviews, such as the one taken from A. A. Hoehling's book *Damn the Torpedoes!* to General P. G. T. Beauregard's 1863 letter proposing abandoning reliance on gunboats and purchasing "swift-going steamers" instead.

The site contains Official Records on several interesting incidents. One set of records covers the unsuccessful Union attempt to destroy the Norfolk Navy Yards in April 1861 to prevent its use by Confederate forces. A report sent to headquarters by General John C. Fremont in August 1861 describes the pro-Southern civilian retaliation in Kentucky against the U.S. capture of the Confederate gunboat *Terry* on the Ohio River: "Yesterday the crew of the Terry, led by the captain and a few citizens, seized the steamer Samuel Orr, from Evansville, the private property of private citizens of Indiana—a retaliation more vindictive than sensible." With material on naval action in distant seas, coastal ports,

and western rivers, the Naval War section of Shotgun's Home of the American
Civil War is an excellent site for novices and experts alike.

CONTENT   ★ ★ ★ ★
AESTHETICS   ★ ★ ★
NAVIGATION   ★ ★ ★ ★

The U.S. Navy in the Civil War: Western Rivers

http://www.webnation.com/~spectrum/usn-cw/index.phtml

FIGURE 4.4
The USS *Argosy*

This privately made site is easily the most comprehensive online source on the
"Brownwater Navy" that secured Union control of western rivers during the
Civil War. The site's contents include images of gunboats, maps of battles, and
outlines of major events in the western rivers.

Four separate chronologies, or timelines, cover the activities of the Union navy
in the lower Mississippi, upper Mississippi, Cumberland and Tennessee Rivers,
and the Gulf Coast blockade. These chronologies carefully record the names
of all of the vessels involved in each action, and users can find images and crew
lists of many of these vessels in another section of the site. Key events in the
chronology are linked to public domain primary sources, and naval terms are
linked to definitions on the site's glossary.

Other contents include the history of the Mississippi Marine Brigade (MMB),
which consisted of infantry, cavalry, and artillery stationed aboard steamships
that patrolled the western waters. These men were to suppress Confederate
guerilla activity along the banks of key rivers. According to the site's account,
the MMB earned a deservedly bad reputation because of its poor discipline and
extensive pillaging of Southern civilian property. When the brigade was even-

tually disbanded, the men refused to leave their boats, arguing that they should not be assigned to duties they had not enlisted for. Only after the forty-eight ring leaders were arrested and placed under armed guard did the unit reluctantly move to their newly assigned camps. In his report to headquarters, the Union officer in charge of the transfer characterized the brigade as "demoralized, insubordinate, undisciplined, and grossly ignorant." As with the chronology, key events and terms in this interesting account are linked to relevant primary documents.

With a wide variety of primary and secondary information about this important aspect of the Civil War, this site is indeed worth a visit.

CONTENT ★ ★ ★ ★ ★
AESTHETICS ★ ★ ★ ★
NAVIGATION ★ ★ ★ ★

Wars and Conflicts of the United States Navy

http://www.history.navy.mil/wars/index.html#anchor4162

The U.S. Department of Navy's history web site includes a large collection of material about the U.S. Navy in the Civil War. Featuring both primary documents and explanatory essays and outlines, the Civil War section of this site is a good starting point for the study of many aspects of the role of navies in the war.

Several pages of the site are of particular value to novice researchers. Battle Streamer gives a brief overview of the role that the U.S. Navy played in securing the Union victory. Another good page for novices is Chronology of Events, a timeline of important Civil War naval events in coastal areas and western rivers. The timeline starts with the Confederate attack on Fort Sumter in April 1861 and ends in December 1865, when Navy Secretary Gideon Welles advocated to President Johnson that the nation maintain a large, permanent naval force.

The site also features pages devoted to three famous Civil War naval craft: the CSS *Alabama*, the USS *Tecumseh*, and the Confederate submarine *H. L. Hunley*. For each of these vessels, the site provides a brief history of its construction and use as well as a description of the current state of the craft's wreckage.

Rounding out the site's offerings is a small collection of primary documents. Included is the 1864 U.S. Navy uniform regulation, which provided detailed requirements on such matters as the sorts of caps that could be worn:

> Cap, of dark blue cloth; top to be one-half inch greater diameter than the base; quarters, one and a half inch wide between the seams; back of the band to be two inches wide between the points of the visor, with a welt half an inch from the lower edge, extending from point to point of the visor; band in front,

one and a half inch wide; bound, black patent leather visor, green underneath, two and a half inches wide, and rounded, as per pattern, inside of the band of heavy duck.

The documents also include Official Records on the Confederate capture of USS *Wachusett* in West Indies and the Union capture of the CSS *Albemarle* off the North Carolina coast. The varied collection of material on the U.S. Navy in the Civil War make this site well worth the visit.

CONTENT   ★ ★ ★ ★
AESTHETICS   ★ ★ ★
NAVIGATION   ★ ★ ★

The *War Times Journal:* Civil War Navies

http://www.wtj.com/archives/acwnavies/

The *War Times Journal* Civil War Navies web site contains full transcriptions of Union and Confederate Official Records on the building of the ironclads USS *Monitor* and CSS *Virginia* and their historic clash at Hampton Roads. The Union records consist of dispatches between naval officers as they nervously monitored the Confederates' transforming of captured USS *Merrimack* into the ironclad CSS *Virginia.* Flag Officer Goldsborough, stationed on a Union blockade ship at Hampton Roads wrote:

> SIR: I have received further minute reliable information with regard to the preparation of the *Merrimack* for an attack on Newport News and these roads, she will, in all probability, prove to be exceedingly formidable. The supposition of the insurgents is that she will be impregnable, and a trial of her sufficiency to resist shot of the heaviest caliber, at a short range, is to take place before she is sent out to engage us.

The records go on to cover the assignment of men to the crew of the Union ironclad USS *Monitor* and the transport of the *Monitor* to the southern Virginia coast.

On March 8, 1862, the CSS *Virginia* ventured out to the Union blockade and sank two ships. Telegrams dispatched between Union officers reveal the fear that the Confederate ironclad created.

To General Wool.

NEWPORT NEWS, March 8, 1862.

We want powder by the barrel. We want blankets sent up to-night for the crews of the Cumberland and the Congress. The *Merrimack* has it all her own way this side of Signal Point and will probably burn the Congress, now aground, with white flag flying, and our sailors swimming ashore. These must come by land tonight.

MANSFIELD.

To General Wool.

NEWPORT NEWS, March 8, 1862.

We have no more ammunition and the *Merrimack* and *Yorktown* are off Signal Point. Send us cartridges and shells for 8-inch columbiad and howitzers by land.

MANSFIELD.

To General Wool.

NEWPORT NEWS, March 8, 1862.

The Congress is now burning. The enemy's steamers have hauled off toward Pig Point. Captain Whipple is here, and so is Max Weber, the Twentieth, and the coast guard, and cavalry. We should have another light battery to resist attack by land if they come.

MANSFIELD. Brigadier-General.

The USS *Monitor* arrived at Hampton Roads just in time to keep the *Virginia* from inflicting further damage. The two ironclads fired at each other for several hours and then retreated.

The Confederate records on this site cover the construction of the CSS *Virginia* and the great confidence that the South had in this powerful vessel. Confederate secretary of navy Stephen R. Mallory even proposed that after the Virginia broke the Union blockade it would steam to Brooklyn and destroy the naval works there. He wrote, "Such an event would eclipse all the glories of the combats of the sea, would place every man in it preeminently high, and would strike a blow from which the enemy could never recover. Peace would inevitably follow."

The *War Times Journal* site does not contain any explanatory narrative. Researchers unfamiliar with the topic may want to first visit the *Monitor*: History and Legacy site before engaging in more in-depth research here. By making these records available for online researchers, the *War Times Journal* has made an important contribution to the World Wide Web.

CONTENT   ★ ★ ★
AESTHETICS   ★ ★ ★ ★
NAVIGATION   ★ ★ ★

SUGGESTED READINGS

Anderson, Bern. *By Sea and by River: The Naval History of the Civil War*. New York, 1962.

Bernath, Stuart L. *Squall Across the Atlantic: American Civil War Prize Cases and Diplomacy*. Berkeley, CA, 1970.

Cooling, Benjamin Franklin. *Forts Henry and Donelson: The Key to the Confederate Heartland*. Knoxville, TN, 1987.

Cunningham, Edward. *The Port Hudson Campaign, 1862–1863*. Baton Rouge, LA, 1963.

Davis, William C. *Duel Between the First Ironclads*. Garden City, NY, 1975.

Fowler, William M. *Under Two Flags: The American Navy in the Civil War*. New York, 1990.

Jones, Virgil Carrington. *The Civil War at Sea*. 3 vols. New York, 1960–62.

McPherson, James. *The Battle Cry of Freedom: The Civil War Era*. New York, 1988.

Niven, John. *Gideon Welles: Lincoln's Secretary of the Navy*. New York, 1973.

Perry, Milton F. *Infernal Machines: The Story of Confederate Submarine and Mine Warfare*. Baton Rouge, LA, 1965.

Wise, Stephen R. *Lifeline of the Confederacy: Blockade Running during the Civil War*. Columbia, SC, 1988.

CHAPTER 5

THE EXPERIENCE OF THE U.S. COLORED TROOPS

Unwelcome at first, discriminated against once in uniform, and in danger of being enslaved if captured by the enemy, more than 180,000 African American men nonetheless joined the effort to save the Union and end slavery. Their contributions to the Union victory have been overlooked for generations, but a recent upsurge of interest among scholars and the public has led to the development of a number of rich web sites devoted to the experience of African American soldiers.

African Americans living in Northern states offered their services to the Union army as soon as President Abraham Lincoln called for troops in April 1861, but local recruiters turned them away. In most white Americans' opinions, the aim of the war was not to end slavery but to save the Union and the conflict was strictly a white man's fight. Furthermore, participation in local and state militias was traditionally seen as a sacred right of citizenship reserved for white men only. Bowing to public sentiment and fearful of antagonizing the slaveholding states that remained in the Union, Lincoln and his cabinet endorsed the official exclusion of black men from Union forces until the war was almost in its third bloody year.

In all parts of the Confederate states, African Americans moved toward the Union armies, ran away from slavery, and tried to enlist to fight the Confederacy. Several Union officers with abolitionist backgrounds welcomed them into their lines. In the spring of 1861, General Benjamin F. Butler protected a group of runaway slaves from their Virginia masters who had come to Butler's outpost at Fortress Monroe to reclaim them. These men, Butler declared, were contraband of war, and their owners had no right to them. Butler put them to work building fortifications and manning supply lines. Other Union generals went even farther. In the spring and summer of 1862, David Hunter on the Georgia coast created armed units of fugitive slaves, but Lincoln, still wary of offending pro-Union slaveholders, declined to recognize these regiments, and they were soon disbanded. In New Orleans, John W. Phelps also organized fugitive slaves into military units. Benjamin Butler, now in command of Louisiana and careful to conform to official policy, overruled Phelps. Yet by the fall of that year, the need for manpower in remote outposts of Union control compelled the Lincoln Administration to accept isolated black regiments.

Meanwhile, abolitionists such as Frederick Douglass, Massachusetts governor John A. Andrew, and former Kansas senator James H. Lane petitioned Washington for the formal acceptance of black troops into the Union army. Lane, acting on his own authority, went ahead and formed two black regiments in Kansas and simply ignored War Department orders to disband the unauthorized units. Only after the Emancipation Proclamation of January 1, 1863, did the military leadership respond affirmatively to abolitionist demands, and even then only haltingly. In February of that year, Secretary of War Edwin M. Stanton authorized the governors of Rhode Island, Massachusetts, Connecticut, and Kansas to raise regiments of African Americans, and he granted formal acceptance to the regiments of runaways and free blacks that had already been formed in areas of the South controlled by the Union. Governor Andrew dispatched black recruiters across the Northern states, and African American men soon flocked to New England to enlist. Dismayed that men were leaving their homes to fill state draft quotas elsewhere, the governors of other Northern states soon demanded the authority to form their own black regiments. Secretary Stanton obliged, and by the end of 1863, black units were being raised across the North.

The movie *Glory* immortalized the 54th Massachusetts Regiment and depicted New England as the heart of the U.S. Colored Troops (USCT) effort, but most men in the USCT did not enlist in New England. In fact, of the approximately 180,000 men in the USCT, only about 38,000 belonged to units raised in Northern free states. A greater number, some 42,000, belonged to units raised in the Union slave states of Delaware, Maryland, Missouri, and Kentucky, and the remainder consisted of men in regiments raised in Confederate territory. In short, the majority of men in the USCT came from slave states. The large numbers of men who ran away from their masters to enlist in black regiments created such an outflow of slave labor that the institution of slavery began to erode throughout the South. Thus, well before the federal government brought official emancipation to Confederate territory, tens of thousands of black men had already freed themselves and the slave system was in the process of disintegration.

In several ways, the day-to-day experiences of African American men in the Union armed services resembled those of white men. Most days were spent marching or in camp. Combat, while infrequent, was terrifying, and death by disease was common. Many enlisted expecting glory on the battlefield and instead found themselves engaged in manual labor.

Shared hardships with their white fellow soldiers did not result in equal treatment, however. White soldiers received $13 per month, plus an allowance for clothing, but African American soldiers were paid only $10, from which $3 was deducted for clothing. In protest against this unfair treatment, the black units from Massachusetts refused to take any pay for more than a year. The men in the 3rd South Carolina Infantry reacted much more forcefully, refusing to perform any duty until pay scales were equalized. This protest was more than Union commanders could swallow, and the protest leader was charged with mutiny and executed. Eventually, dissatisfaction over unequal wages created such unrest that Congress finally equalized compensation in June 1864. Discriminatory promotion rules also hurt black soldiers. African American men were barred from serving as commissioned officers except as doctors and chaplains. Only at the end of the war did pressure from leading Republicans succeed in persuading the War Department to accept black officers.

Compounding the discriminatory policies of their own government was the particularly terrifying possibility of summary execution if captured by the Confederate army. Almost as soon as black soldiers took to the field, the Confederate army announced that it refused to grant prisoner of war status to captured African Americans. As a result, captured men of the USCT faced enslavement or execution. African Americans dreaded the former possibility almost as much as the latter; many had risked their lives to attain freedom.

White soldiers and officers routinely suggested that black soldiers were unfit for combat duty. They variously lampooned, belittled, and maligned black fighting soldiers. For their part, black soldiers quickly perceived that only hard-won victories and bloody sacrifices in action would begin to erode the prejudice against them. The 1st Kansas Colored Troops helped repel a Confederate advance at Honey Springs in Indian Territory in July 1863, and in the same summer African American units participated in the battle of Milliken's Bend and the Siege of Port Hudson, helping to conclude Grant's successful campaign for Vicksburg. Other significant engagements include the attack on Fort Wagner on the coast of South Carolina, also in the summer of 1863, and the 1864 Battle of New Market Heights, Virginia. Five African American men received the Medal of Honor for heroism at this battle.

Because African Americans served the Union and fought in battle for the cause of freedom, they could make the case for equal rights more strongly. Such claims were made most forcefully during the establishment of Reconstruction governments in the Southern states. At first it seemed that they would be successful in their quest. The Fourteenth Amendment, which guaranteed equal protection and due process to all citizens, and the Fifteenth Amendment, which held that the right to vote could not be abridged on account of race, seemed to guarantee black political equality. In many Southern states during Reconstruction, black citizens held state and local offices and represented their districts in the U.S. Congress. The federal government's commitment to protecting African American rights waned in the 1870s, and Southern white politicians soon succeeded in curtailing black political participation.

Despite their initial exclusion from armed service, and despite unequal pay and promotion, members of the USCT fought, suffered, and died for the Union army, and in doing so helped to ensure a Union victory. Their contributions to the war effort have long been overlooked, but now, a generation after another period of African American struggle for equality, historians have begun to examine their experiences and consider their significance. A number of sites on the World Wide Web invite the interested public to join in this endeavor.

WEB SITE REVIEWS

5th Regimental Cavalry, United States Colored Troops

http://members.home.net:80/5thuscc/

Formed in Kentucky in 1864, the 5th Regimental Cavalry was composed of "contraband" slaves and served in southwestern Virginia and eastern Kentucky during the final months of the war. For almost a year after the Confederate surrender, until it was finally mustered out, the 5th patrolled sections of Arkansas. This web site, created by a descendent of a member of the 5th USCT, focuses on the controversy surrounding the first Battle of Saltville and provides a good overall regimental history as well.

The opening page of the site features a brief outline of the experience of the 5th USCT, a list of the six major engagements in which the unit participated, and links to the regimental roster. Four of the battles are linked to detailed information from the National Park Service or historic newspapers. The roster is divided into alphabetical sections and provides each soldier's name, company, original rank, and rank held when mustered out.

The best material on the site is the discussion of the events following the first Battle of Saltville, when a collection of Union forces, including the 5th USCT, made an unsuccessful attempt to capture the southwest Virginia saltworks in October 1864. After the battle, a number of the fallen men of the 5th USCT were shot by Confederate forces. Newspapers across the country reported graphic details, dubbing the episode "The Saltville Massacre." The site designer has presented a balanced account of the controversy over the details of this massacre. As the site explains, one historian maintains that more than forty wounded African American men were shot by Confederate soldiers, whereas another argues that of the list of men missing after the battle, most were eventually accounted for. According to this historian, no more than twelve men could have been murdered. The designer of the site, having conducted his own research, which he makes available on the site, makes a compelling argument that more than forty men were killed.

The 5th Regimental Cavalry USCT site reminds researchers that African American regiments fought under uniquely terrifying conditions and shows that regimental histories are still contested well over a hundred years after the war ended.

CONTENT ★ ★ ★ ★
AESTHETICS ★ ★ ★
NAVIGATION ★ ★ ★

The African American Experience in Ohio, 1850–1920

http://dbs.ohiohistory.org/africanam

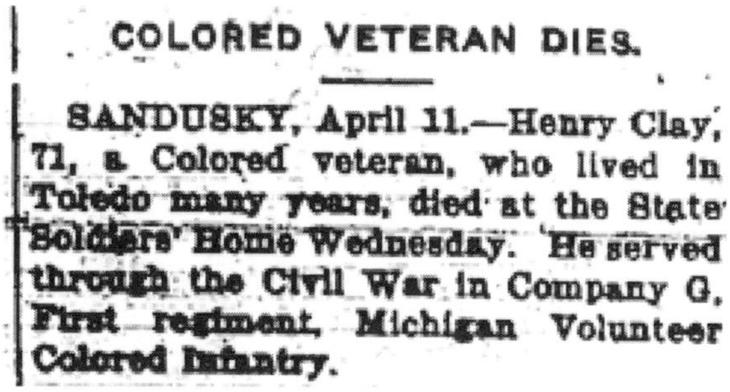
COLORED VETERAN DIES.

SANDUSKY, April 11.—Henry Clay, 71, a Colored veteran, who lived in Toledo many years, died at the State Soldiers' Home Wednesday. He served through the Civil War in Company G, First regiment, Michigan Volunteer Colored Infantry.

FIGURE 5.1
Obituary from the *Cleveland Gazette,* April 20, 1918

This site, created by the Ohio Historical Society, contains a database of materials relevant to African American history in Ohio. Creative and patient use of the search and browse features will reward web users with some fascinating documents on the USCT and its legacy.

Among its most valuable materials related to African American soldiers are scanned articles from late nineteenth-century newspapers, such as the black-owned *Cleveland Gazette*. The *Gazette* articles allow researchers to see how African Americans preserved the memory of the USCT through memorials, meetings, and complimentary obituaries of black veterans. Harry Smith, the fiery editor of the *Gazette*, was particularly defensive against white politicians who claimed credit for ending slavery and who expected black votes in return: "Over 200,000 Negroes were in the rebellion. What for? In whose behalf was their blood shed? To help preserve the Union and save the government and also to gain their freedom. The blood shed by white federal soldiers, republicans and democrats, from '61–'65 was for the preservation of the Union and not in behalf of the Negro."

Smith reminded his readers that African Americans themselves, not the white leadership of the Republican Party, deserved credit for ending slavery.

This site is based on a library model. The material is carefully cataloged, but the search and browse functions are somewhat cumbersome. Like material in the library, the documents in the site are not connected or related to each other in any formal way, and little context or other explanatory material is provided.

Although not friendly to the novice researcher, the African American Experience in Ohio site is excellent. Its documentary content is rich and unique, the materials have been scanned to the highest standards, and download time is quite reasonable, given the high quality of the images.

CONTENT   ★ ★ ★ ★
AESTHETICS   ★ ★ ★ ★ ★
NAVIGATION   ★ ★ ★ ★

The African American Odyssey: A Quest for Full Citizenship

http://memory.loc.gov/ammem/aaohtml/exhibit

FIGURE 5.2
Regimental flag of the 6th USCT

The Library of Congress drew on its extensive American Memory digital collection to build this online exhibit on African American history. Section 4: The Civil War, contains rich material on the USCT, including Frederick Douglass's orders to recruit black soldiers in the Union-held areas around Vicksburg, Mississippi, and a letter from Douglass's son Charles to his father. Charles congratulates his father for doing so much to help fugitive slaves but fearfully warns him to "keep out of the hands of the rebels." Other treasures in this site include an extensive collection of USCT regimental flags, and the portrait and diary of Christian A. Fleetwood of the 4th USCT, who received the Medal of Honor for heroism at the Battle of New Market Heights.

The African American Odyssey site resembles a small museum exhibit. Navigation is straightforward: one proceeds through the site the way a visitor to a museum would walk through the rooms of an exhibit. The documents are arranged thematically and chronologically, and each is accompanied by several paragraphs of explanatory narration. The layout is simple but attractive, and the images are clear. Although not extensive, the Civil War material in the African American Odyssey site is informative, well presented, and carefully documented.

CONTENT   ★ ★ ★ ★
AESTHETICS   ★ ★ ★ ★ ★
NAVIGATION   ★ ★ ★ ★ ★

The Battle of Olustee

http://extlab1.entnem.ufl.edu/olustee/

Typical of many battlefield web sites, the Battle of Olustee site is a labor of love on the part of one passionate individual. It contains everything from photographs of battle reenactments, transcriptions of letters and Official Reports, invitations to join the Olustee Battlefield Citizen's Support Organization, and a poem penned in 1989 ("The mist hung low o'er Ocean Pond / That frosty winter's morn; / Many hopeful hearts at dawnings light, / By night would be forlorn").

The site provides an informative account of a significant Civil War battle and includes a good analysis of the role of the three USCT units there. The narrative on African American soldiers includes the Official Report filed by Captain Romanzo C. Bailey of the 8th USCT. Despite the fact that 343 of his 544 men were casualties in this battle, Bailey was most mortified that his unit's colors were taken by the enemy, and he took great pains to ward off accusations of cowardice and misconduct. Lieutenant Oliver Norton, another white officer in the 8th USCT, wrote to his sister with relief that "a flag of truce from the enemy brought the news that prisoners, black and white, were treated alike. I hope it is so, for I have sworn never to take a prisoner if my men left there were murdered."

The site attests to the ability of energetic private individuals to make valuable contributions to the World Wide Web. Drawing on public domain sources, letters donated by private individuals, and previously published narratives of the battle, the designer has made an informative, rich site.

CONTENT   ★ ★ ★ ★ ★
AESTHETICS   ★ ★ ★
NAVIGATION   ★ ★ ★ ★

The Fight for Equal Rights: Black Soldiers in the Civil War
http://www.nara.gov/education/teaching/usct/home.html

FIGURE 5.3
USCT recruiting poster

Although classroom teachers are the intended audience for the National Archives Teaching With Documents projects, the material in the Fight for Equal Rights lesson plan is so rich that anyone interested in the experience of African American soldiers would benefit from a visit to this site.

The lesson plan begins with a concise history of the USCT. The names of key individuals such as President Lincoln, General John C. Frémont, Harriet Tubman, and Frederick Douglass are linked to their portraits, and topics such as the Emancipation Proclamation and the treatment of black prisoners of war are linked to more detailed explanations and relevant primary documents. An exchange of letters between a Confederate and Union officer provides a vivid illustration of the dangers facing black soldiers if captured. Confederate colonel William P. Hardeman reported to Union forces of the capture of "a negro man named Wilson" and wrote that "if [Wilson's] master lives in the Confederate lines he will be returned to him, if not he will be held to slavery by the government." Other documents include the muster sheets of Douglass's two sons, both of whom fought in the 54th Massachusetts Regiment.

The lesson plan requires students to analyze a USCT recruitment poster and answer a series of questions. Follow-up assignments call on students to read Robert Lowell's poem "For the Union Dead" and to research President Harry S. Truman's 1947 Executive Order desegregating the armed forces.

Although the site is not extensive, the excellent quality of the digital images, the intuitive navigation, and the well-written, informative historic narrative make it valuable for anyone seeking an understanding of the experience and importance of the USCT.

CONTENT   ★ ★ ★
APPEARANCE   ★ ★ ★
NAVIGATION   ★ ★ ★ ★

Fort Scott National Historic Site

http://www.nps.gov/fosc/

This is a very small site, with few documents and only minimal narration, but it is one of the few web projects by a National Park Service historic or battlefield site with good content on African American soldiers. The Site History section contains a page on African American units raised in the area of Fort Scott, Kansas. Noting with pride that Kansas was the first state officially to raise units of black soldiers, the site also provides quotations from the unit's leaders on the bravery of their men as well as a brief explanation of how the units were raised and later incorporated into the USCT.

CONTENT   ★ ★ ★
AESTHETICS   ★ ★ ★
NAVIGATION   ★ ★ ★ ★

Freedmen and Southern Society Project: The Black Military Experience

http://www.inform.umd.edu/ARHU/Depts/History/Freedman/bmepg.htm

The Freedmen and Southern Society Project, based at the University of Maryland, edits the excellent multivolume series *Freedom: A Documentary History of Emancipation, 1861–1867*. Although the primary purpose of the web site is to advertise the series, which can be purchased online, it provides visitors with selected documents from the series, seven of which are relevant to the African American Civil War military experience.

The amount of material at this site is small, but the documents are extremely powerful. A letter to President Lincoln from the mother of a member of the 54th Massachusetts Infantry expresses her outrage at the Confederate practice of killing black prisoners: "Will you see that the colored men fighting now, are fairly treated. You ought to do this, and do it at once, Not let the thing run along, meet it quickly and manfully, and stop this, mean cowardly cruelty." Another document shows the outrage that black soldiers felt against slave owners and the sense of power that came from being in uniform. A soldier whose daughter remained in slavery wrote to her master that "my Children is my own and I expect to get them and when I get ready to come after mary I will have bout a powrer and autheri- ty to bring hear away and to exacute vengencens on them that holds my Child."

The site design is strictly utilitarian and consists only of a few paragraphs of historic background and a small collection of documents. The selection of doc- uments, however, makes it worth the visit.

CONTENT   ★ ★ ★ ★
AESTHETICS   ★ ★ ★
NAVIGATION   ★ ★ ★ ★

Museum of the Kansas National Guard: Historic Units

http://skyways.lib.ks.us/kansas/museums/kng/kngunits.html

Two regimental histories on this site make it a valuable complement to the Fort Scott web site described earlier. Developed by the Kansas National Guard, the Historic Kansas National Guard Units site contains the histories of every Kansas-based military regiment. Included in these histories are the 1st Kansas (Colored) Volunteer Infantry and the 2nd Kansas (Colored) Volunteer Infantry, which are considered by some to be the first "officially" raised troops of African American soldiers in the Civil War.

The histories, which are drawn from out-of-copyright books, Official Reports of the War of the Rebellion, and contemporary newspaper accounts of battles, provide vivid accounts of the dangers faced by African American men in bat- tle. The Official Report for the 1st Kansas (Colored) Infantry describes the exe- cution of a captured black soldier by Confederate forces at Poison Springs and the killing of a Confederate prisoner in retaliation: "Determined to convince the rebel commander that that was a game at which two could play [Captain James M. Williams] directed that one of the prisoners in his possession be shot, and within 30 minutes the order was executed." Later, Williams found the mas- sacre site: "I visited the scene of this engagement the morning after its occur- ance and for the first time beheld the horrible evidences of the demoniac spirit of these rebel fiends in their treatment of our dead and wounded. Men were found with their brains beaten out with clubs, and the bloody weapons left by their sides, and their bodies most horribly mutilated."

At the Battle of Jenkins Ferry, the 2d Kansas (Colored) Infantry sought to avenge the deaths of their comrades in the 1st. This site provides a dramatic account of this engagement:

> Col. S. J. Crawford, of the Second Colored . . . asked Gen. Rice where he should bring his regiment into action. "What regiment do you command?" was the immediate inquiry. To which the prompt reply was, "2d Kansas Colored Infantry." "They won't fight," responded Gen. Rice. To which the Colonel, in language much more emphatic than Christian, replied that they could and would go as far as it was possible for any others to go. . . . The rebel battery was taken. . . . The men of the 2d, as they rushed for the battery, nerved each other for the deadly work before them by exclaiming, "Remember Poison Springs!"

The Historic Kansas National Guard Units site is modest, with few images and no searchable databases, and it is limited almost entirely to public domain documents. But by providing hard-to-find historical material on a subject of great interest, it is a small gem.

CONTENTS   ★ ★ ★ ★
AESTHETICS   ★ ★ ★
NAVIGATION   ★ ★ ★ ★

National Park Service Civil War Soldiers and Sailors System: History of African Americans in the Civil War

http://www.itd.nps.gov/cwss/history/aa_history.htm

The National Park Service has embarked on an ambitious project to make an online, searchable database of the compiled military service records for all men in the U.S. Army and Navy during the Civil War. The USCT records are already available, making the Soldiers and Sailors System web site a required stop for anyone studying African American Civil War soldiers.

In its current state the database can be searched by name, unit, and function. It took a few minutes using a phone modem to search the database and to compile the results for the 1,422 men in the USCT with the last name Green.

The list that is generated from the search provides the first and last names of the soldiers and the name of their regiments. The soldiers' names are linked to a page with basic information such as unit and company name, rank when enlisted and discharged, and National Archives record number for other material on that soldier. The names of the regiments are linked to brief unit histories.

In addition to the searchable database, this web site also contains a brief history of the USCT as well as biographical sketches and portraits of African American Congressional Medal of Honor recipients. One of these men was First Sergeant Powhatan Beaty. According to his medal citation, Beaty, of the 5th USCT, "took command of his company, all the officers having been killed or wounded, and gallantly led it" at the Battle of New Market Heights. The National Park Service Soldiers and Sailors System site contains the most extensive individual-level records on the USCT found on the web, and it should prove of great value to genealogists, students, and historians alike.

CONTENT   ★ ★ ★ ★
AESTHETICS   ★ ★ ★ ★
NAVIGATION   ★ ★ ★ ★

The Valley of the Shadow: Two Communities in the American Civil War

http://valley.vcdh.virginia.edu

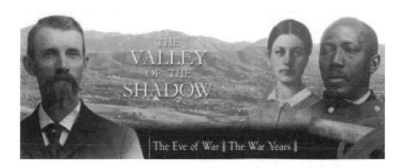

FIGURE 5.4

Image from the home page of The Valley of the Shadow

The Valley of the Shadow site is an extensive multimedia archive created at the University of Virginia. It takes two communities—Augusta County, Virginia, and Franklin County, Pennsylvania—through the experience of the Civil War. The War Years section contains rich material on the USCT.

Included in Student Projects is an in-depth analysis of Franklin County men in the USCT. The project, made by a group of undergraduate students at the University of Virginia, includes a fully searchable database of the compiled military service records of 138 men. It can be searched by name, age, occupation, and type of record. Searching for all Franklin County USCT soldiers who were wounded in action, for example, yields the dossier for Thomas J. Keith. As his records show, Keith was actually wounded twice—first in Williamsburg, Virginia, in February 1864, and later that same year at Fair Oaks, Virginia.

The Newspapers section details how black soldiers were perceived by white citizens on both sides of the Mason–Dixon line. Reporting on the recruitment of black men into the Union army in West Virginia, the Augusta County, Virginia, *Republican Vindicator* patronizingly expressed sympathy for "the poor deluded African[s]." In a similar vein, the *Valley Spirit*, a Democratic Party paper in Franklin County, Pennsylvania, saw the Union army's recruitment of

African Americans as proof of the ineptness of Republican military leadership. In contrast, the Republican Party newspaper, the *Franklin Repository*, commended the bravery of black men in action and condemned their inhumane treatment at the hands of Confederate forces.

Searching the database in Images allows web visitors to examine portraits of African American soldiers as well as dozens of magazine illustrations showing African Americans in camps, on the battlefield, and on the home front. Among the *Harper's Weekly* illustrations are also dramatic depictions of the 1863 New York City draft riots, during which mobs of white protesters attacked the homes and institutions of blacks and murdered black individuals.

Visitors to this site will benefit from lengthy and patient exploration. Consisting almost entirely of documents and containing little explanatory material, the site may be overwhelming to those entirely unfamiliar with the Civil War or with nineteenth-century American life. But no Civil War site matches the Valley of the Shadow for its depth, its scholarly focus, and its emphasis on the experiences of everyday people.

CONTENT   ★ ★ ★ ★
AESTHETICS   ★ ★ ★
NAVIGATION   ★ ★ ★

SUGGESTED READINGS

Blackerby, H. C. *Blacks in Blue and Gray: Afro-American Service in the Civil War*. Tuscaloosa, AL, 1979.

Cornish, Dudley Taylor. *The Sable Arm: Negro Troops in the Union Army, 1861–1865*. New York, 1966.

Crane, Elaine, and Jay David. *The Black Soldier from the American Revolution to Vietnam*. New York, 1971.

D'Entremont, John. *White Officers and Black Troops, 1863–1865*. Charlottesville, VA, 1974.

Glatthaar, Joseph T. *Forged in Battle: The Civil War Alliance of Black Soldiers and White Officers*. New York, 1990.

Gooding, James Henry. *On the Altar of Freedom: A Black Soldier's Civil War Letters from the Front*. Amherst, MA, 1991.

Quarles, Benjamin. *The Negro in the Civil War*. Boston, 1953.

Redkey, Edwin S. *A Grand Army of Black Men: Letters from African-American Soldiers in the Union Army, 1861–1865*. New York, 1992.

CHAPTER 6

SLAVERY AND EMANCIPATION

Historians have debated the importance of slavery as a cause of the American Civil War since the first shots were fired on Fort Sumter. Many have maintained that slavery was the central issue dividing the Union. But others have minimized slavery's role, arguing that the conflict grew out of irreconcilable economic differences, the breakdown of the second party system, or disagreements over issues such as states' rights and tariffs. Whether a direct or indirect cause, *the* issue dividing the Union or one of many issues dividing the Union, the role of slavery has generated an intense controversy that points to its importance. In fact, it is impossible to understand the Civil War without understanding the institution of slavery.

Slaves could be found throughout the North and South during the colonial period, but by the early nineteenth century, slavery had become a distinctly Southern institution. At the same time that Northern states began outlawing the practice in the 1790s, economic developments made Southern slave labor more profitable than ever. The invention of the cotton gin and power loom meant that cotton could be produced in greater quantities and sold at higher prices than ever before. Slave labor was a crucial component of this equation. In the noncotton South, slaves were valued not only for their labor but for the price they could command from traders purchasing slaves for cotton growers in the deep South. At the eve of the Civil War, one in three Southerners was enslaved.

In the first half of the nineteenth century, Southern slaveholders passionately defended the institution against abolitionists' increasingly strident charges. Slaveholders insisted that American slaves lived more comfortably than Northern factory laborers and pointed to the care given to sick and elderly slaves. Owners often referred to slaves as members of their family and demonstrated their commitment to their human property by giving gifts, holding occasional parties and festivals, and seeing to their religious instruction.

But gestures of kindness could not mask the harsh reality that slaves were legally chattel, with no rights that owners or governments were obligated to respect. State laws prohibited slaves from learning to read and write and from traveling without a pass. Slaves could be—and were—brutally beaten and sold against their will. Families were separated by sale and by being hired out by their owners to distant employers. Slave women had no protection against being raped by their masters and bearing their children.

In these harsh conditions, enslaved people established for themselves whatever autonomy and comfort they could. Despite the dangers of forced and permanent separations, slaves married and had children. Family names were passed down through generations, and ties of kinship were carefully documented and maintained. Slaves also developed a sustaining spiritual Christianity with distinct African American traditions that continue today.

Some slaves fought against their enslavement. The most well-known and violent example took place in Virginia in 1831. In what became known as Nat Turner's rebellion, a group of more than thirty slaves killed about sixty whites before they were apprehended. The most common form of resistance, however, was not armed rebellion but running away. Southern newspapers commonly carried offers of reward for the return of missing slaves. Slaves, free blacks, and sympathetic whites formed a secret network of support for runaways known as the Underground Railroad, which provided safe stopping points and assistance to slaves escaping bondage.

Slaves found increased opportunities for resistance when the Civil War began. They took advantage of the absence of masters and overseers by slowing the pace of their work and refusing to exhibit the same deference that they had before the war. As Union forces approached their homes, authority broke down further. Many slaves left their masters' farms and crossed Union lines.

Congress originally designated these runaways "contraband of war." Because slave labor helped the Confederate war effort, Congress stated, escaped slaves could legitimately be withheld from their masters. In the Sea Islands of Georgia and South Carolina, thousands of additional slaves came under federal control when their white owners fled approaching Union forces. Government officials and missionary men and women came to the Sea Islands to raise cotton and educate the black men and women working in the fields in what became known as the Port Royal Experiment. For the first years of the war, however, the permanent status of the growing population of human "contraband" and "abandoned property" remained unsettled.

But by the fall of 1862, a number of developments persuaded President Lincoln to adopt a policy of emancipation. When it became clear the war would last for years rather than months, Northerners increasingly favored completely destroying the Southern slave system. Emancipation, Northerners knew, would also lead to black enrollment in the Union army, thereby relieving the enlistment pressure on Northern whites. European diplomacy played a role as well. Lincoln was aware that the North's official neutrality over slavery hampered U.S. diplomatic efforts to prevent European aid to the South. By issuing the preliminary Emancipation Proclamation in the fall of 1862, Lincoln altered the aims of the war and turned Union forces, which would soon contain dozens of black regiments, into an army of liberation.

It soon became clear that emancipation raised as many questions as it settled. Many in the Republican Party hoped that emancipation would be only the first step in a permanent and fundamental remaking of Southern society into one in which African Americans would have the same political and economic opportunities enjoyed by whites. Some Republicans advocated a program of land redistribution, in which the property of former Confederates would be divided in small landholdings and given to freed slaves.

Many elements of this reform agenda were carried out. In 1865, Congress established the Freedmen's Bureau to assist ex-slaves, and the Thirteenth Amendment, which permanently outlawed slavery everywhere in the United States, was ratified. When Southern states enacted Black Codes that reinstituted many features of slavery, Congress passed a series of Civil Rights Acts, which declared all persons born in the United States to be U.S. citizens with equal rights to enter into contracts, hold property, and receive protection from the government. The Fourteenth Amendment, ratified in 1868, prohibited any state from abridging the privileges and immunities of citizens or depriving any person of life, liberty, or property without due process. Finally, the Fifteenth Amendment, ratified in 1870, declared that the right to vote could not be denied on account of race.

These reforms led to impressive gains for Southern African Americans in the decades after the Civil War. Thousands became landowners, and black men could be found holding local office, serving in Southern statehouses, and representing their districts in the halls of the U.S. Congress. Black men and women established thousands of schools and churches, often with the help of the Freedmen's Bureau or private freedmen's relief organizations. African Americans rebuffed white landowners' attempts to force ex-slaves into yearlong labor contracts. Landowners and landless blacks instead settled on a system of sharecropping, in which tenants lived and worked on sections of land and gave the landowner a large share of their crop in exchange.

Still, the change was neither as fundamental nor as permanent as many reformers had wished. Sharecropping tended to ensnare African Americans in a cycle of debt. A series of Supreme Court decisions weakened the guarantees of the Fourteenth

Amendment and gave Southern states the go-ahead to enact discriminatory legislation. Constitutional conventions across the South curtailed access to the ballot through measures such as the poll tax and literacy tests, and black voting and office holding fell dramatically.

Today, Americans are seeking to come to terms with the legacy of slavery and emancipation by learning about life during those times. Many are finding excellent research materials on the World Wide Web, and some are creating their own sites for the benefit of other researchers. By allowing people to read about slavery through the eyes of slaves, slaveholders, military commanders, and Freedmen's Bureau officials, the Internet has put the raw materials of history into the hands of the general public.

WEB SITE REVIEWS

The African American Odyssey: A Quest for Full Citizenship

http://memory.loc.gov/ammem/aaohtml/exhibit

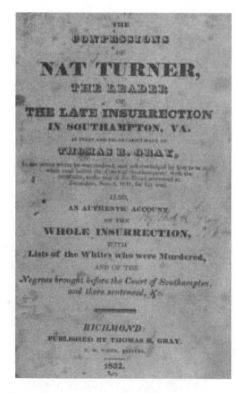

FIGURE 6.1

Title page from *The Confessions of Nat Turner*

Part of the Library of Congress's extensive American Memory project, the African American Odyssey site tells the story of slavery and emancipation through important Library of Congress documents and explanatory narrative.

The section titled Slavery—The Peculiar Institution shows various liberation strategies employed by slaves as well as white reactions to them. The discussion of Nat Turner's 1831 rebellion features Virginia governor John Floyd's explanation of the forces behind the uprising. In his letter to South Carolina governor James Hamilton, which has been partially transcribed, Floyd blamed the rebellion on "Yankee pedlers and traders" who "began first by making them religious" and telling slaves "that all men were born free and equal." The section also describes how slaves sought freedom by running away and features a runaway notice offering a reward for the return of an entire slave family that has left its master.

The African American Odyssey site conveys a sense of the promise of Reconstruction as well. Digitized magazine illustrations show African American men at the voting booth, in the South Carolina legislature, and in the U.S. Congress. Documents about numerous freedmen's schools established after the Civil War give a vivid sense of the importance that former slaves placed on education.

Web visitors proceed through each section of this site as they would through a museum exhibit. Most documents have been digitized but not transcribed, so researchers who wish to conduct more in-depth research will be better served at other sites. The material is arranged along a chronological narrative, and each section opens with several paragraphs of background information. The featured documents are accompanied by explanatory text describing their context and significance.

The site's material on slavery and emancipation, although not extensive, makes it a good starting point, especially in the areas of slave resistance and Reconstruction.

CONTENT ★ ★ ★ ★
AESTHETICS ★ ★ ★ ★ ★
NAVIGATION ★ ★ ★ ★ ★

African American Women: On-line Archival Collections

http://scriptorium.lib.duke.edu/collections/african-american-women.html

This Duke University Library site consists of entirely transcribed texts as well as digital images of documents themselves. With letters from slave women to their owners and members of their families, this site makes an extremely valuable contribution to the body of online material about slavery.

One letter, from Vilet Lester to Patsey Patterson, her former owner, is a heartbreaking testament to the suffering brought about by the slave trade. After being sold away from the Patterson family, Lester had at least four different owners. In her letter, she expresses longing to see the family she was forced to leave behind: "I have thaugh[t] that I wanted to See mother but never befour did I [k]no[w] what it was to want to See a parent and could not. . . . I wish to [k]now what has Ever become of my Presus little girl. I left her in goldsborough with Mr. Walker and I have not herd from her Since."

The site also features a collection of letters written by two slave women to their owners and family members living in far-off Richmond. Left in charge of running the western Virginia household while their owner, John Campbell, served his term as Virginia governor, Hannah Valentine and Lethe Jackson expressed longing to see their owners as well as their own family members taken by the Campbells to Richmond.

CONTENT   ★ ★ ★ ★ ★
AESTHETICS   ★ ★ ★
NAVIGATION   ★ ★ ★ ★ ★

American Slave Narratives: An Online Anthology
http://xroads.virginia.edu/~HYPER/wpa/wpahome.html

In the 1930s, writers working for the Works Progress Administration (WPA) interviewed thousands of former slaves. These interviews have provided historians with rich material for the study of slavery, and historian Bruce Fort has made many of these narratives available to the public over the World Wide Web.

American Slave Narratives: An Online Anthology contains transcriptions of thirteen WPA interviews. A useful index page summarizes the interviews and provides thumbnail photographs of the subjects, when available. The interview with Fountain Hughes is accompanied by sound files of the recording taken during the interview. Hughes described his memories of slavery: "We were slaves. We belonged to people. They'd sell us like they sell horses an' cows an' hogs an' all like that. Have a auction bench, an' they'd put you on, up on the bench an' bid on you jus' same as you bidding on cattle you know." After the war, Hughes's family was homeless and destitute, and his mother hired him out to white employers for one-year contracts. Hughes lived with these employers, and his mother would come by once a month to collect the money. "We didn' have no property. We didn' have no home. We had nowhere or nothing. We didn' have nothing only just, uh, like your cattle, we were jus' turned out. An' uh, get along the best you could."

Mary Reynolds's memories testify to slavery's effect on families. Her father, a free black man traveling in the South, sought to buy Reynolds's mother and marry her, but her owner refused. To stay with his bride, Reynolds's father lived and worked on the plantation as a slave. Reynolds's mother nursed the owner's daughter along with Mary, and the two girls spent their first years side by side and formed a lifelong bond. When she was old enough, Reynolds was taught to work a hoe in the field. Summoned to work before sunrise by the blowing of a conch shell, Reynolds worked in fear of the brutal driver, who would whip slaves until their bones were exposed. Reynolds also recalled secret nighttime prayer meetings, in which the preacher told the slaves that the day was coming that they would be slaves only of God.

In general, the men and women interviewed by the WPA had not spent any of their adult lives as slaves, so their experiences under the institution were limited. The transcriptions can be difficult to read, because the interviewers attempted to capture their subject's dialect in their transcriptions. Despite their limitations as historic sources, the WPA slave narratives are essential reading for anyone seeking an understanding of slavery.

CONTENT ★ ★ ★ ★ ★
AESTHETICS ★ ★ ★ ★
NAVIGATION ★ ★ ★ ★ ★

"Been Here So Long": Selections from the WPA American Slave Narratives
http://newdeal.feri.org/asn/

"Been Here So Long": Selections from the WPA American Slave Narratives is a part of the New Deal Network, an online project dedicated to teaching the legacy of the public works projects carried out during the New Deal. The seventeen narratives reproduced on this site are accompanied by explanatory essays and three lesson plans suitable for secondary school history classes. The site provides two gateways to the narratives: one lists the interviews by subject, the other by topic.

As with the American Slave Narratives site reviewed above, the interviews here allow researchers to construct a sense of the African American experience during slavery, emancipation, and Reconstruction. Especially helpful for researchers is this site's topical index, which provides subject links directly to the appropriate section of each relevant interview. Under the heading Runaways, for example, are links to particular passages in five separate interviews. Some interviewees remembered the sound of hounds chasing runaways in the woods. Scott Bond recalled that "when you went to bed at night you could hear the blood hounds, and in the morning when you would wake up, you could hear them running colored people. The white folks said the music they made was the sweetest music in the world."

Several of the ex-slaves recalled the day they were told that they were free. Andy Anderson's owner gathered his slaves and announced that they were free but that they could stay on the plantation and work for shares or wages. Anderson remembered his response: "I's says to myse'f, not loud 'nough fo' anyone to heah, I's thinks, but de Marster heahs me w'en I's says, 'Lak hell I's will.' Now, I's don't mean anything 'gainst de Marster. W'at I's mean am dat I's gwine to take my freedom, but he took it to mean something else."

Jerry Moore recalled the political strength enjoyed by African Americans during Reconstruction: "The 'publican party had a 'Loyal League' for to protect the cullud folks. First the Negroes went to the league house to get 'structions and ballots and then marched to the court house, double file, to vote. My father was a member of the 11th and 12th legislature from this county." But James Green pointed out that few things actually changed: "No great change come about in de way we went on. We had de same houses, only we all got credit from de store and bought our own food. We got shoes and what clothes we wanted, too. Some of us got whipped just de same but nobody got nailed to a tree by his ears." Extremely well designed, "Been Here So Long" is a valuable site for teachers and researchers at all levels.

CONTENT	★ ★ ★ ★ ★
AESTHETICS	★ ★ ★ ★
NAVIGATION	★ ★ ★ ★ ★

Documenting the American South: North American Slave Narratives

http://metalab.unc.edu/docsouth/neh/neh.html

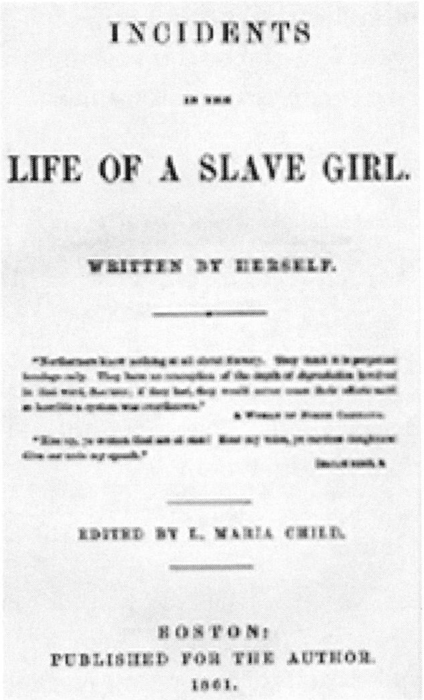
INCIDENTS

IN THE

LIFE OF A SLAVE GIRL.

WRITTEN BY HERSELF.

[illegible]

EDITED BY L. MARIA CHILD.

BOSTON:
PUBLISHED FOR THE AUTHOR.
1861.

FIGURE 6.2

Title page from Harriet Jacobs's *Incidents in the Life of a Slave Girl*

In contrast to the WPA slave narrative sites, Documenting the American South: North American Slave Narratives consists of written works by former slaves published up to 1920. According to the essay that accompanies this collection, until 1930 slave narratives outnumbered any other type of African American literature.

The collection contains widely known works such as the *Narrative of the Life of Frederick Douglass, an American Slave*, Harriet Ann Jacobs's *Incidents in the Life of a Slave Girl*, Nat Turner's 1831 *Confessions*, and Booker T. Washington's *Up from Slavery*. In addition, the site includes accounts not well known today, such as *The Life of Isaac Mason as a Slave*.

Mason's *Life* includes a dramatic story of his escape from slavery. He and two other men paid a free black man twelve dollars for helping them get to Pennsylvania. Their escape would not have been possible had it not been for a network of safe havens provided by sympathetic whites and blacks. Mason acquired work as a farmhand in New Jersey and married. When his master, armed with the terms of the newly passed Fugitive Slave Law, arrived at his new home, Mason and his wife fled to Massachusetts. Later, Mason took part in an ill-fated scheme in which several thousand black men and women emigrated to Haiti. Mason became extremely ill there, quickly recognized that the emigrants had been duped by their leader, and returned to Massachusetts. He published an account of the misadventure in several newspapers, and the Haiti scheme collapsed as a result.

Testaments to the humanity of the slave, the horrors of slavery, and the fruits of full American citizenship, slave narratives such as Mason's fueled the antislavery and freedmen's aid movements and constitute an important body of American protest and reform literature. As with all of the Documenting the American South collections, the North American Slave Narratives is a true digital library. Apart from one scholarly essay, the site contains no annotations or explanatory material. Users not familiar with the authors or the genre of slave narratives may be overwhelmed by the long list of works to choose from. But with the largest online collection of material written by African Americans, this site is extremely valuable.

CONTENT   ★ ★ ★ ★
AESTHETICS   ★ ★ ★
NAVIGATION   ★ ★ ★

Excerpts from Slave Narratives
http://vi.uh.edu/pages/mintz/primary.htm

This course web site developed by University of Houston history professor Steven Mintz contains transcriptions of forty-six previously published, public domain, firsthand accounts of slavery. The narratives are listed under eleven subject headings: Enslavement, the Middle Passage, Arrival, Conditions of Life, Child-hood, Family, Religion, Punishment, Resistance, Flight, and Emancipation.

Many of the documents are not true slave narratives, but are valuable nonetheless. One is a transcription of an 1863 magazine article about Harriet Tubman, which is found in the Flight category. The Emancipation documents include a wonderful 1865 letter from Jordan Anderson to his former master in Tennessee, who has asked Anderson and his wife to return to the old plantation. Anderson wrote, "[W]e have concluded to test your sincerity by asking you to send us our wages for the time we served you. This will make us forget and forgive old scores, and rely on your justice and friendship in the future. I served you faithfully for thirty-two years and Mandy twenty years. At $25 a month for me, and $2 a week for Mandy, our earnings would amount to $11,680." It is unlikely that Anderson returned to Tennessee.

Free of images, frames, and menu bars, this simple site would serve as a good starting point for students of slavery. The documents are well chosen, carefully excerpted, and clearly presented.

CONTENT   ★ ★ ★ ★
AESTHETICS   ★ ★ ★
NAVIGATION   ★ ★ ★

Freedmen and Southern Society Project
http://www.inform.umd.edu/ARHU/Depts/History/Freedman/home.html

The Freedmen and Southern Society Project, based at the History Department at the University of Maryland, is editing a nine-volume documentary book series titled *Freedom: A Documentary History of Emancipation, 1861–1867*, published by Cambridge University Press. The primary purpose of this site is to promote the book, but the volume and quality of the material made available here make it a complete site in its own right.

The section titled Chronology of Emancipation During the Civil War provides a timeline in which key events and terms are linked to explanatory material and documents on other pages. The timeline traces the federal government's halting steps toward full-scale emancipation. It includes the proposal of a constitutional amendment (not passed) that forbade the federal government from interfering with the institution of slavery and the first Confiscation Act of 1861, which nullified Confederate owners' claims to slaves who abandoned their plantations for Union army lines. The second Confiscation Act, passed in July 1862, freed the slaves of owners who were assisting the Confederate government. The next step was Lincoln's Emancipation Proclamation, which freed all slaves in areas still under Confederate control. The timeline concludes with the ratification of the Thirteenth Amendment, which abolished slavery in all parts of the United States.

The Sample Documents page consists of a list of annotated links to documents selected from the book series. In one, Maryland slave Annie Davis impatiently demands that President Lincoln clarify the status of slaves there (because Maryland was not part of the Confederacy, the terms of the Emancipation Proclamation did not apply): "Mr president[,] It is my Desire to be free. to go to see my people on the eastern shore. my mistress wont let me[.] you will please let me know if we are free. and what i can do. I write to you for advice. please send me word this week. or as soon as possible and oblidge." Other documents include the full text of federal measures such as the Conscription Acts and Emancipation Proclamation, as well as General William T. Sherman's remarkable 1865 order to distribute thousands of acres of seized land to African American families.

The timeline and document collection make the Freedmen and Southern Society Project site a valuable aid for researchers seeking a sense of the complex story of emancipation and its aftermath.

CONTENT ★ ★ ★ ★
AESTHETICS ★ ★ ★
NAVIGATION ★ ★ ★

Jesuit Plantation Project: Maryland's Jesuit Plantations, 1650–1838

http://www.georgetown.edu/departments/amer_studies/jpp/coverjpp.html

This is a challenging site for anyone not already familiar with the history of the Jesuit-owned Maryland plantations, but the material on it is truly fascinating. The site consists primarily of diaries and correspondence of the Jesuit priests who oversaw six plantations in eastern Maryland. The story that unfolds from these documents illustrates the fundamental paradox of slave owner paternalism: how could a person participate in an institution that deprived people of their very humanity while still being a good Christian?

The earliest documents on the site give a sense of the dissatisfaction some priests felt over the Jesuit practice of owning slaves. Although one of the priests defended the institution and portrayed abolitionism as just another heresy propagated by Protestants, he later argued that the Jesuit plantations rid themselves of their troublesome human property: "1st Because we have their souls to answer for— 2nd Because Blacks are more difficult to govern now, than formerly—and 3rd Because we shall make more & more [profit] to our satisfaction." Seeking to establish uniform and just practices for their plantations that would still be in line with Catholic teachings, the corporation issued regulations for the treatment of slaves. They included "5. That this chastise[ment] should not be inflicted on any female in the house, where the priest lives—sometimes they have been tied up in the priests own parlour, which is very indecorous" and "7. To devise more effectual means to promote morality & the frequentation of the sacram[ents]."

In 1833, when the Jesuits of Maryland opted to sell all their slaves to owners in Louisiana, paternalism was put to the test. The priests set strict conditions on their sale. Their new owners had to promise that the slaves would be able to practice Catholicism with the assistance of a priest and that families would not be separated. The slaves' new owners did not keep their obligations, however, and a Jesuit priest in Louisiana wrote his brothers in Maryland asking for funds to set up a church for their former slaves: "I am taking the liberty to write to you again to pledge the cause of these poor negroes, who used to belong to your Province and who find themselves now deprived of almost any religious (support) in Louisianna. I might be wrong, but it appears to me that the province of Maryland is morally obliged to provide them with this support and to make some sacrifices for this purpose."

Not designed for the lay researcher, the site has extremely confusing navigation. Visitors would be best served by going to the Resource Chronology page, which lists all the documents in chronological order. Despite the site's weak navigation, the designers should be congratulated for making these Georgetown University Library manuscripts available to the general public.

CONTENT   ★ ★ ★ ★
AESTHETICS ★ ★ ★ ★
NAVIGATION ★ ★

Levi Jordan Plantation Project
http://www.webarchaeology.com

Focusing on the period from 1848 to 1900, the Levi Jordan Plantation Project site invites visitors to participate in an ongoing archaeological project to reconstruct the lives of the black and white residents of a Texas plantation before and after emancipation. The site represents the work of a unique collaboration of university scholars, local historians, and genealogists.

Census manuscripts and plantation papers indicate that the Levi Jordan plantation was home to 150 slaves in 1862 and that many of these individuals remained there as tenants at least until the 1890s. A variety of findings, such as a shell carved with a Kongo symbol and an intricately decorated staff, suggest that the black residents on the plantation maintained strong African traditions. Additional evidence of direct African influence is provided by 1870 census manuscripts, which list Africa as the birthplace of several of the plantation's tenants.

Visitors to the site can examine small photographs of dozens of objects uncovered by the excavation, such as tools, eyeglasses, eating utensils, and decorative shell and bone carvings. Transcriptions of personal papers have also been made available by Levi Jordan's descendents. The site is dominated not by the archaeological findings or historic documents but by papers, interviews, and other material prepared by the scholars engaged in the research. In fact, the site is as much about the process of archaeological inquiry as it is about the plantation and its residents.

Archaeology provides an important window into the world of slaves and ex-slaves, and the Levi Jordan Plantation Project makes make this window available to the general public.

CONTENT   ★ ★ ★ ★
AESTHETICS   ★ ★ ★
NAVIGATION   ★ ★ ★

Race and Place: African American Community Histories
http://www.vcdh.virginia.edu/afam

Created at the University of Virginia by the Virginia Center for Digital History, Race and Place: African American Community Histories explores the world of slaves and slave owners in Augusta County, Virginia, just before, during, and after the American Civil War. Drawing on the rich African American material found in the Valley of the Shadow web site, Race and Place allows researchers to get a sense of how slavery and its demise shaped and were in turn shaped by its larger community.

The section titled Enslaved and Free African Americans provides online researchers with a sense of antebellum slavery and slave life in the Upper South. The government documents include the 1860 Augusta County Slaveowner Census, which can be searched by the names of owners and employers and by the numbers of slaves owned. Unfortunately for researchers, census takers did not record the names of any slaves.

The section also contains dozens of newspaper articles pertaining to slavery. One, titled "Desperate Negro Woman," reports on an Augusta County slave who chopped off three of her fingers to prevent her sale. Newspapers did not often provide such unblemished accounts of slavery. Their articles generally served to bolster white Southerners' confidence in the institution. Papers gleefully reported instances of freed and runaway slaves who voluntarily returned to their masters after suffering terribly in Northern states.

The Letters section contains several powerful documents from manuscript collections at the University of Virginia, Yale University, and other sources. In one document, a slave residing in a nearby county wrote to her husband that she and her children were about to be sold to a trader. She begged her husband to find someone to purchase them instead: "Dear Husband, I write you a letter to let you know of my distress. My master has sold Albert to a trader on Monday court day and myself and other child is for sale also." The McCue Papers, a collection from the University of Virginia Library's Special Collections, show how slavery was woven into the business and personal lives of an extended family in Augusta County. This collection contains contracts for the hiring of slaves as well as letters between family members concerning their slaves' behavior. One such letter reports on a slave who has run away: "Dear John, I write this evening, to inform you that Wilson has run off. . . . You know he is such a sly negro that he may have more in his head than we know of. . . . [H]e was once taken up in Augusta and has so many acquaintances that he may be harbored . . . or perhaps may aim for a free state." For most of the documents in this collection, only the transcriptions are available although a few have been scanned.

The section titled African Americans on the Civil War Battlefield and Home front documents the disintegration of slavery over the course of the conflict. In 1863, the Staunton *Spectator* boasted that the high price of slaves confirmed that slavery was as strong as ever. The frequent runaway notices, however, suggest a different story.

The work of a group of University of Virginia undergraduate students as a class project, Reconstruction and the Freedmen's Bureau uses transcribed newspaper articles and Freedmen's Bureau Records to document how former slaves in Augusta County worked with federal officials to earn fair wages, reunite their families, build churches and schools, and protect themselves from violence. The newspaper transcriptions in this exhibit are filled with notices about freedmen's fairs to raise money to start churches and schools, as well as a Freedmen's Bureau notice to whites regarding labor contracts with ex-slaves: "It is a fact which all should bear in mind, that contracts for service between white and colored persons for any time longer than two months are required to be in writing, signed by both parties, and acknowledged before a justice, notary public, or two witnesses, who shall certify, on their oaths, that the contract was read and explained to the colored parties." The exhibit also contains correspondence between the local Bureau agent and his superiors. Following the experiences of one county's slaves and slaveholders before, during, and after the Civil War, Race and Place is an excellent source of material on slavery and emancipation.

A fourth section of Race and Place not discussed in detail here focuses on the African American community of Charlottesville and neighboring Albermarle County, Virginia, from 1870 to 1930. An ongoing collaboraton with the Carter G. Woodson Institute for Afro-American and African Studies, this section is already the largest single source of online material about African American life during the Jim Crow era.

CONTENT ★ ★ ★ ★ ★
AESTHETICS ★ ★ ★ ★
NAVIGATION ★ ★ ★ ★

Third Person, First Person: Slave Voices from the Special Collections Library

http://scriptorium.lib.duke.edu/slavery/

This web version of a physical exhibit at Duke University's Special Collections Library contains fascinating documents that capture the complexities of the master–slave relationship. One section, titled Caesar, contains a slave named Caesar's 1785 bill of sale to William Gibbons of Georgia. In a document dated 1794, Gibbons authorized an agent to retrieve Caesar, who had run away. Caesar was found in Connecticut, and the person he was living with told Gibbons that Caesar would return if he were allowed to work on his own time and earn money to buy his freedom. A plantation document from several years later showed that Caesar had returned to Gibbons plantation, but whether his terms were met is unknown.

The section titled Black Southerners in the Old South— The Slave Community features the records of slave owner Louis Manigault, in which he lists the cholera deaths among his slaves and describes the remedy he gave to slaves suffering from the disease (alternating doses of castor oil with a mixture of calomel and opium).

An online exhibit rather than an archive for researchers, Third Person, First Person does not contain full transcriptions of the documents, and only the description is given for some of the items due to the fragility of the original documents.

CONTENT ★ ★ ★ ★
AESTHETICS ★ ★ ★ ★ ★
NAVIGATION ★ ★ ★

SUGGESTED READINGS

Berlin, Ira, Barbara J. Fields, Thavolia Glymph, Joseph P. Reidy, and Leslie S. Rowland, eds. *The Destruction of Slavery*. New York, 1985.

Blassingame, John W. *The Slave Community: Plantation Life in the Antebellum South.* Rev. and enl. New York, 1979.

Elkins, Stanley M. *Slavery: A Problem in American Institutional and Intellectual Life*. 3d ed., rev. Chicago, 1976.

Fogel, Robert W. *Without Consent or Contract: The Rise and Fall of American Slavery*. New York, 1989.

Fogel, Robert W., and Stanley L. Engerman. *Life on the Cross: The Economics of American Negro Slavery*. Boston, 1974.

Foner, Eric. *Reconstruction: America's Unfinished Revolution*. New York, 1989.

Fox-Genovese, Elizabeth. *Within the Plantation Household: Black and White Women of the Old South*. Chapel Hill, NC, 1988.

Franklin, John Hope, and Loren Schweninger. *Runaway Slaves: Rebels on the Plantation*. New York, 1999.

Genovese, Eugene. *The Political Economy of Slavery*. New York, 1965.

———. *Roll Jordan Roll: The World the Slaves Made*. New York, 1974.

Gutman, Herbert G. *The Black Family in Slavery and Freedom*. New York, 1976.

Lane, Ann J., ed. *The Debate Over Slavery: Stanley Elkins and His Critics*. Urbana, IL, 1971.

Litwack, Leon F. *Been in the Storm So Long: The Aftermath of Slavery*. New York, 1979.

McFeely, William S. *Frederick Douglass*. New York, 1995.

Rose, Willie Lee. *Rehearsal for Reconstruction: The Port Royal Experiment*. Indianapolis, 1964.

Stampp, Kenneth M. *The Peculiar Institution: Slavery in the Ante-Bellum South*. New York, 1956.

CHAPTER 7

WOMEN
IN THE
CIVIL WAR

Women were barred from the polls in the mid-nineteenth century, but they had strong partisan and regional attachments, and they followed closely the political developments that precipitated the secession crisis. When the war began, women fought for victory by organizing soldiers' aid societies and serving as nurses in military hospitals. More adventurous women served as spies, disguised themselves as men to enlist in the army, and moved south to teach freed slaves. In Maryland, Pennsylvania, and most of the South, women did not need to travel to the war; the war came to them. Standing at their doorsteps, women saw wounded soldiers by the thousands staggering away from battlefields, and many women were forced to live under enemy occupation. The lives of slaveholding women, left first to manage their slaves on their own and then to see their slaves emancipated, were fundamentally and irreversibly altered. Until recently, to explore the varied experiences of Civil War women in their own words, researchers had to comb through manuscripts and academic books. Today, they can turn to the World Wide Web, where they will find a variety of excellent material.

It is possible that there were dozens of women who disguised themselves as men and fought with the military. Searching the Compiled Military Service Records in the National Archives, historian DeAnn Blanton has found discharge orders for several soldiers who had been discovered to be female. She has also located nineteenth and early twentieth century newspaper accounts of six other women who enlisted, either on their own or to accompany their husbands. One woman,

Sarah Emma Edmonds, deserted from the 2nd Michigan Infantry to avoid discovery when she contracted malaria after serving more than two years. After the war, Edmonds received a veteran's pension for her service. Private Albert D. J. Cashier of the 95th Illinois lived as a man until an accident in 1910 led to the discovery of her gender. It is entirely likely that there are dozens of additional women who assumed male identities and enlisted in the military.

Women also served as spies during the Civil War. Informal social networks made women well positioned to glean secret military information, cross military lines, and pass the information on to friendly ears. Rose O'Neal Greenhow, a well-connected Washington hostess, organized the network that informed General P. T. G. Beauregard of the Union advance on Manassas Station in the summer of 1861. Beauregard reinforced his lines in time to ensure a Confederate victory. Imprisoned in her home and in a Washington jail for several months, Greenhow was released to Richmond, where she received a hero's welcome. Belle Boyd of Front Royal, Virginia, passed on the location of federal troops to General Stonewall Jackson during his famous Valley campaign. Tennessee Unionist Sarah Thompson rode to Union lines with the secret location of famous Confederate cavalry raider John Hunt Morgan. She personally led Union soldiers to his hiding place.

For most women, aiding the war effort did not involve becoming a spy or soldier. Typically, female war work consisted of gathering and manufacturing supplies for the army. Tapping into the strong tradition of antebellum women's voluntary associations, women across the country formed aid societies to knit gloves, sew regimental flags, and gather food and medical supplies.

Women soon realized that local aid societies alone could not improve the health and safety of men in the army. The overburdened military transportation system left them languishing at shipping docks and railway stations for months. Military medical bureaus employed unsanitary and outdated medical techniques. Camps housing thousands of men were built without proper latrines and water supplies. In response, Northern women allied with civilian physicians to form organizations such as the U.S. Sanitary Commission. Its leaders bypassed hostile officers of the Army Medical Bureau, appealed directly to President Lincoln, and received official authority to inspect camp conditions and advise on proper sanitary practices. The Commission also trained nurses, arranged for the transport of supplies and nurses to army hospitals, and set up food and medical stations for furloughed soldiers at railway stops. Recognizing the quality of the female nurses trained by the U.S. Sanitary Commission, Surgeon General William Hammond appointed the noted reformer Dorothea Dix to recruit and train women nurses, and he ordered that at least one-third of army nurses be women. According to Civil War historian James McPherson, more than three thousand women worked as paid nurses for the Union army, and thousands more served as volunteers and paid agents for the Commission.

Southern women also mobilized to address the poor care given to sick and wounded soldiers, volunteering as nurses and establishing their own infirmaries. As in the North, the superiority of female volunteers over regular military hospital staff inspired the Confederate Congress to pass a law encouraging the hiring of women as nurses.

As the Union army took over more and more Southern territory, the care and education of freed slaves became a concern for many Northern women. These women, many of whom were veterans of the antislavery movement, sought to ensure that ex-slaves had education and skills to provide for themselves and to ward off the accusation that black men and women were inherently ill-suited for freedom. In 1862, dozens of female volunteers traveled to the Sea Islands of South Carolina to teach the slaves there, in the hopes that their success would spur Lincoln to adopt a policy of emancipation. Other women reformers, such as Josephine Griffin, worked to improve conditions of freedmen refugees in Washington, DC.

Most women remained in their homes during the war, assuming sole responsibility for running farms and shops in addition to meeting their prewar responsibilities of raising children and keeping house. Southern women on the home front faced particular hardships. By the final year of the war, Confederate currency was practically worthless, and women could acquire needed goods only by barter. As federal control over Southern territory expanded, women faced the ordeal of life under enemy occupation. Looting and destruction of property, whether the work of undisciplined troops or the result of official military policy, created extreme hardship as well as intense humiliation.

Slaveholding women were in particularly precarious positions. With husbands, sons, and overseers gone, these women found it difficult to force their slaves to work as they had before. In their diaries, they expressed mortal fear of violent insurrection and bitter disappointment at the exodus of many of their slaves to Union lines. Historian Drew Gilpin Faust argues that the ordeal of slaveholding women led to their disaffection with the Confederate cause and helped bring about Confederate defeat. Faust's interpretation is not universally accepted, but there is no question that female slaveholders faced profound difficulties during the Civil War.

Many women remained active in the public sphere when the war ended. Clara Barton, a nurse in the Union army, headed the national effort to locate and return missing soldiers and later founded the American Red Cross. Other nurses fought for and received government pensions for their wartime services. Many freedmen's teachers remained at their schools for the rest of their lives, often campaigning actively for equal rights and improved education for Southern African Americans.

Women's rights advocates, many of whom had participated actively in aiding the war effort, hoped that social revolution brought about by the end of slavery would expand to bring about increased rights for women. Bitterly disappointed when the Fifteenth Amendment guaranteed suffrage to black men only, women's rights activists returned to the suffrage campaign with renewed determination. It took more than sixty years of intense activity for the constitutional amendment guaranteeing votes for women to pass.

Thanks to the efforts of historians and archivists across the country, dozens of Civil War women's letters, diaries, and memoirs are available to the public on the web. Online researchers can read about the experiences of nurses, spies, and freedmen's schoolteachers in their own words, and they can examine the private thoughts of Southern women living under enemy occupation.

WEB SITE REVIEWS

Civil War Women: On-line Archival Collections

http://scriptorium.lib.duke.edu/collections/civil-war-women.html

FIGURE 7.1
Rose O'Neal Greenhow, spy for the Confederacy

This small archive, part of Duke University's Digital Scriptorium project, features three significant sets of manuscripts that portray key aspects of women's experience in the American Civil War. All are from the manuscript collection of Duke University Library.

Rose O'Neal Greenhow, one of the more well-known spies for the Confederacy, ran a spy network out of her home in Washington, DC. Her messages informed General P. G. T. Beauregard of the Union movements toward Manassas in 1861, enabling him to amass troops and defeat the Northern army there. Imprisoned for her activities, Greenhow still managed to pass on information about Union military and diplomatic activities to the South. After her release and exile to the Confederate states, Greenhow traveled to Britain and France to lobby for their support of the Confederate cause.

The Greenhow collection consists of scans and transcriptions of thirteen documents. Most of the material is correspondence from Greenhow to her Confederate colleagues, much of which was sent from Europe. She describes her impatience with her lack of diplomatic success in many of her letters: "I had the honor of an audience with the Emperor . . . and altho the Emperor was lavish of expressions of admiration of our President and cause there was nothing upon which to hang the least hope of aid unless England acted simultaneously—the French people are brutal ignorant and depraved to a degree beyond description and have no appreciation of our struggle they believe it is to free the slaves and all their sympathies are really on the Yankee side." In 1864, the British blockade runner that carried Greenhow home from Europe ran aground off the coast of North Carolina, and Greenhow drowned while fleeing from an approaching Northern gunboat.

Sixteen-year-old Alice Williamson, an ardent Confederate partisan, kept a journal while her town of Gallatin, Tennessee, was under Union military occupation. Her diary records the summary executions and looting carried on by Northern forces under notorious Brigadier General Eleazar Arthur Paine, whom she sarcastically referred to as "our King" and "his lordship." Paine's harsh occupation was later replaced by a Unionist East Tennessee regiment, who directed their hostility not against white civilians, as Paine had, but against freed slaves living in the "contraband camp."

Williamson's journal captures many aspects of Southern women's Civil War experience. As more and more Confederate territory fell under Union military control, Southern women, usually with husbands, fathers, and brothers away fighting, had to conduct their daily lives under enemy occupation. Unable to express openly her hatred of her Unionist occupiers, Williamson poured out her defiance in her diary: "Our king (old Payne) has just passed. I suppose he has killed every rebel in twenty miles of Gallatin and burned every town. Poor fellow! you had better be praying old Sinner! His Lordship left Tuesday. Wednesday three wagons loaded with furniture came over. I do not pretend to say that he sent them. No! I indeed, I would not. I would not slander our king. . . . He always goes for rebels but invariably brings furniture. I suppose his task is to furnish the contraband camp, i.e. the camp of his angels (colored)."

Other Southern women, such as Sarah E. Thompson, were active Unionists. Thompson spent the first years of the war helping her husband raise Union regiments in Tennessee. After her husband was assassinated by pro-Southern elements in his town, Thompson became a spy for the Union army. Her most notable achievement was in 1864, when she informed Union forces that Confederate general John Hunt Morgan was in Greeneville, Tennessee. According to her personal testimony, she led Union troops to his hiding place, where Morgan was shot and killed. In addition to her spy activity, Thompson also served as a military nurse. After the war, Thompson supported herself by giving speeches about her wartime experiences and with occasional Washington, DC, government jobs.

Most of the documents in the Thompson collection consist of postwar correspondence from supporters who sought to award her a government pension for her services. In 1878, Captain S. G. Carter wrote, "She undertook the long and dangerous journey from her love for the cause of the Union and her hatred of the rebellion. . . . I take pleasure in recommending Mrs. Thompson to the favorable consideration of the proper authorities as one who deserves well of her country from her fearless devotion to its interests under circumstances of trial and danger." After decades of effort, Thompson was finally awarded a nurse's pension in 1898.

The manuscripts have been transcribed in full and are also available as high-quality digital images. Links to documents are accompanied by summaries of their contents. Each collection features a biographical sketch of the woman. The names of important people and groups mentioned in Alice Williamson's diary are linked to pages that provide additional background information.

CONTENT   ★ ★ ★ ★
AESTHETICS   ★ ★ ★
NAVIGATION   ★ ★ ★ ★

Clara Barton: National Historic Site

http://www.nps.gov/clba/

This small National Park Service site chronicles the life of Clara Barton, the founder of the American Red Cross. Presented in the form of a timeline, with no analysis or documents, the site serves as a good introduction to her life and times, although it will not satisfy researchers seeking a deep understanding of this complex woman and her role in the Civil War. The timeline covers her prewar struggles against discrimination as an educator and federal government worker. The section on the Civil War years recounts the assistance she provided out of her home to soldiers wounded in the 1861 Baltimore riots as well as her hospital work in Virginia and South Carolina. In 1865, President Lincoln appointed

Barton to lead the effort to locate missing soldiers, an undertaking that lasted four years. Barton established the American Red Cross in 1881, having become aware of the international organization while in Europe aiding soldiers wounded in the Franco-Prussian War. The timeline also includes entries that show Barton's connection with Christian Science and the women's suffrage movement.

CONTENT   ★ ★ ★
AESTHETICS   ★ ★ ★
NAVIGATION   ★ ★ ★ ★

Documenting the American South

http://metalab.unc.edu/docsouth/

Documenting the American South, sponsored by University of North Carolina, is a digital collection of more than 300 historic sources on Southern history. Although it does not contain a separate collection pertaining exclusively to women in the Civil War, there are numerous documents that illustrate their varied experiences. These documents are generally in the form of memoirs and diaries, some of which were published in the decades after the war.

A *Confederate Girl's Diary*, by Sarah Morgan Dawson gives a vivid account of the home front experience of women. Dawson struggled to assert her identity as an ardent Confederate women after her home town of Baton Rouge fell under Union occupation in 1862. "'All devices, signs, and flags of the Confederacy shall be suppressed.' So says Picayune Butler. Good. I devote all my red, white, and blue silk to the manufacture of Confederate flags. As soon as one is confiscated, I make another. . . . [T]he man who says take it off will have to pull it off for himself; the man who dares attempt it—well! a pistol in my pocket fills up the gap. I am capable, too." As the war progressed, however, Dawson's efforts shifted from maintaining her feminine defiance to ensuring the physical survival of her family as they became refugees fleeing Union shelling of their home.

Several documents at this site chronicle women's experiences as Civil War spies and soldiers. The archive includes the memoirs of the famous Confederate spy Belle Boyd as well as a fascinating book titled *The Woman in Battle: A Narrative of the Exploits, Adventures, and Travels of Madame Loreta Janeta Velazquez, Otherwise Known as Lieutenant Harry T. Burford, Confederate States Army.*

Documenting the American South consists entirely of full-text digital versions of manuscripts and published works. With no summaries or explanatory background information, the site can be challenging for researchers unfamiliar with Civil War history. Furthermore, there is no easy way to identify which among the more than 300 documents are about women in the Civil War. The best option is simply to scroll through the long lists of authors and titles. The search option is confusing for anyone not familiar with digital archive terminology. Although difficult to use, Documenting the American South is the largest collection of full-text Civil War era manuscripts, and researchers will find it extremely valuable.

CONTENT   ★ ★ ★ ★
AESTHETICS   ★ ★ ★
NAVIGATION   ★ ★ ★

Hearts at Home: Southern Women in the Civil War

http://www.lib.virginia.edu/exhibits/hearts/

FIGURE 7.2

"General Stuart's New Aid," from *Harper's Weekly*, April 4, 1863

A companion to the museum exhibit at the University of Virginia Library, the Hearts at Home site contains extensive material on Southern women in the American Civil War. Organized around themes such as spies, war work, patriotism, religion, education, refugees, and slavery and freedom, the site invites online researchers to explore many aspects of Southern women's wartime experience.

The documents feature rare books, letters and diaries, and Civil War–era periodicals from the University of Virginia's Special Collections Library. A *Harper's Weekly* cartoon of a uniformed Confederate female spy on horseback shows Northern public indignation against the Southern practice of relying on female spies. The section called Hard Times at Home contains a letter written by a Henry County, Virginia, resident describing the economic upheaval created by the war: "Times are very hard here every thing is scarce and high ... corn is selling for ten dollars, bacon 45 cents per pound, brandy is selling about here from 4 to 5 dollars per gallon, in Danville it sells for eight dollars. We cannot get a yard of calico for less than one dollar we cannot get a pound of copperas [a sulfate used in making ink] for less than a dollar and 25 cents."

Designed as an online exhibit and not as an archive, the site does not contain full-text transcriptions of any of the items on display, which may frustrate some online researchers. But like a good exhibit, each item is accompanied by explanatory text that provides context as well as brief excerpts of the document.

CONTENT   ★ ★ ★ ★
AESTHETICS   ★ ★ ★ ★ ★
NAVIGATION   ★ ★ ★

Illinois Alive! Illinois in the Civil War: Private Albert D. J. Cashier (Jennie Hodgers)

http://www.rsa.lib.il.us/~ilalive/files/iv/htm2/ivtxt002.html

Among the many stories of women who disguised themselves as men and enlisted in the Confederate and Union armies, Albert D. J. Cashier's story stands out. Born in Ireland with the name Jennie Hodgers, Cashier apparently lived her entire adult life as a man. She enlisted in the 95th Illinois Regiment, which participated in the siege of Vicksburg and Mobile. In 1910, Cashier was admitted to a Soldier's and Sailor's Home. Four years later, her gender was discovered, and Cashier was discharged to an insane asylum, where she died a year after that.

This site, sponsored by the Illinois State Library, features an excellent exhibit on this interesting individual. It contains several photographs, a brief biography, newspaper articles, and scans of Cashier's military, pension, and hospital records. According to the essay titled "Union Maid," Cashier's grave is marked by a monument with this inscription: "Albert D. J. Cashier, Co. G, 95. Inf., Civil War, Born: Jennie Hodgers in Clogher Head, Ireland, 1843–1915."

CONTENT   ★ ★ ★ ★
AESTHETICS   ★ ★ ★
NAVIGATION   ★ ★ ★

Prologue: Women Soldiers of the Civil War

http://www.nara.gov/publications/prologue/women1.html

In this National Archives publication article, historian DeAnne Blanton tells the stories of women who disguised themselves as men and fought in the Union and Confederate armies. Combing through the National Archive's Compiled Military Service Records, Blanton found discharge records of soldiers whose true gender had been discovered, one of whom was discharged for reasons of "sextual [sic] incompatibility." She also recounts the cases of Albert D. J. Cashier and Sarah Edmonds Seelye, both of whom received federal pensions for their military service carried out under false identities. Blanton's article is illustrated by photographs of women soldiers and military documents.

CONTENT   ★ ★ ★ ★
AESTHETICS   ★ ★ ★ ★
NAVIGATION   ★ ★ ★ ★

United States Sanitary Commission

http://www.netwalk.com/~jpr/index.htm

FIGURE 7.3
U.S. Sanitary Commission seal

Created by Civil War reenacter Jan P. Romanovich with contributions from a network of volunteers, this extensive web site can be explored for hours. A varied collection of documents and helpful explanatory text make this the by far the largest and best site on the U.S. Sanitary Commission and on the role of women in this important organization.

The material includes an 1861 New York City newspaper announcement signed by more than a hundred women on the "importance of systematizing and concentrating the spontaneous and earnest efforts now being made by the women of New York" and for establishing a program of selecting, training, and compensating female nurses to care for wounded soldiers in military hospitals. Other documents consist of camp inspection reports, transcriptions of the *U.S.S.C. Bulletin*, and patterns for making bandages and hospital gowns.

The site also contains excerpts of an 1865 history of the U.S. Sanitary Commission. Describing the Commission's work at Shiloh, the author of the publication made special mention of the crucial role women played there: "After the battle, the Commission established a depot at the Landing. . . . [T]he stores issued from this depot amounted in all to 160,143 articles . . . . During the period that this depot was kept open, a great service was rendered to the Sanitary Commission by two women who volunteered for the work, and to whom its thanks are due. (One of whom is familiarly known among the soldiers as 'The Cairo Angel.')"

With its large collection of transcribed documents, Romanovitch's United States Sanitary Commission site is of immense value to anyone seeking to understand the experience of Northern women's war work during the American Civil War.

CONTENT   ★ ★ ★ ★
AESTHETICS ★ ★ ★ ★
NAVIGATION ★ ★ ★ ★

The Valley of the Shadow: Two Communities in the American Civil War
http://valley.vcdh.virginia.edu

Created by historians at the University of Virginia, this site assembles a wide variety of documents from one Northern county and one Southern county. With its rich archival content, the Valley of the Shadow allows visitors to get a broad sense of how women worked within their communities in the midst of war.

The War Years Letters and Diaries section contains several documents that cast light on women's home front experience during the war. Nancy Emerson, an unmarried woman living in her brother's home in Augusta County, Virginia, sadly recorded news of casualties from distant and not-so-distant battles. Emerson wrote of the humiliations she and her sister-in-law endured when the war came to her doorstep in the form of occupying Union soldiers in 1864. Anna Mellinger, a young Mennonite woman living in Franklin County, Pennsylvania, during the war, wrote of hiding her family's livestock from approaching Confederate raiders in the summer of 1864. Both of these documents are transcribed and searchable, and beautiful scans of the originals are also available.

Aid societies in both counties assembled supplies to send to the war front, which was never very far from home, and women frequently cared for wounded and hungry soldiers in their own houses. Both counties' newspapers gave complimentary reports of women's war work, and these can be read by clicking Newspapers: Transcriptions by Topic and Date.

With its deep, varied archival content on two counties, the Valley of the Shadow site allows online researchers to gain a sense of how women's war work took place in a society that saw respectable women's lives as properly suited for the domestic sphere only. Articles reporting on women's active relief work were accompanied by pieces such as this one, titled "A Wife!": "A wife! she must be the guardian angel of his footsteps on earth, and guide them to Heaven; so firm in virtue that should he for a moment waver, she can yield him support and place him upon its firm foundation; so happy in conscious innocence that, when from the perplexities of the whole world, he turns to his home, he may never find a frown where he sought a smile." These women, supposedly "so happy in conscious innocence," labored all day to care for wounded and hungry men and faced enemy soldiers at their doorsteps.

The population census database in the section titled The Eve of War provides another means to explore women's experience during the war. With occupational and economic data on every Augusta and Franklin County woman recorded in the 1860 census, this database can be searched by first or last name, race, gender, age, occupation, wealth, and birthplace.

The newspapers, letters and diaries, and public documents on the Valley of the Shadow site allow visitors to explore the Civil War experiences of women from a number of different perspectives. The content is largely archival, with material taken from microfilmed newspapers, documents in the University of Virginia Library, and local historical societies. There is little explanatory material, so some visitors may initially find the site overwhelming. But patient exploring will be rewarded with an excellent sense of women's Civil War experience.

CONTENT   ★ ★ ★ ★ ★
AESTHETICS   ★ ★ ★ ★ ★
NAVIGATION   ★ ★ ★ ★

Women and the Freedmen's Aid Movement
http://womhist.binghamton.edu/projects.htm#aid

Part of the excellent site titled Women and Social Movements in the United States, 1830–1930, Women and the Freedmen's Aid Movement is the work of SUNY Geneseo history professor Carol Faulkner. The site opens by posing a question: How did white women aid former slaves during and after the Civil War and what obstacles did they face?" Visitors are then invited either to read the introductory essay, which provides useful background information and many thought-provoking questions, or to proceed directly to an annotated list of eighteen documents. The documents are from the Freedmen's Bureau Records in the National Archives and from the Josephine White Griffing Papers at Columbia University.

Included in the documents is the 1864 appeal made by Freedmen's Bureau agent Josephine Griffing in the *Liberator* and other reform papers. In it, she described in vivid detail the suffering of thousands of freed people living as refugees in Washington, DC. The documents that follow trace the response of the Freedmen's Bureau to this unwelcome publicity. Jacob R. Shipherd of the Freedmen's Aid Commission wrote to the head of the Freedmen's Bureau, "Mrs. Griffing is simply irrepressible: & yet she must be repressed, so far as you & I have to do with her, or else we must bear the odium of her folly. She still represents the '20,000 utterly destitute' as needing outright support from northern charity. Located as she is, & endorsed by the head of the Bureau, she sends her appeal everywhere, to the glee of the copperheads, who want no better reading to confirm their 'I told you so!'" Alarmed at the public suggestion that the efforts of the Bureau and its allies were inadequate, the Bureau removed Griffing from its ranks and publicly denied her allegations.

The postwar letters between Griffing and Lucretia Mott express the women's frustration at their exclusion from freedmen's aid efforts. Mott described an argument she had with the organizer of the "Reconstruction Union" being formed by Northern reformers: "I told him it was objected, that woman was ignored in their new organization, and if it really were a reconstruction for the nation, she ought not so to be, and that it would be rather humiliating for our antislavery women and Quaker women to consent to be thus overlooked." Other postwar documents include reports from Caroline Putney, a freedmen's teacher who remained in Virginia after the war to help African Americans there.

This site, with its excellent background material, well-chosen documents, and central unifying question, has immediate applications to the high school and college level classroom. It is also of immense value to anyone seeking an understanding of how the Civil War gave women opportunities to play a role in public life at the same time that it reminded women of the limits to their participation.

CONTENT   ★ ★ ★ ★
AESTHETICS   ★ ★ ★
NAVIGATION   ★ ★ ★ ★

SUGGESTED READINGS

Attie, Jeanie. *Patriotic Toil*. Ithaca, NY, 1998.

Clinton, Catherine, and Nina Silber, eds. *Divided Houses: Gender and the Civil War*. New York, 1992.

Ginzburg, Lori D. *Women and the Work of Benevolence: Morality, Politics, and Class in the Nineteenth-Century United States*. New Haven, CT, 1990.

Faust, Drew Gilpin. *Mothers of Invention*. New York, 1997.

Leonard, Elizabeth. *Yankee Women: Gender Battles in the Civil War*. New York, 1994.

————. *All the Daring of the Soldier: Women of the Civil War Armies*. New York, 1999.

Rable, George. *Civil War: Women and the Crisis of Southern Nationalism*. Urbana, IL, 1991.

Rose, Willie Lee. *Rehearsal for Reconstruction: The Port Royal Experiment*. New York, 1976.

CHAPTER 8

CIVIL
WAR
REGIMENTS

In the film *Gettysburg*, based on Michael Shaara's Pulitzer Prize–winning novel *The Killer Angels*, the 20th Maine almost single-handedly changes the course of the battle of Gettysburg. Americans love the idea that one regiment can make a decisive difference in the outcome of so large a battle as Gettysburg, which took place over three days of hard fighting and twenty-five square miles of ground. The idea appeals to our natural sense that a close band of soldiers might break through the chaos of a modern battle and that the smaller unit—the regiment—harbors our aspirations and glories.

The regiment was the basic fighting unit in the Civil War and its men often came from the same locality. In 1861 men rushed to sign up and join regiments that were forming in their area. Most expected a short war, full of quick glory and limited opportunity. These vigorous volunteers did not want to be left out of the fight. Volunteer and militia units went into service already organized. They boasted nicknames from before the war, such as the Palmetto Guards, the Fire Zouaves, the Floyd Rifles, and the Chambers Artillery. Often, the newly formed regiments took the name of their organizing captain or colonel. Regiments were sometimes organized by ethnicity in both North and South, as volunteers took great pride in their heritage. Examples include the fiery 6th Louisiana Irish Regiment and the stout 69th New York, which was a mostly Irish regiment.

Some states, particularly those along the border between North and South, produced regiments for both the Confederacy and the Union.

Divided loyalties in an area were common. Virginia raised hundreds of regiments for the Confederacy, second in the Confederacy only to North Carolina in its proportion of white men enlisted in the army. Almost twenty regiments of Virginia soldiers fought for the Union, however. They came from the western areas of Virginia where unionism ran strong. The pattern was similar in Missouri, Kentucky, Maryland, Tennessee, and Illinois.

Each Civil War regiment consisted of approximately one thousand men in ten companies, but units rarely fought at full strength. By the middle of the war, many regiments in both the Union and Confederate armies went into battle with fewer than five hundred men. Diseases such as dysentery hospitalized and killed many new recruits, while medical discharges, leaves, and battle deaths further reduced the ranks in short time.

Initially, officers of the regiment were elected in both Union and Confederate forces. A colonel commanded the regiment and a lieutenant colonel served as second in command. Each regimental commander had a staff of officers, including a surgeon, a chaplain, adjutants, quartermasters, and musicians. Captains commanded each of the ten companies in a regiment, and lieutenants served under them. The regiment fought as a part of a larger unit, the brigade, which was made up of four or five regiments. Three or four brigades formed a division, and two or more divisions constituted an army corps.

Enlistment in regiments ran high in the first year of the war, but began to slow as the war became perceived as less of a freewheeling jaunt and more of a hellish duty. The Confederacy was the first to use conscription to raise regiments. It declared that all able-bodied men between the ages of eighteen and thirty-five were required to serve three years. The volunteers who had already served a year had to remain in the army for two more. Some exemptions to the draft were allowed: state and Confederate officials, railroad employees, clergy, teachers, and eventually overseers of plantations. Substitutes were allowed as well, so richer men could pay another to serve, although the practice was outlawed in the Confederacy after a year. The North enacted a conscription law a year after the South did. The main purpose of these laws was to stimulate volunteering with the threat of a draft.

The regiments that were formed after 1862 differed markedly from their volunteer predecessors. In the North, draftees and new volunteers were brought into new units, not mixed in with depleted veteran units. These units went into battle green and untested without experienced veterans in them to lead and guide them. In the South, however, the opposite practice developed. New recruits were interspersed with the remaining veterans in old units, bringing depleted units up to full strength. The practice of electing officers was abandoned, and the regiments became more professional.

Regimental histories of the war abound. Veterans published many memoirs, regimental accounts, diaries, and histories. Veterans associations commissioned many histories as a way of ensuring the preservation of their unit's history. Sons of veterans followed these with regimental histories and edited accounts. Some examples of the wide range of regimental histories include Sam Watkins' fascinating *Co. Aytch*, John B. Gordon's overblown *Reminiscences of the Civil War*, and John Obreiter's turgid *The Seventy-seventh Pennsylvania at Shiloh*.

These veterans and writers might be surprised by how little their work is read or taken seriously by academics. Regimental histories, especially those commissioned by associations, tended to offer bland accounts of movement and abbreviated, generic battle descriptions, punctuated by lively, humorous stories of camp life or buffoonery on the march. Rarely did these histories cover tactics, overall strategy, the exact movement of troops in battle, or the emotions of the men involved in these actions. These histories had little to offer scholars of military history and even less to scholars of social history. As a result, regimental histories as a source of information and as a means of viewing the war have languished on library bookshelves, rarely checked out or loaned.

The World Wide Web offers a rich collection of regimental sites. Indeed, it has revived the genre of regimental history. Followers of a particular unit's history have produced online versions of what once were commonplace volumes. Surprisingly, sites for hundreds of units can be found online, with the obscure far outnumbering the well-known. Individuals maintain most of these sites, which consequently vary in quality and sophistication. As a group, the sites impress any researcher with their dedication, attention to detail, and care for their subject. More significantly, most have moved beyond the limited usefulness of the old regimental histories and instead have created complex social and military histories.

WEB SITE REVIEWS

MASSACHUSETTS

The Harvard Regiment: 20th Regiment of Massachusetts Volunteer Infantry 1861–1865

http://www.people.Virginia.EDU/~mmd5f/

This site was created by an independent researcher at the University of Virginia to honor the men of the 20th Massachusetts Volunteer Infantry, which was known as the Harvard Regiment because of the preponderance of Harvard graduates among its officers. The 20th Massachusetts played a prominent role in most of the major battles of the eastern theater, including Fair Oaks/Seven Pines, Antietam, Fredericksburg, Chancellorsville, Gettysburg, and the Wilderness, and it lost more men than any other regiment from its state.

Secondary accounts of the 20th Massachusetts on this site include excerpts from Fox's *Regimental Losses in the Civil War* and Dyer's *Compendium* as well as a summary of the unit's history written by the site designer. Key details in the summary are linked to explanatory notes elsewhere in the site. As the summary explains, the unit is most renowned for its contribution in two battles. At Fredericksburg, the regiment led a deadly advance through the streets of the town while under fierce fire from Confederate sharpshooters. At the Battle of Gettysburg, men of the 20th formed the front line against Confederate general George E. Pickett's famous July 3 charge. In addition to the general overviews, the site features biographical sketches of many of the officers, including future Supreme Court justice Oliver Wendell Holmes, Jr., and Paul Revere, the grandson of the midnight rider.

The site also contains extensive primary sources. Many of these sources, such as Official Reports, are in the public domain, and others come from manuscripts housed in the Boston Public Library that have been transcribed by the site's designer. The Letters page contains links to a variety of correspondence, including one written by General Robert E. Lee to thank Colonel W. Raymond Lee of the 20th Massachusetts for returning the sword of a Confederate officer who had died while in custody of the 20th: "I have caused your kind and considerate communication to be transmitted to the father of the deceased, to whom I doubt not it will afford a great satisfaction to know that his son, in his last moments, enjoyed the care and attention of a humane and generous enemy." The documents also include several famous Memorial Day speeches given by Oliver Wendell Holmes, Jr., after the war. In one, Holmes made his famous pronouncement about the men who fought for the Union: "The generation that carried on the war has been set apart by its experience. Through our great good fortune, in our youth our hearts were touched with fire."

The Battles page contains links to a variety of documents and secondary accounts about Ball's Bluff, Yorktown, Fair Oaks, Antietam, Chancellorsville, and Gettysburg, but the most dramatic accounts are of the Battle of Fredericksburg. A. W. Greeley, a member of the 19th Massachusetts who witnessed the 20th's desperate advance toward Caroline Street, wrote, "Thrown into platoon fronts I saw the 20th make this desperate march, with no definite end in view as far as anyone could see, into the most useless slaughter I ever witnessed. It was a wonderful display of orderly movement by a body of men of unsurpassed courage and coolness."

The Harvard Regiment web site does an excellent job conveying the heroism and sacrifice made by the men of this famous unit.

CONTENT ★ ★ ★ ★ ★
AESTHETICS ★ ★ ★
NAVIGATION ★ ★ ★ ★

28th Massachusetts Volunteer Infantry

http://www.28thmass.org/

A predominantly Irish regiment when it was raised in the fall of 1861, the 28th Massachusetts served in the Sea Islands of South Carolina and Georgia before engaging in its first major battle at Manassas in August 1862. At Fredericksburg, while attacking Marye's Heights, the regiment lost 38 percent of its men. By the end of the war, having participated in every major battle in the eastern theater after the Peninsular Campaign, the 28th had suffered enough casualties to qualify for designation as one of the "Fighting 300" in historian William F. Fox's *Regimental Losses in the Civil War.*

In addition to a concise regimental history, this web site features the complete rosters for the regiment, providing name, occupation, enlistment date, and remarks for each man. The selected Official Records contained in the section titled Life in the 28th gives a sense of the regiment's combat experience, and a small collection of letters allows researchers to explore the stories of men of the 28th in their own words. Private Dennis Ford's letter to his wife and neighbors shows how ethnic identity shaped soldiers' sense of themselves and their regiment: "Do pray for us, we look shabby and thin, though we were called a clean regiment. I saw a great deal (of) shot and wounded. . . . Our regiment stood the severest fire that was witnessed. . . . [W]e ran through what we did not shoot. We bayoneted them. One man begged and got no mercy, a yankee ran him through. Thank God it was not an Irishman (that) did it." According to the notes accompanying the letter, Ford survived many more battles and spent several months as a prisoner of war. He returned to Massachusetts after his enlistment expired in December 1864.

One of the several impressive features of this site is the careful analysis of Irish-born Americans and the Civil War. The designer has devoted an entire section to this topic, describing immigration, Democratic Party allegiance, and the uneasy relationship between Irish and African American residents in Northern cities before the war. Confounding the expectations of many, Irish men enlisted in great numbers during the war's early years. But by 1863 Lincoln's emancipation policy combined with general war weariness to create disaffection. Antiwar and antiblack sentiment peaked in the New York City draft riots of the summer of 1863. Still, the 28th Massachusetts and other members of the Irish Brigade fought fiercely through the entire war and made important contributions to the Union victory.

Sponsored by a 28th Massachusetts reenacting organization, this site is one of the few that clearly separates historic material from reenactment news. Easily navigated, it is a beautifully designed site with a great deal of interesting content.

CONTENT   ★ ★ ★
AESTHETICS   ★ ★ ★ ★
NAVIGATION   ★ ★ ★ ★

N E W   Y O R K

5th New York Volunteer Infantry: Duryée's Zouaves
http://www.zouave.org/

FIGURE 8.1
Reunion of the 5th New York Zouaves

The 5th New York Volunteer Infantry was one of dozens of Zouave regiments fighting on both sides in the American Civil War. This web site, sponsored by a 5th New York reenacting group, provides both a thorough account of the Zouave craze that swept the divided nation in 1861 and an excellent history of the 5th New York.

According to the site's designer, French Zouave units, inspired by the distinctive garb worn by Algerian and Moroccan fighters, were first formed under the reign of Louis Napoleon. During the Crimean War, these Zouave units received a great deal of coverage in the American press. Illinois politician Elmer Ephraim Ellsworth raised a militia based on the Zouave model that toured the country in the 1850s, inspiring imitators in its wake. At the beginning of the Civil War, Ellsworth raised a new Zouave regiment in New York and led it against secessionist strongholds in Alexandria, Virginia, where he was shot. The first Union officer killed in the war, Ellsworth became an instant martyr, inspiring the creation of numerous Zouave regiments across the Union.

One of these units was the 5th New York Volunteer Infantry, also known as Duryée's Zouaves. Composed of men from New York City, Long Island, and Poughkeepsie, the unit's first major engagement was at Gaines' Mill, part of the Seven Days Battle near Richmond. The regiment also faced enemy fire at the Second Battle of Manassas, where more than half the unit was killed or wounded. Replenished with new recruits, Duryée's Zouaves fought at Antietam, Fredericksburg, and Chancellorsville before the men's enlistment terms expired.

In addition to the fascinating history, the 5th New York Volunteer Infantry site features an image gallery, a list of all the men who fought, and an account of the many reunions that took place after the war. Although not strong in terms of documentary content, this is a well-made site that deserves a visit.

CONTENT   ★ ★ ★
AESTHETICS   ★ ★ ★ ★
NAVIGATION   ★ ★ ★ ★

PENNSYLVANIA

77th Pennsylvania Volunteers: On the March

http://jefferson.village.virginia.edu/vshadow2/HIUS403/77pa/main.html

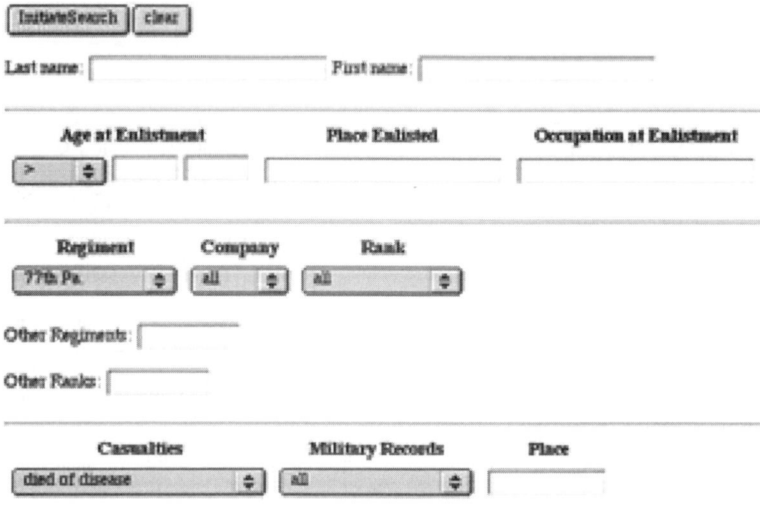

FIGURE 8.2

Searchable compiled military service database

As the only regiment from Franklin County, Pennsylvania, that did not fight in the Eastern theater during the Civil War, the 77th Pennsylvania Volunteers received little of the public attention given to other units from that state. This innovative web site, created as a class project by a group of students at the University of Virginia, corrects this imbalance by making the rich record of this unit available to the public.

Visitors may want to start with the Timeline page, which is divided into The War and The Regiment, because it outlines the larger context of the regiment's activities. The timeline reveals that the same month (February 1862) that the 77th Pennsylvania was marching through Kentucky on its way to Pittsburg Landing, Jefferson Davis was sworn in as the president of the Confederate States of America. The timeline takes the unit through the entire war and beyond. In May 1865, a month after Lee's surrender at Appomattox, the 77th boarded a steamer for Texas, where the troops were on duty until the beginning of 1866.

The site presents a variety of options for exploring certain aspects of the experience of the 77th Pennsylvania Volunteers in greater detail. The map on the home page serves as a gateway to collections of documents about the unit's activities in those regions. Clicking Chickamauga takes the visitor to photographs, maps, and a list of casualties printed in the unit's hometown newspaper. At the bottom of the home page is a link for the Documents section, which contains letters, newspaper articles, and official military documents. The documents include letters from the Compiled Military Service Records at the National Archives (which have been scanned but not transcribed). One of these letters is an 1866 appeal from Private H. Metchley that his name be cleared of the desertion charges against him. Documents also includes the record of death for Adam Lautenschlager, a German-born eighteen-year-old resident of Chambersburg, Pennsylvania, who was killed by a gunshot wound to the knee at Murfreesboro, Tennessee.

The most sophisticated feature of the 77th Pennsylvania web site is the searchable database, which contains the records of all the men from Franklin County, Pennsylvania, who enlisted in Union regiments. The database can be queried in countless ways. A search for all the men in the 77th whose records indicate that they died of disease resulted in eleven matches, including John Wetzel, who was captured at Chickamauga and who died at Andersonville Prison a year later. Five men in the database died of their wounds, and seven were killed in action, including Captain John A. Walker, shot during the campaign for Atlanta.

This site, drawn largely from local newspapers and National Archives records, successfully portrays the experience of a group of Pennsylvania men drawn far from their homes to defend the Union. With rich material tucked away in every corner, it invites hours of exploration.

CONTENT   ★ ★ ★ ★ ★
APPEARANCE   ★ ★ ★ ★ ★
NAVIGATION   ★ ★ ★

TENNESSEE

20th (Russell's) Tennessee Cavalry

http://home.olemiss.edu/~cmprice/cav.html

The 20th Tennessee Cavalry was formed in late 1863 by West Tennessee veterans whose original terms had ended or who had deserted their infantry regiments, and it fought under Lieutenant General Nathan Bedford Forrest in the Confederate Department of Alabama, Mississippi, and East Louisiana. This thorough online history of the 20th Tennessee Cavalry was created by a professor at University of Mississippi.

The home page includes a detailed table of contents and a brief summary of the history of the 20th Tennessee Cavalry. Key terms on this page are linked to explanatory notes, maps, and images. From the home page, visitors can choose a number of ways to learn more about the experience of this regiment. The most helpful starting point is the Chronology of Movements and Activities, which lists recruiting and organizational developments along with troop movements and engagements with the enemy. The regiment's first major engagement was in Estenula, Tennessee, in the winter of 1863. The following spring, the 20th participated in the Confederate capture of Fort Pillow. Although the designer of the site does not recount the controversy over the Confederate's firing on retreating Union soldiers, many of whom were African American, the description of Fort Pillow has links to sites that discuss the issue in some detail. The chronology follows the unit into Mississippi and Alabama, where it engaged in numerous small skirmishes as well as major attacks on Union positions at Franklin and Nashville, Tennessee.

The Biographical Notes section covers officers and enlisted men alike. For each member of the regiment, the information from the Compiled Military Service Record is provided. For example, the following is provided about D. F. Bullock, of Company K: He enlisted in the 20th Cavalry on May 1, 1863, with a bay horse valued at $1,100. Although present on both muster rolls recorded for 1863, Bullock's name appeared on the list of absentees and deserters made on February 28, 1865.

The site has few images and makes minimal use of colors. But the 20th Tennessee Cavalry site compensates for its utilitarian design with extensive documentary content and careful editing. It is extremely informative and worth a long visit.

CONTENT   ★ ★ ★ ★ ★
AESTHETICS   ★ ★ ★
NAVIGATION   ★ ★ ★ ★

TEXAS

Official Historic Website of the 10th Texas Infantry
http://members.aol.com/SMckay1234/

This site, created by a private historian and reenactor, invites online researchers to construct a history of the 10th Texas Infantry, which saw action in Arkansas, Georgia, and Tennessee in 1863 and 1864. Rosters, letters, and official military correspondence make this one of the best sites for documentary content on a Confederate unit.

Visitors may want to start by going to the Battle Reports section and skimming the contents to see when and where the 10th Texas Infantry operated. Clicking the name of a battle accesses a detailed report of the unit's actions there. One of the more interesting reports is the one for Tunnel Hill, Tennessee, which was defended from attacking Union forces during the Battle of Chattanooga. The anonymous author of the report, which was printed in the *Memphis Daily Appeal*, wrote to exonerate the 10th Infantry and other units in his command from the Confederate disaster there: "To sum up—we lost no prisoners, lost no artillery, held our position against five times our numbers, took two hundred prisoners and five stands of colors, repulsed the enemy and charged them twice from our works, driving them from the field. That night we crossed the Chickamauga, learning . . . every where of our disaster at other points on the line." Other battles covered in the Battle Reports section include Chickamauga, Pickett's Mill, Atlanta, and Franklin. Many of the reports are accompanied by links to additional information about that battle, such as casualty lists, letters, and ordnance records.

The site features an impressive collection of transcribed personal papers that have been assembled in chronological order. Some of the documents in this section have been contributed by descendents of members of the original regiment. Others are previously published works, and still others have been located in different repositories by the site's designer. One letter, written by First Lieutenant Overton F. Davenport to his brother in December 1863, echoes the defensiveness of the Tunnel Hill report that appeared in the Memphis *Appeal:* "I notice that the papers give all the credit of the fight on Missionary Ridge on the right to the 2nd Tenn & 5th Arkansas. I like to see honor given to whom honor is due but our Brigade done the fighting that day on the right the others might have done equally as well if they had been there but they were held in reserve & I never saw them on the field & if they are to receive the honor, I would like for them to share the danger."

Additional contents on the 10th Texas Infantry site include rosters, casualty lists, and ordnance reports. The rosters list the men by company, and since each company was recruited from a particular Texas county, the men in each company were likely to be neighbors. For each man, the rosters provide the rank, age, date of enlistment, and "remarks." The Official Historic Website of the 10th Texas Infantry is one of the few regimental history sites that feature casualty reports, which give the name of men killed, wounded, or captured during every engagement. Interesting details from personal papers and published accounts have been inserted into the lists. Ordnance reports, filed by officers after every engagement to record the loss of equipment, allow researchers to see the kinds of rifles and ammunition the men of the 10th used. After the Battle of Tunnel Hill, Captain Jonathan Kennard recorded the following losses:

> 103 Austrian Rifles, Cal. 54
>   14 Mississippi Rifles, Cal. 54
> 204 Rifle Bayonets
> 104 Cartridge Boxes
> 112 Cap Boxes
> 122 Waist Belts & Plates
> 153 C B Belts
> 224 Bayonet Scabbards
>   31 Knapsacks
> 144 Haversacks
>   56 Canteens & Straps
>   8 Ammunition Boxes

Innovative and extensive use of primary sources on this site compensates for distracting background images and proofreading errors. Anyone seeking a deep understanding of the experience of a Confederate infantry unit will be well served by a visit to this interesting site.

CONTENT   ★ ★ ★ ★
AESTHETICS   ★ ★ ★
NAVIGATION   ★ ★ ★ ★ ★

U.S. COLORED TROOPS

5th Regimental Cavalry, United States Colored Troops

http://members.home.net:80/5thuscc/

See Chapter 5 for a description.

WISCONSIN

The 26th Wisconsin Infantry Volunteers

http://www.agro.agri.umn.edu/~lemedg/wis26/26pgmain.htm

FIGURE 8.3

**Image from The 26th Wisconsin—the official web site of the
26th Wisconsin Infantry Volunteers**

This site, sponsored by the Sons of the 26th Wisconsin Infantry Volunteers, is a compelling documentary account of the 26th Wisconsin Infantry. Composed primarily of German immigrants, the 26th Wisconsin fought at Chancellorsville,
Gettysburg, and Atlanta, and it participated in Sherman's March to the Sea.
Heavy casualties suffered by the unit during these battles and campaigns led
William F. Fox, in his influential *Regimental Losses in the Civil War*, to include
the 26th Wisconsin in his Fighting 300. Only four other units lost a greater
proportion of men.

The section titled History opens with an illustrated summary of the 26th's Civil
War record, with key terms linked to other pages on the site or to outside sites.
Clicking Day to Day History accesses a chronological compilation of excerpts
from letters, diaries, reports, and newspaper articles. On August 13, 1862, for

example, the Milwaukee *Sentinel* printed this announcement: "'GERMAN AMERICANS' FOR GEN. SIGEL'S COMMAND. All are invited, without regard to nationality, to serve under that gallant commander. F. C. Winkler, Francis Lackner, Chas. Doerflinger, Louis C. Heide and others are combining their efforts to raise a first rate company. Fall in for the army of Virginia!" On the same day, Karl Karsten wrote in his diary, "I signed up as a solder for the U.S.A. for three years." In addition to this innovative timeline, the material in History also includes a reprint of a regimental history written in 1866, the memoirs of Generals Carl Schurz and Oliver Otis Howard, and descriptions of rifles used by the men of the 26th.

Visitors who choose to go directly to the documents themselves can read the Letters/Diaries, Documents, or Newspaper section. One of the letters was written by Adam Muenzenberger to his wife. Muenzenberger, along with many others in his unit, was captured at the Battle of Gettysburg and held at Richmond's Libby Prison, where he died a few months later. The letters in this section have been transcribed from the originals in the University of Wisconsin Milwaukee Library, the Wisconsin State Historical Society, and other sources. Documents include the Official Records for the Battle of Chancellorsville, the Battle of Gettysburg, and the Atlanta and Savannah campaigns. Writing from North Carolina in March 1865, Captain Fred Winkler recorded the damage his Wisconsin men had inflicted on the Southern countryside: "The whole amount taken from the country may be about as follows: Eight hundred pounds of wheat flour, 4,000 pounds of corn meal, 550 bushels of sweet potatoes, 13,000 pounds of meat, 900 pounds of lard, 150 pounds of dried fruit."

The site's newspaper transcriptions show how leaders jealously protected their units' reputations. Major General Franz Sigel wrote to the *Daily Wisconsin* in November 1862 that rumors of 26th's cowardice at Thoroughfare Gap were entirely false: "The whole story about throwing away arms . . . is a most malicious and infamous miss ticket misrepresentation and lie, brought up by some treacherous scoundrel."

The 26th Wisconsin site has augmented the traditional rosters featured in most regimental web sites. In addition to providing the rank, company, place enlisted, and "remarks" for every member of the regiment, the Interactive Roster links many men's names to documents, photographs, and biographical narratives. Clicking the name of Henry Fink, a private in Company B, reveals that Fink was a Milwaukee store clerk before the war. After his discharge due to wounds received at Chancellorsville, Fink became a traveling salesman and later became active in state politics and veterans' organizations.

The memoirs linked to Major General Oliver Otis Howard's name in the roster list shed light on the centrality of ethnicity in recruitment and command.

Since Howard's appointment as commander of the 11th Corps was accompanied by the demotion of German-born commanders Franz Sigel and Carl Schurz, there was resentment in the ranks. Howard wrote, "The corps . . . had about 5,000 Germans and 8,000 Americans. . . . Outwardly I met a cordial reception, but I soon found that my past record was not known here; that there was much complaint in the German language at the removal of Sigel."

The 26th Wisconsin is an excellent model of a regimental web site. Rich and extensive documents and secondary narrative are creatively linked in ways that invite visitors to explore for hours.

CONTENT   ★ ★ ★ ★ ★
AESTHETICS ★ ★ ★
NAVIGATION ★ ★ ★ ★

SUGGESTED READINGS

Driver, Robert J. *The First and Second Rockbridge Artillery*. Virginia Regimental Histories Series. Appomattox, VA, 1987.

———. *Fourteenth Virginia Cavalry*. Virginia Regimental Histories Series. Appomattox, VA, 1988.

———. *First Virginia Calvary*. Virginia Regimental Histories Series. Appomattox, VA, 1991.

Dyer, Frederick H. *A Compendium of the War of the Rebellion*. 1908. Reprint. Dayton, OH, 1979.

Fox, William F. *Regimental Losses in the Civil War*. 1898. Reprint. Dayton, OH, 1993.

Gaff, Alan D. *On Many a Bloody Field: Four Years in the Iron Brigade*. Bloomington, IN, 1997.

Gordon, John B. *Reminiscences of the Civil War*. 1888. Reprint. Baton Rouge, LA, 1993.

Hagerty, Edward J. *Collis' Zouaves: The 114th Pennsylvania Volunteers in the Civil War*. Baton Rouge, LA, 1997.

Johansson, M. Jane. *Peculiar Honor: A History of the 28th Texas Cavalry, 1862–1865*. Fayetteville, AR, 1998.

Krick, Robert E. L. *40th Virginia Infantry*. The Virginia Regimental Histories Series. Appomattox, VA, 1985.

McGowen, Stanley S. *Horse Sweat and Powder Smoke: The First Texas Cavalry in the Civil War*. Texas A & M University Military History Series, no. 66. College Station, TX, 1999.

Miller, Edward A., Jr. *The Black Civil War Soldiers of Illinois: The Story of the Twenty-ninth U.S. Colored Infantry*. Columbia, SC, 1998.

Morris, W. S., L. D. Hartwell, and J. B. Kuykendall. *History 31st Regiment Illinois Volunteers.* Carbondale, IL, 1998.

Morrison, Marion, and John Y. Simon. *A History of the Ninth Regiment Illinois Volunteer Infantry, with the Regimental Roster.* Carbondale, IL, 1997.

Mullholland, St. Clair A. *The Story of the 116th Regiment, Pennsylvania Volunteers in the War of the Rebellion: Pennsylvania Volunteers in the War of Rebellion.* New York, 1996.

Norman, Douglas Hale. *The Third Texas Cavalry in the Civil War.* Norman, OK, 1992.

Overmyer, Jack K. *A Stupendous Effort: The 87th Indiana in the War of the Rebellion.* Bloomington, IN, 1997.

Washington, Versalle F. *Eagles on Their Buttons: A Black Infantry Regiment in the Civil War.* Shades of Blue and Gray Series. Columbia, MO, 1999.

Watkins, Sam R. *Co. Aytch: A Confederate's Memoir of the Civil War.* 1880. Reprint. New York, 1997.

Wilkinson, Warren. *Mother, May You Never See the Sights I Have Seen: The Fifty-seventh Massachusetts Veteran Volunteers in the Army of the Potomac 1864–1865.* New York, 1990.

PART II

SITES
WORTH
A VISIT

A

TOPICAL

INDEX

GENERAL SITES

Civil War

http://www.civilwar.com

Created by a web design company as a public service; features an illustrated timeline of the war with brief accounts of major battles.

The Civil War Artillery Page

http://www.cwartillery.org

Extremely thorough explanation of artillery technology, organization, and strategy, with excellent diagrams and other illustrations.

The Civil War Home Page

http://www.rugreview.com/cw/cwhp.htm

Part of an advertisement for an antiques dealer; features digital reproductions of illustrations and articles from *Harper's* and *Century* magazines written during the Civil War about important battles.

Civil War Sites Advisory Commission Battle Summaries

http://www2.cr.nps.gov/abpp/battles/tvii.htm

National Park Service site; provides brief summaries of hundreds of Civil War battles divided into campaigns and listed in chronological order.

Civil War Traveler

http://civilwartraveler.com/

Made by a small Virginia publishing company; provides a guide to Civil War tourist attractions in Maryland, Virginia, West Virginia, and Washington, DC.

Confederate States Armory Homepage

http://www.geocities.com/Athens/Delphi/1880/csarmory/csarmory.html

Privately made site; contains a brief history of Confederate armories, with letters from the National Archives Compiled Military Service Records, maps, biographical sketches, and drawings.

Selected Civil War Photographs in the American Memory Collection

http://memory.loc.gov/ammem/cwphome.html

Database of hundreds of battlefield photographs taken by Matthew Brady and other notable photographers as well as a timeline linked to key photographs in the collection; part of the Library of Congress's American Memory Project.

Shotgun's Home of the American Civil War

http://www.civilwarhome.com

The most comprehensive single online source for Orders of Battle, Official Records, and other firsthand accounts of practically every major Civil War battle.

This Week in the Civil War

http://www.civilweek.com/

Privately made site; contains Official Records and other documents pertaining to military events "this week" in the war.

United States Civil War

http://www.us-civilwar.com/

Privately made site; provides a timeline of major military events in the Civil War.

The Valley of the Shadow: Two Communities in the American Civil War, The War Years

http://jefferson.village.virginia.edu/cwhome.html

University of Virginia site; contains an interactive theater-level map showing battles fought by regiments from two counties, one in the North and one in the South, with each battle linked to information about that unit's experience there. Also, features newspapers, letters and diaries, Official Records.

The *War Times Journal*: The American Civil War Series

http://www.wtj.com/wars/civilwar/

Commercial site; includes memoirs and other primary sources about Shiloh, Antietam, Fredericksburg, Gettysburg, and other battles.

ANTIETAM/SHARPSBURG

Antietam—A Photographic Tour

http://www.enteract.com/~westwood/

Privately made site; contains photographs, topographical maps, and a brief narrative of the Battle of Antietam.

Antietam: The Bloodiest Day

http://www.alleghenymountain.org/antmain.htm

Created by a local historian and part of a larger site on the Civil War in the Allegheny Highlands; contains an illustrated summary of the battle and an animated map.

Antietam National Battlefield

http://www.nps.gov/anti/home.htm

National Park Service site; provides a brief overview of the Battle of Antietam, with emphasis on the battle's role in Lincoln's Emancipation Proclamation.

Brian Downey's Antietam on the Web

http://www.geocities.com/Athens/Olympus/1845

Well-designed, privately made site; provides in-depth analysis as well as interesting primary sources.

APPOMATTOX

See Richmond

CHANCELLORSVILLE

See Fredericksburg

CHICKAMAUGA AND CHATTANOOGA

The Battle of Chickamauga: An Alabama Infantry Regiment's Perspective

http://www.19thalabama.org/battles/chickamauga/index.html

Created by a Civil War reenactment group; has good overview of the Battle of Chickamauga as it was experienced by one regiment.

Chattanooga: A Road Trip Through Time

http://www.mediaalchemy.com/civilwar/

Created by a team of professional web designers; contains an excellent narrative, artistic photographs, and informative maps.

COLD HARBOR

See Richmond

CORINTH
See Western Theater

FLORIDA

Battle of Olustee
http://extlab1.entnem.ufl.edu/olustee

Created by a University of Florida entomologist and battlefield preservationist; provides a capsule history as well as detailed analysis, primary documents, and regimental histories.

FREDERICKSBURG

Battle of Fredericksburg
http://members.aol.com/lmjarl/civwar/frdrksburg.html

Created by a private researcher; home to a nicely detailed description of the Battle of Fredericksburg and its effect on Union command.

Fredericksburg and Spotsylvania National Military Park Visitor Center
http://www.nps.gov/frsp/vc.htm

National Park Service site; has good overviews and excerpts of firsthand accounts of the four major battles fought around the Fredericksburg area.

GEORGIA
See also Chickamauga and Chattanooga

Pickett's Mill Battlefield Historic Site
http://www.geocities.com/Athens/Rhodes/8540/pickettsmillpg.html

Created to promote tourism in the area around the battlefield; features an extensive collection of documents, a narrative of battle, and biographical sketches of the generals in command of the Battle of Pickett's Mill, part of Sherman's Atlanta campaign.

GETTYSBURG

The Battle of Gettysburg by Brock Bourgase
http://www.geocities.com/Athens/Delphi/4633/

Privately made site; consists of a one-page essay on the battle, with key terms and names linked to pages with more detailed information.

Carl Reed's Gettysburg Revisited

http://home.sprynet.com/~carlreed/

Well-designed, privately made site; contains interesting essays, Official Records, and excerpts of previously published accounts.

The Gettysburg Address

http://lcweb.loc.gov/exhibits/gadd/

Part of the Library of Congress's American Memory project; provides an overview of the Battle of Gettysburg and the commemoration of the National Cemetery established there.

Gettysburg Discussion Group

http://www.gdg.org

Created by a Civil War history association; consists of essays and articles by association members as well as a small collection of primary sources.

Gettysburg National Military Park

http://www.nps.gov/gett/home.htm

National Park Service site; provides an exhaustive virtual tour covering each day of the battle in great detail.

Military History Online—Battle of Gettysburg

http://www.militaryhistoryonline.com/gettysburg

High-quality commercial site; a section on the Battle of Gettysburg contains essays, documents, and highly detailed descriptions of the battle.

MANASSAS/BULL RUN

A Last Salute

http://www.espdesigns.com/salute/

Made by an educational technology design firm; documents ongoing archeological excavations of human remains and armaments at the Manassas Battlefield.

Manassas National Battlefield Park

http://www.nps.gov/mana/home.htm

National Park Service site; includes a good overview of the First and Second Battles of Manassas, with much of the material designed especially for students.

MARYLAND

See also Antietam

Monocacy National Battlefield

http://www.nps.gov/mono/home.htm

Nicely designed National Park Service site; contains an informative, well-written overview about the "battle to save Washington."

MISSOURI

See Western Theater

NEW MARKET

The Battle of New Market, Virginia, May 15, 1864

http://www.vmi.edu/~archtml/cwnm.html

Part of a larger Civil War site; contains fascinating documentary account of the Virginia Military Institute's role in this battle.

NORTH CAROLINA

Bentonville Battleground

http://www.ah.dcr.state.nc.us/sections/hs/bentonvi/bentonvi.htm

Part of a large web site on North Carolina historic places; contains an overview of the battle as well as outstanding maps.

PENINSULAR CAMPAIGN

See Richmond

PETERSBURG

Petersburg National Battlefield

http://www.nps.gov/pete/mahan/PNBhome.html

National Park Service site; provides a thorough overview of the important events in and around Petersburg during the Civil War.

The Siege of Petersburg

http://members.aol.com/siege1864/

Privately made site; contains highly detailed information about armies and leaders during the Union Army's Siege of Petersburg.

RICHMOND

Appomattox Courthouse National Historic Park

http://www.nps.gov/apco/

Created by the National Park Service; provides an overview of the events leading up to Lee's surrender at Appomattox as well as an interesting explanation of how Confederate soldiers were paroled.

The Battle of Staunton River Bridge: June 25, 1864

http://www2.halifax.com/county/battle/stauntpk.htm

Created by the Staunton River Battlefield State Park; contains a description of this battle fought in southeast Virginia and a map of troop movements in the region.

Richmond National Battlefield Park Homepage

http://www.nps.gov/rich/home.htm

National Park Service site; contains material on the Peninsular Campaign of 1862 as well as Grant's overland campaign of 1864, with an especially powerful section on Cold Harbor.

SOUTH CAROLINA

Civil War @ Charleston

http://www.awod.com/gallery/probono/cwchas/cwlayout.html

Created by a Charleston Civil War reenactor; contains information on naval and land battles fought around Charleston, South Carolina.

SPOTSYLVANIA

See Fredericksburg

VICKSBURG

See Western Theater

V I R G I N I A

See also Fredericksburg, Manassas, and Richmond

Civil War in the Shenandoah Valley, 1863–1865

http://www.rockingham.k12.va.us/EMS/Civil_War_in_the_Shenandoah/Civil_
War_in_the_Shenandoah.htm

Made by a Virginia public schoolteacher; includes brief narratives of the Shenandoah military campaigns that took place from 1863 to 1865.

Harpers Ferry National Historic Park

http://www.nps.gov/hafe/home.htm

National Park Service site; provides brief overviews of the military campaigns in and around Harpers Ferry, (West) Virginia.

W E S T E R N   T H E A T E R

The Battle of Galveston (1 January 1863)

http://www.lsjunction.com/events/galvestn.htm

Part of a commercial web site on Texas history; provides a one-page description of the Confederate recapture of the port of Galveston.

The Battle of Mill Springs/Fishing Creek

http://www.geocities.com/Pentagon/Quarters/1864/Default.htm

Privately made site; features Orders of Battle, Official Records, photographs, diagrams of weapons, casualty lists, and unit rosters pertaining to the Battle of Mill Springs, Kentucky, in 1862.

Britton Lane Battlefield Association: "The Battle That History Forgot"

http://www.brittonlane1862.madison.tn.us/

Made by a local preservation agency; contains a brief secondary account, reenactment photographs, and an interesting map of this "forgotten" battle in Tennessee.

The Civil War in Arkansas

http://www.civilwarbuff.org

Made by the Arkansas Civil War Round Table; features a searchable (by location and date) database of Civil War events that took place in Arkansas.

Corinth: Crossroads of the Confederacy

http://www.corinth.org/

Created by local tourist agency; provides an excellent overview of the Civil War battles and skirmishes fought around Corinth, Mississippi.

Fort Scott National Historic Site

http://www.nps.gov/fosc/home.htm

National Park Service site about a Union outpost in Kansas and the battles fought in the area.

Vicksburg National Military Park

http://www.nps.gov/vick/home.htm

National Park Service site; covers the Vicksburg campaign and contains a database of paroled Confederate soldiers.

The *War Times Journal*: Visiting the Battle of Picacho Pass Historic Site

http://www.wtj.com/articles/picacho/

Part of a larger commercial site; provides an interesting account of this little-studied New Mexico battle.

Wilson's Creek National Battlefield

http://www.nps.gov/wicr

National Park Service site; provides a lively account of this battle as well as a good analysis of the political and military events in Missouri throughout the war.

WILDERNESS

The Battle of the Wilderness: A Virtual Tour

http://home.att.net/~hallowed-ground/wilderness_tour.html

Created by two Civil War enthusiasts to tell the story of the Wilderness through the use of photographs and explanatory narrative.

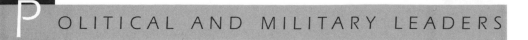

POLITICAL AND MILITARY LEADERS

GENERAL SITES

Biographies of North Georgia

http://ngeorgia.com/people

Brief histories of dozens of Civil War leaders who were from North Georgia or who had a "profound effect" on the region.

Germans in the American Civil War

http://www.geocities.com/Athens/Atlantis/2816/germans/heimat.html

Made by a genealogist; contains biographies of well-known German-born Civil War leaders.

Pearce Civil War Documents Collection

http://www.nav.cc.tx.us/lrc/Homepg2.htm

Based on a collection of Civil War papers donated to Navarro College by a private collector; includes transcriptions and scans of letters by Civil War leaders ranging from Joshua Chamberlain to Nathan Bedford Forrest.

Selected Civil War Photographs

http://lcweb2.loc.gov/ammem/cwphome.html

Part of the Library of Congress's American Memory project; houses photographs of dozens of Civil War leaders.

Shotgun's Home of the American Civil War

http://www.civilwarhome.com

Privately made site; contains material excerpted or paraphrased from previously published sources on more than a hundred Civil War leaders.

United States Civil War

http://www.us-civilwar.com/

Brief biographical sketches of dozens of Civil War notables.

The *War Times Journal*: The Civil War Series: Longstreet, Sherman, Hood, and Gordon

http://www.wtj.com/wars/civilwar/

Commercial site; features lengthy excerpts from the public domain memoirs of four important Civil War generals: James Longstreet, William Tecumseh Sherman, John B. Hood, and John B. Gordon.

A R M I S T E A D ,   L E W I S   A .

Brig. General Lewis A. Armistead, C.S.A.

http://pw2.netcom.com/~buck1755/laa.htm

Privately made site; contains a very brief biographical sketch of this leader of the 9th Virginia Infantry.

B E A U R E G A R D ,   P .   G .   T .

General P. G. T. Beauregard

http://www.beau.lib.la.us/~belflowr/bgard/pgtbgard.htm

Created by the public library of Beauregard Parish, Louisiana; offers a short overview of Beauregard's life, with an emphasis on his Confederate military career and his postwar political activity.

B R A G G ,   B R A X T O N

General Braxton Bragg

http://www.ils.unc.edu/nc/BraxtonBragg.html

Part of a North Carolina history web site created at the University of North Carolina for elementary school students; contains a short sketch of the life of Bragg.

C H A L M E R S ,   J A M E S   R .

General James R. Chalmers

http://members.aol.com/danhaire/chalmer1.htm

Privately made site by fan of Chalmers, who fought in the western theater with Bragg and Forrest; consists of an excerpt from Ezra Warner's *Generals in Gray*.

C H A M B E R L A I N ,   J O S H U A   L .

Chamberlain Biography

http://www.curtislibrary.com/pejepscot/joshbiog.htm

Made by a Maine historical society; features a scholarly, concise essay on the life of the Hero of Little Round Top.

CLEBURNE, PATRICK R.

Confederate States of America: General Patrick R. Cleburne

http://www.westga.edu/~cscott/general.html

Made by a professor at the State University of West Georgia; contains a brief biographical sketch of Cleburne and a transcription of his letter advocating the enlistment of slaves in the Confederate army.

The Patrick Cleburne Society

http://www.patrickcleburne.com

Privately made site by a group of Cleburne fans; features a one-page highly complimentary biography of this Irish-born lawyer who led the defense of Tunnel Hill in the Battle of Missionary Ridge and who was one of the first to propose emancipating slaves in return for their enlistment in the Confederate army.

COOPER, SAMUEL

General Samuel Cooper

http://www.generalcooper.com/

Privately made site; contains extensive information about Cooper, who served as the adjutant and inspector general of the Confederate army, as well as information on Cooper's ancestors and descendants.

DAVIS, JEFFERSON

The Papers of Jefferson Davis

http://www.ruf.rice.edu/~pjdavis/jdp.htm

Made at Rice University, offers selections from the multivolume series of Jefferson Davis's collected papers.

EARLY, JUBAL A.

Jubal A. Early Homeplace Preservation, 1816–1894

http://www.jubalearly.org

Designed primarily to solicit support for preserving the Jubal A. Early Homeplace; features quotations by Civil War historians Gary Gallagher and Douglas Southall Freeman about this important Confederate general.

F A R R A G U T , D A V I D G L A S G O W

Admiral David Glasgow Farragut (1801–1870)

http://www.encompass.net/ctyson/civwar/farmain.htm

Privately made site; reprints Alfred Thayer Mahan's biography of this famous Union admiral.

F O R R E S T , N A T H A N B E D F O R D

The Forrest Preserve

http://nbforrest.com

Privately made site; contains transcripts of speeches by Nathan Bedford Forrest and an essay on his Civil War career.

Forrest's Headquarters

http://members.aol.com/GnrlJSB/index.html

Made by an avid Forrest partisan; consists largely of complimentary essays about this notorious general.

G R A N T , U L Y S S E S S .

An SR Books
BEST CIVIL WAR SITE
Selection

The Ulysses S. Grant Association

http://www.lib.siu.edu/projects/usgrant

Made by a group affiliated with Southern Illinois University; features a link to Grant's memoirs, a chronology of Grant's life, and an essay by Bruce Catton, as well as other resources.

Ulysses Grant *Memoirs*

http://home.nycap.rr.com/history/grant.html

Part of a larger site titled Scholars' Guide to WWW, made by a retired professor; contains memoirs transcribed in full with a hyperlinked table of contents.

Ulysses S. Grant Home Page

http://www.mscomm.com/~ulysses/

Made by a private organization; contains reprints of public domain sources on Grant.

Ulysses S. Grant Network

http://saints.css.edu/mkelsey/gppg.html

Maintained by the Ulysses S. Grant Network, an organization seeking to preserve Grant's tomb and other landmarks; offers a variety of primary documents and secondary narratives.

JACKSON, THOMAS J. "STONEWALL"

Stonewall Jackson Resources at the Virginia Military Institute Archives

http://www.vmi.edu/~archtml/jackson.html

Extensive collection of primary documents about this famous general, who
had been a professor at the Virginia Military Institute.

JOHNSON, EDWARD "ALLEGHANY"

Edward Alleghany Johnson World Wide Web Page

http://www.fsu.edu/~ewoodwar

Made by a Florida State University researcher; contains extensive reprints of
public domain sources on Johnson's life.

LEE, ROBERT E.

The Apotheosis of Robert E. Lee

http://xroads.virginia.edu/~CAP/LEE/lee.html

Made by University of Virginia students for a class project; features interesting account of Lee's postwar deification as well as original documents
that include late nineteenth- and early twentieth-century poems and essays
about the Confederate general.

Robert E. Lee Memorial

http://www.nps.gov/gwmp/arl_hse.html

National Park Service site; consists of one page of historic material focused
on the history of the Arlington house, Lee's home seized by the U.S. government during the Civil War.

The Robert E. Lee Papers at Washington and Lee University

http://miley.wlu.edu/LeePapers/

Beautiful digital reproductions of selections of Lee's official correspondence as Confederate general and as president of Washington College (now Washington and Lee University).

Stratford Hall Plantation: The Birthplace of Robert E. Lee

http://www.stratfordhall.org

Made to encourage visits to Lee's birthplace; paints a complimentary picture of Lee through the use of primary documents and essays.

LINCOLN, ABRAHAM

Abraham Lincoln Online

http://www.netins.net/showcase/creative/lincoln.html

A volunteer effort by a group of Lincoln partisans; features Lincoln This Week as well as the transcripts of numerous well-known speeches and writings by Lincoln.

Abraham Lincoln Research Site

http://members.aol.com/RVSNorton/Lincoln2.html

Made by a retired history teacher; features a wealth of material on Lincoln's family life as well as a well-documented and fascinating account of the national mourning that followed Lincoln's assassination.

Assassination of President Lincoln and the Trial of the Assassins (Brigadier-General Henry Lawrence Burnett)

http://www.tiac.net/users/ime/famtree/burnett/lincoln.htm

Made by a genealogist; contains reprints of General Henry L. Burnett's previously published account of the trail of John Wilkes Booth and his co-conspirators; Burnett assisted in the capture and prosecution of Booth.

Ford's Theatre National Historical Site

http://www.nps.gov/foth/index2.htm

National Park Service site; contains an interesting hyperlinked narrative on Lincoln's assassination.

Lincoln: Man, Martyr, Myth

http://xroads.virginia.edu/~CAP/LINCOLN/lincoln.htm

Made a group of University of Virginia students as a class project; examines the process by which Lincoln became a national icon and also contains late nineteenth-century poems, essays, and art work.

Lincoln/Net: The Abraham Lincoln Digitization Project

http://lincoln.lib.niu.edu/

Focused on Lincoln's Illinois years; first installment consists of a searchable database of campaign songs from 1860 and 1864; promises to be the largest source of research material on Abraham Lincoln. Based at the University of Northern Illinois.

Mr. Lincoln's Virtual Library

http://lcweb2.loc.gov/ammem/alhtml/

Part of the Library of Congress's American Memory project; consists of online exhibits about the Gettysburg Address and the Emancipation Proclamation.

Sheet Music about Lincoln, Emancipation, and the Civil War

http://memory.loc.gov/ammem/scsmhtml/scsmhome.html

Part of the Library of Congress's extensive American Memory project; features a searchable collection of hundreds of song lyrics and scans of sheet music about Lincoln, emancipation, and the Civil War.

LONGSTREET, JAMES

The Longstreet Chronicles

http://tennessee-scv.org/longstreet/

Created by a Longstreet fan intent on rehabilitating Longstreet's reputation; contains essays and an impressive collection of primary sources.

LORING, WILLIAM WING

The William Wing Loring World Wide Website: 50 Years a Soldier

http://home.earthlink.net/~atomic_rom/loring.htm

Privately made site; features a long hyperlinked biography of this general who fought in the Seminole Wars, Texan war for independence, and Mexican-American War before leaving the U.S. Army to serve as brigadier general of the Confederate Army of Northern Virginia and then becoming an advisor to the Egyptian army after the war; contains public domain documents, essays, and maps.

MCCLELLAN, GEORGE B.

The McClellan Society's MG George B. McClellan Pages

http://www.civilwarreader.com/McClellan/index.html

Features exhaustive research by avid McClellan partisans; refutes "frequently asserted claims" against McClellan and reviews several books assessing McClellan's generalship.

MEADE, GEORGE GORDON

The Meade Archive

http://adams.patriot.net/~jcampi/welcome.htm

Made by a group of Meade fans; contains a nice collection of documents as well as interesting essays about this Union general.

THOMAS, GEORGE

The George H. Thomas Home Page

http://home.att.net/~dmercado/index.htm

Privately made site; features a chronology and essay about this Virginian who fought for the Union.

WHEELER, JOSEPH

Pond Spring and the Joe Wheeler Home

http://www.wheelerplantation.org

Made to encourage visits to the Wheeler Plantation; consists of a brief, illustrated biography of this lieutenant general of cavalry for the Army of the Tennessee.

LIFE OF THE SOLDIER

GENERAL SITES

Revised Regulations for the Army of the United States, 1861

http://members.tripod.com/howardlanham/unireg.htm

Made by a lay historian; contains the complete Revised Regulations for the Army of the United States, published in 1861.

CAMP LIFE

An SR Books
BEST CIVIL WAR SITE
Selection

Camp Life: Civil War Collections from Gettysburg National Military Park

http://www.cr.nps.gov/csd/gettex/

National Park Service site; features beautiful images of artifacts from the Gettysburg National Military Park museum as well as informative explanatory narrative.

Civil War Music of the Western Border

http://www.mid-mo.net/dpara/civilwar/

Created by team of Missouri musicians to advertise their recordings; contains full lyrics of Civil War songs as well as liner notes from their albums.

Poetry and Music of the War Between the States

http://users.erols.com/kfraser/

Privately made site; contains lyrics and names of lyricists for hundreds of songs about the Civil War, most of which were composed during the war itself; songs can be heard with the proper plug-in.

United States Civil War

http://www.us-civilwar.com/

Contains an unusual assortment of material, including camp recipes, one of which is for a substitute for coffee made with acorns and bacon fat.

ETHNIC GROUPS

Jews in the Civil War

http://www.jewish-history.com/civilwar.htm

Part of a large Jewish history and genealogy site; contains a fascinating collection of firsthand accounts of the war by Jewish soldiers as well as correspondence about Jewish soldiers by high commanders on both sides.

HOSPITALS AND MEDICINE

Civil War Medicine

http://www.powerweb.net/bbock/war/

Privately made site; consists largely of illustrated essays by the designer discussing developments in medical technology and hospital design over the course of the war; includes complete bibliography suggesting avenues for further research.

Images from: *Photographic Atlas of Civil War Injuries* and *Orthopaedic Injuries of the Civil War*

http://www.iserv.net/~civilmed/images.html

Made by the Medical Staff Press to publicize its books; consists of graphic photographs of Civil War battle wounds and accompanying case descriptions on how the wounds were treated.

Medicine in the Civil War

http://www.cl.utoledo.edu/canaday/quackery/quack8.html

Part of a large web site on the history of medicine created by the University of Toledo Library; describes wounds inflicted by different types of ammunition and explains how they were treated; contains drawings taken from *Medical and Surgical History of the War of the Rebellion.*

United States Sanitary Commission

http://www.netwalk.com/~jpr/index.htm

Made by a Civil War reenactor; an excellent source of material on medical care for Civil War soldiers.

Whitman's *Drum Taps* and Washington's Civil War Hospitals

http://xroads.virginia.edu/~CAP/hospital/whitman.htm

Made by a University of Virginia student as a class project; a compelling documentary account of military hospitals in Washington, DC, during the Civil War.

LETTERS AND DIARIES

American Civil War Resources in the Special Collections Department, University Libraries, Virginia Tech

http://spec.lib.vt.edu/civwar/cwhp.htm

Maintained by the Virginia Polytechnic Institute; contains an impressive collection of Civil War letters—some transcribed and scanned, some transcribed but not scanned, and some only described.

The Calvin Shedd Papers

http://www.library.miami.edu/archives/shedd/index.htm

Made by the University of Miami Archives; contains the transcribed letters of a Union soldier stationed in Florida.

Civil War Diaries

http://sparc5.augustana.edu/library/civil.html

Created by the library of Augustana College in Rock Island, Illinois; contains two Civil War diaries, one of which, by Basil H. Messler of the Mississippi Marine Brigade, has been painstakingly transcribed and annotated.

Civil War Diary of Bingham Findley Junkin, 100th Pennsylvania Volunteer Infantry ("Roundheads")

http://www.iwaynet.net/~lsci/junkin/

Diary of Bingham F. Junkin transcribed by his descendents; covers Junkin's experiences in the battles of the Wilderness and Cold Harbor with important terms linked to explanatory notes.

Dwight Henry Cory Letters and Diary

http://homepages.rootsweb.com/~lovelace/cory.htm

Made by a descendent of Cory; features transcription of letters written by Cory, 6th Ohio Volunteer Cavalry, as he took part in most of the major battles of the Eastern theater.

Electronic Text Center: Subject: American Civil War

http://etext.lib.virginia.edu/subjects/American-Civil-War.html

Massive, searchable collection of Civil War letters, diaries, and memoirs, all transcribed in full and with beautifully digitized scans of many of the originals.

Illinois Greyhounds

http://www.ketzle.com/diary/

Made by a descendent of Henry Ketzle, who served in the 37th Illinois Volunteer Infantry; contains Ketzle's postwar memoirs.

Letters from an Iowa Soldier in the Civil War

www.civilwarletters.com

Created by descendents of the letters' authors; features transcriptions of more than a dozen letters (scan available for one) written by Newton Robert Scott of the 36th Iowa Infantry to friends and family at home, with links from names and places mentioned in the letters to explanatory information.

Letters of the Civil War (from the Newspapers of Massachusetts)

http://www.geocities.com/Pentagon/7914/

Privately made site; compilation of letters written by Massachusetts soldiers to their hometown newspapers.

The Memoirs, Diary, and Life of Private Jefferson Moses, Company G, 93rd Illinois Volunteers

http://www.ioweb.com/civilwar/

Made by a descendent; contains the diary of Private Jefferson Moses, Company G, 93rd Illinois Volunteers, which has been transcribed and broken down by date and which covers events in 1864 and 1865 in South Carolina and North Carolina.

Overall Family Civil War Letters

http://www.geocities.com/Heartland/Acres/1574/

Created by descendents of the Overall family to share the letters of Isaac Overall, a member of the 36th Ohio Volunteer Infantry, and his family at home; contains both transcriptions and scanned images of the letters as well as a helpful summary page.

Prisoner of War Letters of Brigadier General Montgomery Dent Corse

http://www.alexandria.lib.va.us/corse/corse.htm

Created by a public library in Alexandria, Virginia; provides biographical information on Corse, who commanded the 17th Virginia Infantry, and contains transcriptions and images of five letters he wrote while a prisoner of war in Boston.

Samuel S. Dunton Civil War Letters

http://home.pacbell.net/dunton/SSDletters.html

Made by a descendent of Dunton; contains twelve letters written by Dunton while he was stationed near Washington, DC, and in Louisiana.

The Steubing Letters: The Civil War Letters of W. J. and Nancy Steubing

http://www.geocities.com/Athens/Cyprus/6533/

Privately made site; contains transcriptions of sixteen letters written between William J. Steubing, a German immigrant who served as a blacksmith in the 26th Texas Cavalry, and his wife.

PRISONS

Alton in the Civil War: Alton Prison

http://www.altonweb.com/history/civilwar/confed/index.html

Part of the community web site for the city of Alton, Illinois; contains a brief history of the prison as well as a database of approximately thirteen hundred men who died while held there.

Andersonville National Historic Site

http://www.corinthian.net/mccc/aville.html

Made by the Chamber of Commerce of Macon County, Georgia; features a brief history of Andersonville Prison and a searchable database of the men imprisoned there.

Archeology at Andersonville

http://www.cr.nps.gov/seac/andearch.htm

National Park Service site; contains a brief history of the notorious prison for captured Union soldiers and a description of the ongoing excavations at the site.

Camp Ford, C.S.A.

http://www.gower.net/Community/campford/campford.htm

Sponsored by a local historical society; contains a short history of Camp Ford, the largest Confederate prisoner of war camp west of the Mississippi River, a list of Union units to which the men imprisoned there belonged, and the number in each unit who died or escaped.

Famous Trials: The Trial of Captain Henry Wirz, Commandant Andersonville Prison, 1865

http://www.law.umkc.edu/faculty/projects/ftrials/wirz/wirz.htm

Created by a team of law students at the University of Missouri–Kansas City; contains a detailed analysis of the trial and execution of the captain of Andersonville Prison.

Salisbury Confederate Prison

http://www.ci.salisbury.nc.us/prison/csprison1.htm

Made by the town of Salisbury, North Carolina; features original drawings and other documents about the Confederate prison there and a description of a disastrous escape attempt.

NAVAL OPERATIONS

Admiral David Glasgow Farragut (1801–1870)

http://www.encompass.net/ctyson/civwar/farmain.htm

Privately made site; consists of a reprint of Alfred Thayer Mahan's biography of this famous Union admiral.

American Coast Defense Forts

http://www.geocities.com/~jmgould/seacoast.html

Aerial photographs and descriptions of Civil War era coastal fortifications made by a lay historian.

Battle Between the *Monitor* and the *Virginia*

http://www.ironclads.com/

Privately made site; features an illustrated description of this famous naval battle.

The Charles Read Home Page

http://www.fortunecity.com/meltingpot/cavendish/779/

Shortened version of the designer's previously published article about Read, who was lieutenant in the Confederate States Navy and later a captain in the British Merchant Marine.

Civil War @ Charleston

http://www.awod.com/gallery/probono/cwchas/cwlayout.html

Made by a Civil War reenactor; describes naval battles in and around the Charleston harbor.

Confederate Navy Collection Index at the Virginia State Library

http://image.vtls.com/collections/CN.html

Made by the Virginia State Library in Richmond; contains the digitized records of Confederate navy veterans.

C.S.S. *Alabama* Digital Collection

http://www.slis.ua.edu/tgtest/cssala/MAIN.HTM

Made by the University of Alabama W. S. Hoole Special Collections Library; features extensive resources about this famous Confederate raiding ship.

CSS *Albemarle*

http://www.cronab.demon.co.uk/alb.htm

Part of a large maritime history web site made by a naval history buff in Britain; describes the famous Confederate ram that was destroyed by a Union torpedo.

CSS *Neuse* State Historic Site

http://www.ah.dcr.state.nc.us/sections/hs/neuse/neuse.htm

Created by the North Carolina Department of Cultural Resources; covers the CSS *Neuse,* a Confederate ironclad built in eastern North Carolina but destroyed before it could be put to use against the enemy; considers the problems the Confederacy faced in building a strong naval fleet; contains a description and photographs of the ship's remains.

CSS *Virginia* Home Page

http://members.aol.com/vacsn/index.htm

Made by a descendant of an officer aboard the CSS *Virginia* during its battle with the USS *Monitor;* contains public domain documents as well as links to content on other sites.

The *Denbigh* Project

http://nautarch.tamu.edu/projects/denbigh/index.htm

Maintained by the Institute of Nautical Archaeology at Texas A&M University, which has embarked on a project to identify, document, and preserve the wreck of *Denbigh,* one of the most successful blockade runners of the American Civil War; contains a capsule history, a small collection of documents, and photographs of the wreckage.

Florida State University: Underwater Archaeology Projects

http://www.adp.fsu.edu/uw_proj.html

Description of Florida State University's underwater exploration of sunken Civil War vessels in the Mobile Harbor, including ruins of the Confederate blockade runner *Ivanhoe* and the Confederate ironclad CSS *Phoenix.*

Hunley Update

http://www.cla.sc.edu/sciaa/hunley1.html

Made by the University of South Carolina Institute of Archaeology and Anthropology; uses photographs, diagrams, and narrative to document the ongoing project to recover the remains of this Confederate submarine.

The *Hunley* Web Site

http://members.aol.com/litespdcom/index.html

Made by a Sons of Confederate Veterans chapter; disputes the claim made by the designers of the Official Site of the *H. L. Hunley* that they have found the ship's wreckage; most of the content cannot be viewed through a browser but must be downloaded.

Index of Civil War Naval Forces: Confederate and Union Ships

http://www.tarleton.edu/~kjones/navy.html

Exhaustive collection of links assembled by a professor at Tarleton University in Texas.

Ironclads and Blockade Runners of the American Civil War

http://www.ameritech.net/users/maxdemon/ironclad.htm

Privately made site; features an extensive collection of facts and frequently asked questions about naval aspects of the Civil War; also contains a bibliography, excerpts of public doman documents, lists of commanders, and photographs.

The Legacy of the USS *Monitor*

http://home.att.net/~iron.clad/

Made by a researcher at the *Monitor* National Marine Sanctuary to inform the public about the history of the USS *Monitor* and the status of the ongoing recovery effort; features underwater photographs, the *Monitor*'s crew list, and an essay on the history of this most famous of the Union ironclads.

Maple Leaf Shipwreck

http://www.mapleleafshipwreck.com/

Online collection of essays contributed by marine engineers, curators, amateur historians, and archaeologists about the *Maple Leaf,* a Union army transport ship sunk in 1864 by a Confederate torpedo; also features a lengthy bibliography.

Monitor: History and Legacy

http://www.mariner.org/monitor/

Created by the Mariners' Museum in Newport News, Virginia, which was chosen by the National Oceanic and Atmospheric Administration to be the official museum of the USS *Monitor;* provides an informative history of the *Monitor a*s well as an overview of Union naval strategy.

The Official Site of the H. L. *Hunley*

http://www.hunley.org

Professionally designed site; provides an informative history of the *Hunley* and solicits financial support for the continued excavation of this Confederate combat submarine.

Shotgun's Home of the American Civil War: Naval War

http://www.civilwarhome.com/navalwar.htm

Section of a large privately made site; contains a large collection of excerpts of out-of-print books and public domain primary sources.

St. Louis' Ships of Iron

http://www.usgennet.org/~ahmostlu/ironclads.htm

Exploration of the history of the St. Louis shipyard of James B. Eads and Company, which constructed the famous gunboats designed by Samuel Pook; contains digital photographs and drawings of the ships built there as well as a number of crew rosters.

Steam Machines

http://www.archaeology.org/online/features/steam/index.html

Created by the Museum of the Rockies; consists of an essay by a professor of historical archeology at Montana State University describing the USS *Monitor,* the CSS *H. L. Hunley,* and other famous Civil War naval vessels.

U.S. Marine Detachment: Washington Navy Yard (1859–1865)

http://www.geocities.com/Heartland/Plains/4198/

Made by a historical reenacting group; dedicated to documenting the contributions made by the U.S. Marine Corps in the Civil War.

The U.S. Navy in the Civil War: Western Rivers

http://www.webnation.com/~spectrum/usn-cw/index.phtml

Privately made site; the most comprehensive source on the "Brownwater Navy"; includes images of gunboats, descriptions of battles, and a chronology of major events in the western rivers.

U.S.S. *Harvest Moon*

http://members.aol.com/WaltESmith/hmhome.htm

Sponsored by the Harvest Moon Historical Society in Wilmington, Delaware; documents the history of the blockade ship USS *Harvest Moon,* now resting on the ocean floor off the South Carolina coast, where the ship was sunk by a Confederate torpedo.

Vicksburg National Military Park

http://www.nps.gov/vick/home.htm

National Park Service site; provides a good description of the role of the "Brownwater Navy" in the Union capture of Vicksburg and other important Mississippi River outposts.

Wakulla County, Florida: Some Civil War Action

http://www.polaris.net/~rblacks/st-marks.htm

Privately made site; contains reprints of two previously published articles by the site's designer.

Wars and Conflicts of the United States Navy

http://www.history.navy.mil/wars/index.html#anchor4162

Made by the U.S. Navy; all aspects of the navy in the Civil War; includes a brief discussion of the CSS *Alabama,* a detailed chronology, and transcriptions of many public domain documents.

The *War Times Journal:* Civil War Navies

http://www.wtj.com/archives/acwnavies/

Part of a large commercial site dedicated to military science and history; consists of extensive excerpts from the Official Records about the clash between the CSS *Virginia* and USS *Monitor.*

Yazoo Naval Preservation Foundation

http://www.geocities.com/Pentagon/5106/index.html

Made by the Yazoo Naval Preservation Foundation; contains a brief history of naval action in Yazoo, Mississippi.

THE EXPERIENCE OF THE U.S. COLORED TROOPS

GENERAL SITES

5th Regimental Cavalry, United States Colored Troops

http://members.home.net:80/5thuscc/

The African American Experience in Ohio, 1850–1920

http://dbs.ohiohistory.org/africanam

Made by the Ohio Historical Society; contains a searchable database of newspaper articles written by and about African American Union veterans.

The African American Odyssey: A Quest for Full Citizenship

http://memory.loc.gov/ammem/aaohtml/exhibit

Part of the Library of Congress's American Memory Project; provides explanatory narrative about the experience of African American Union soldiers; includes letters written by the sons of Frederick Douglass to their father.

African Americans at Petersburg

http://www.nps.gov/pete/mahan/eduhistafam.html

Section of the National Park Service site about Petersburg; describes the role of the USCT in the Union siege.

The Battle of Olustee

http://extlab1.entnem.ufl.edu/olustee

Made by a private researcher employed by the University of Florida; contains a detailed discussion of the role played by USCT regiments in this Florida battle.

Black Civil War Soldiers of the Trans Mississippi West

http://www.angelfire.com/md/usctwest/

Made by a private researcher; features a large collection of primary documents and brief secondary accounts about the experience of the USCT fighting in the far Western theater.

Blacks in the Union Army of Tennessee (1861–1866)

http://www.tnstate.edu/library/digital/Blacks.htm

Part of a Tennessee history site made by the Tennessee State University Library; consists of a one-page essay on African American Union soldiers.

Christine's Genealogy Website

http://ccharity.com/

Privately made African American genealogy site; contains a vast collection of USCT regimental history documents.

The Fight for Equal Rights: Black Soldiers in the Civil War

http://www.nara.gov/education/teaching/usct/home.html

National Archives site designed primarily for teachers and students; contains background material and digitized primary sources valuable for researchers at all levels.

Fort Scott National Historic Site

http://www.nps.gov/fosc/

National Park Service site; contains a page on African American units raised in the Fort Scott, Kansas, area.

Freedmen and Southern Society Project: The Black Military Experience

http://www.inform.umd.edu/ARHU/Depts/History/Freedman/bmepg.htm

Made by the University of Maryland History Department to publicize the multi-volume book series *Freedom: A Documentary History of Emancipation, 1861–1867;* contains a powerful collection of transcribed documents.

Images of African Americans from the 19th Century

http://digital.nypl.org/schomburg/images_aa19/

Part of the New York Public Library's Digital Schomburg Project; consists of a searchable database of digitized nineteenth-century magazine illustrations depicting African Americans, many of which pertain to the USCT.

Museum of the Kansas National Guard: Historic Units

http://skyways.lib.ks.us/kansas/museums/kng/kngunits.html

Developed by the Kansas National Guard; contains the histories of every Kansas-based military regiment, including the 1st Kansas (Colored) Volunteer Infantry and the 2nd Kansas (Colored) Volunteer Infantry, which are considered by some to be the first officially raised troops of African American soldiers in the Civil War.

National Park Service Civil War Soldiers and Sailors System: History of African Americans in the Civil War

http://www.itd.nps.gov/cwss/history/aa_history.htm

National Park Service site; consists of a searchable database of all the men who served in the USCT, brief histories of every USCT regiment, and biographical sketches of USCT Congressional Medal of Honor recipients.

Serving the Union: U.S. Colored Troops in the Retreat to Appomattox

http://www.nps.gov/apco/blacks.htm

Section of the National Park Service Appomattox Courthouse web site; discusses the experience of African American men serving in both the Union and Confederate forces during the final weeks of the Civil War.

United States Colored Troops at Camp Nelson, Kentucky

http://www.campnelson.org/colored

Made by the Camp Nelson Restoration and Preservation Foundation; describes the history of Camp Nelson, which during the Civil War served as an American Missionary Society school and a refugee center for African American soldiers' families as well as a recruiting place for more than ten thousand men for the USCT.

United States Colored Troops in the Civil War

http://www.coax.net/people/lwf/data.htm

Part of a large African American history site made by a private researcher; features an extensive collection of documents in addition to interesting timelines.

The USCT Ring

http://afamgenealogy.ourfamily.com/usct/usct.html

Segment of an African American genealogy web ring site; allows visitors to take a tour of many privately made sites about the USCT.

The Valley of the Shadow: Two Communities in the American Civil War

http://valley.vcdh.virginia.edu

Made at the University of Virginia; features an in-depth exploration of USCT regiments from Franklin County, Pennsylvania, as well as transcriptions of newspaper articles showing northern and southern reactions to the raising of African American soldiers.

U.S. COLORED TROOPS REGIMENTAL HISTORIES

Like the sites listed in the Civil War Regiments index, these sites generally contain a combination of one or more of the following: rosters, Official Records, letters and diaries, and photographs.

1st Regiment Colored Infantry/55th U.S. Colored Troops

http://members.aol.com/Blountal/55th.html

4th USCT

http://members.castles.com/p-mir-l/

A History of the 4th United States Colored Troops

http://www.ncwa.org/4thUS.html

7th Regiment Colored Infantry/11th Regiment

http://members.aol.com/Blountal/7th.html

8th United States Colored Troops

http://extlab1.entnem.ufl.edu/olustee/8th_USCI.HTML

15th United States Infantry Unit History

http://extlab1.entnem.ufl.edu/olustee/15th_US_infantry.html

35th United States Colored Troops (First North Carolina Colored Volunteers)

http://extlab1.entnem.ufl.edu/olustee/35th_USCI.html

54th Massachusetts Company B

http://www.54thmass.org/

54th Massachusetts Infantry Casualty List

http://www.nara.gov/exhall/originals/54thmass.html

History of 73rd U.S.C.T.

http://www.siteone.com/tourist/blakeley/73rdUSCT.htm

106th Regiment Colored Infantry

http://members.aol.com/Blountal/106th.html

111th Regiment Colored Infantry

http://members.aol.com/Blountal/111th.html

The Louisiana Native Guards

http://www2.netdoor.com/~jgh/

National Park Service Civil War Soldiers and Sailors System: History of African Americans in the Civil War

http://www.itd.nps.gov/cwss/history/aa_history.htm

SLAVERY AND EMANCIPATION

An SR Books
BEST CIVIL WAR SITE
Selection

The African American Odyssey: A Quest for Full Citizenship

http://memory.loc.gov/ammem/aaohtml/exhibit

Part of the Library of Congress's extensive American Memory project; tells the story of slavery and emancipation through important Library of Congress documents and explanatory narrative.

An SR Books
BEST CIVIL WAR SITE
Selection

African American Women On-line: Archival Collections

http://scriptorium.lib.duke.edu/collections/African American-women.html

Made at Duke University; features letters written by three slave women to their masters and former masters.

Africans in America

http://www.pbs.org/wgbh/aia/

Made by the Public Broadcasting Service to serve as a companion to the television series of the same name; designed primarily for classroom teachers as an interactive textbook on the rise and fall of slavery in the United States.

An SR Books
BEST CIVIL WAR SITE
Selection

American Slave Narratives: An Online Anthology

http://xroads.virginia.edu/~HYPER/wpa/wpahome.html

Created by a graduate student at the University of Virginia; contains transcriptions and some audio recordings of Works Progress Administration interviews with former slaves.

Antietam National Battlefield

http://www.nps.gov/anti/home.htm

National Park Service site; considers the Union victory at Antietam, which played an important role in the timing of Abraham Lincoln's Emancipation Proclamation; also traces the evolution of Lincoln's policy on slavery and emancipation.

"Been Here So Long": A Selection from the WPA American Slave Narratives

http://newdeal.feri.org/asn/

Collection of Works Progress Administration slave narratives that is part of the larger New Deal Network site; uses thematic organization of transcripts, with an eye toward classroom use.

Black Resistance: Slavery in the United States

http://www.afroam.org/history/slavery/main.html

Part of AFRO-Americ@'s online Black History Museum; considers the tradition of African Americans' resistance against their enslavement; features a listing of slave revolts and excerpts from slave memoirs.

Boston African American National Historic Site: Underground Railroad

http://www.nps.gov/boaf/ugrrho~1.htm

National Park Service site; features a map of common Underground Railroad routes as well as descriptions of places in and around Boston that may have been Underground Railroad stopping points.

Christine's Genealogy Website

http://ccharity.com/

Designed by an avid genealogist; contains transcriptions of a variety of primary sources from many localities, including census manuscripts and Freedmen's Bureau marriage documents.

The District of Columbia Emancipation Act

http://www.nara.gov/exhall/featured-document/dcact/dcproc.html

Small National Archives and Records Administration site; contains a scan of the original 1862 District of Columbia Emancipation Act, the only case of compensated emancipation in the United States, as well as a transcription and a brief explanatory essay.

Documenting the American South: North American Slave Narratives

http://metalab.unc.edu/docsouth/neh/neh.html

Made by the University of North Carolina; features what is probably the most extensive online collection of nineteenth- and early twentieth-century slave narratives, which have been transcribed in full and which are fully searchable.

Emancipation Proclamation

http://memory.loc.gov/ammem/alhtml/almintr.html

Part of the Library of Congress's American Memory project; features a time-line that traces the evolution of federal emancipation policy over the course of the Civil War; also contains scans of early drafts of the Emancipation Proclamation as well as the official order issued in January 1863.

The Emancipation Proclamation

http://www.nara.gov/exhall/featured-document/eman/emanproc.html

National Archives online exhibit; contains explanatory narrative, a scan and transcription of the National Emancipation Act, an essay by John Hope Franklin, and audio files of Works Progress Administration slave interviews.

Excerpts from Slave Narratives

http://vi.uh.edu/pages/mintz/primary.htm

Developed by University of Houston history professor Steven Mintz; contains thematically organized transcriptions of forty-six previously published, public domain, firsthand accounts of slavery.

Exploring *Amistad* at Mystic Seaport

http://amistad.mysticseaport.org/main/welcome.html

Created by the Mystic Seaport Museum in Connecticut; contains a narrative, timeline, and collection of primary documents about the *Amistad* rebellion and subsequent trial.

Free at Last: A History of the Abolition of Slavery in America

http://www.gliah.org/exhibits/free/index.html

Created by the Gilder Lehrman Institute of American History; serves as an interactive textbook on the history of slavery and emancipation; features mostly secondary narrative written by prominent historians.

Freedmen and Southern Society Project

http://www.inform.umd.edu/ARHU/Depts/History/Freedman/home.html

Contains selections from the multivolume documentary book series by the same name, edited by scholars at the University of Maryland and other institutions; features a detailed timeline showing the development of emancipation policy over the course of the Civil War in addition to a rich collection of documents.

Jesuit Plantation Project: Maryland's Jesuit Plantations, 1650–1838

http://www.georgetown.edu/departments/amer_studies/jpp/coverjpp.html

Created by the American Studies program at Georgetown University; documents the experience of Jesuit slave ownership in early nineteenth-century Maryland.

Levi Jordan Plantation Project

http://www.webarchaeology.com

Uses the tools of archeology and history to explore the lives of black and white residents of a Texas plantation before, during, and after the Civil War; includes descriptions of artifacts found at the plantation, which show evidence of direct African influence. A collaboration between university scholars, local historians, and descendants of plantation residents.

Race and Place: African American Community Histories

http://www.vcdh.virginia.edu/afam

Created at the University of Virginia; allows visitors to re-create the world of slaves and slaveholders before, during, and after the Civil War through documents such as newspapers and letters, Freedmen's Bureau Records, and the 1860 Augusta County, Virginia, slaveowner census.

Sheet Music about Lincoln, Emancipation, and the Civil War

http://memory.loc.gov/ammem/scsmhtml/scsmhome.html

Section of the Library of Congress's American Memory project; consists of a searchable collection—both scans of the original sheet music and transcriptions of the lyrics—of hundreds of Civil War era songs, many of which are about the end of slavery.

Slave Data Collection: Wills, Inventories, Bible Records, Slave Manifests, and more

http://www.afrigeneas.com/slavedata/

Created by the organization AfriGeneas and designed with the needs and interests of genealogists in mind; contains a collection of plantation, federal census, Freedmen's Bureau, and other records.

Third Person, First Person: Slave Voices from the Special Collections Library

http://scriptorium.lib.duke.edu/slavery/

Online version of a Duke University Library exhibit; features scans of plantation records and slaveowner correspondence.

Turner's Confession

http://www.melanet.com/nat/nat.html

Section of the MelaNet site, which is a platform for intellectual, economic, and spiritual expression of peoples throughout the African diaspora; features the full text of Nat Turner's jail cell confession as it was printed in newspapers at the time.

The Underground Railroad

http://www.nationalgeographic.com/features/99/railroad/index.html

Designed by the National Geographic Society; highly interactive site that invites visitors to pretend they are slaves escaping on the Underground Railroad by presenting them with a series of difficult choices similar to the ones that escaping slaves had to make while fleeing to freedom.

The Underground Railroad in the National Park Service

http://www.cr.nps.gov/history/ugrr.htm

National Park Service site; provides a gateway to its online material about the Underground Railroad.

WOMEN IN THE CIVIL WAR

American Civil War Civilians

http://reality.sgi.com/dianeg_corp/civil_war_civ/

Privately made site; concentrates on female nurses—notably Dorothea Dix—as well as the Women's Loyal League; consists largely of essays by the site's designer.

The Civil War Comes to Hardin County

http://www.hardinhistory.com/history/war.htm

Created by the Hardin County Historical Society in Tennessee; includes a pension application filed by a widow whose husband was killed by bushwhackers while he was visiting home on furlough.

Civil War Richmond

http://www.mdgorman.com/

Privately made site; contains a discussion of women's work in Richmond's Civil War hospitals.

Civil War—War Crimes: Rape During the War

http://hometown.aol.com/cwrapes

Made by a private researcher; contains transcriptions from soldiers' compiled military service records showing disciplinary actions taken against soldiers found guilty of raping civilian women.

Civil War Women: On-line Archival Collections

http://scriptorium.lib.duke.edu/collections/civil-war-women.html

Created by Duke University; features the diaries and correspondence of Rose O'Neal Greenhow, the well-known Confederate spy; Sarah Thompson, an active pro-Union partisan in Tennessee; and Alice Williamson, a young pro-Confederate woman living under federal occupation in Gallatin, Tennessee.

Clara Barton: National Historic Site

http://www.nps.gov/clba/

National Park Service site; contains a chronology of Barton's life.

Documenting the American South

http://metalab.unc.edu/docsouth/

Made by the University of North Carolina; contains dozens of memoirs and other fully transcribed and searchable documents chronicling the experiences of Southern women during the Civil War.

Fredericksburg and Spotsylvania National Military Park Visitor Center

http://www.nps.gov/frsp/vc.htm

National Park Service site; includes an excerpt from the diary of a local woman whose world was turned upside down by occupying federal forces.

Hearts at Home: Southern Women in the Civil War

http://www.lib.virginia.edu/exhibits/hearts/

Created by the University of Virginia; features digitized letters, magazine illustrations, and rare books that capture the experience of Southern women during the Civil War.

Illinois Alive! Illinois in the Civil War: Private Albert D. J. Cashier (Jennie Hodgers)

http://www.rsa.lib.il.us/~ilalive/files/iv/htm2/ivtxt002.html

Sponsored by the Illinois State Archive; tells the story of a woman who assumed a male identity, fought in the 95th Illinois, and maintained her disguise for decades after the war.

Manassas National Battlefield Park

http://www.nps.gov/mana/home.htm

National Park Service site; contains a history of the First Battle of Manassas, including a description of the death of eighty-year-old Judith Henry, killed in her bed when Union forces opened fire on Confederate sharpshooters in her house.

Prologue: Women Soldiers of the Civil War

http://www.nara.gov/publications/prologue/women1.html

Online version of a National Archives publication; contains a scholarly article about women who disguised themselves as men to fight in the Civil War.

Richmond National Battlefield Park Homepage

http://www.nps.gov/rich/home.htm

National Park Service site; discusses women's work in Richmond's Civil War hospitals.

Sarah S. Sampson, 1832–1907

http://www.state.me.us/sos/arc/archives/military/civilwar/sampson.htm

Section of the Maine State Archives site; contains a biographical sketch of Sarah S. Sampson, who served in the Maine Soldiers' Relief Agency, based in Washington, DC; also features a report she filed after her return from Gettysburg, where she had helped to care for the wounded and bury the dead.

Shotgun's Home of the American Civil War: Civil War Biographies

http://www.civilwarhome.com/biograph.htm

Privately made site; includes short biographies of notable Civil War women, including Clara Barton, Belle Boyd, Varina Howell Davis, and Sojourner Truth.

The Steubing Letters: The Civil War Letters of W. J. and Nancy Steubing

http://www.geocities.com/Athens/Cyprus/6533/

Privately made site; includes letters written by Nancy Steubing to her husband in the 26th Texas Cavalry that depict of the difficulties faced by women left to run the household economy on their own.

United States Sanitary Commission

http://www.netwalk.com/~jpr/index.htm

Made by a Civil War reenactor; consists of a thorough documentary account of this soldiers' aid organization staffed largely by women volunteers.

The Valley of the Shadow: Two Communities in the American Civil War

http://valley.vcdh.virginia.edu

Created at the University of Virginia; features letters and diaries, government documents, and transcriptions of newspaper articles from two communities—one in the North and one in the South—that capture the experience of women living at home in areas never far removed from the fighting.

Women and the Freedmen's Aid Movement

http://womhist.binghamton.edu/projects.htm#aid

Created by the State University of New York at Geneseo; considers how women, who played an active role in the antislavery movement, also led efforts to help freed slaves build their new lives after the war; shows how freedmen's aid workers Josephine Griffing and others were frustrated by cautious officials and an apathetic public.

CIVIL WAR REGIMENTS

In general, regimental history sites are similar in their sponsorship and types of content. Most have been created by private individuals working on their own time, often with the sponsorship of a living history or reenactment organization. For the most part these sites contain at least two of the following types of material: rosters, Official Records, and excerpts from previously published public domain histories of the unit. Some also contain photographs, letters, and diaries. Because these sites tend to be so similar, individual-level descriptions have not been provided.

The regiments below are listed by state. In most cases, if one site featured a number of regimental histories from the same state, that site was listed only once. U.S. Colored Troop units also occasionally had state names; in these cases, a cross-reference is provided.

A L A B A M A

See also The Experience of the U.S. Colored Troops

1st Alabama Cavalry
http://adpservices.com/1st_Ala_Cav/index.html

4th Alabama "Roddey's" Cavalry, Confederate States Army
http://www.geocities.com/BourbonStreet/Delta/3843/4thalabama.htm

6th Alabama Infantry Regiment Home Page
http://home.att.net/~al_6th_inf/

8th Alabama Emerald Guard, Company I
http://www.37thtexas.org/html/Col8thAla.html

Mobile German Fusiliers, Co. H, 8th Alabama Infantry, CSA
http://www.37thtexas.org/html/gerfus1.html

The 17th Alabama Regimental History
http://www.fred.net/stevent/17AL/17al.html

19th Alabama Infantry Regiment, C.S.A.
http://www.19thalabama.org

The 23rd Alabama Volunteer Infantry Regiment C.S.A.
http://members.aol.com/armyoftenn/23_ala_inf/23-home.htm

25th Alabama Infantry Regiment
http://home.earthlink.net/~sdriskell/25th/25th.htm

O'Neal's 26th Alabama
http://www.rootsweb.com/~alcw26/26thala.htm

27th Alabama Infantry, Confederate States Army
http://www.datasync.com/~jtaylor/27th.htm

28th Alabama Infantry Regiment
http://members.aol.com/publishcon/index.html

32nd Alabama Volunteer Infantry: McKinstry's Regiment
http://acan.net/~dixie/32nd.Alabama.htm

History of the 33rd Alabama Infantry, CSA
http://members.aol.com/wwhitby/33rd.html

42nd Alabama Infantry
http://www.alaska.net/~bearpaw/Alabama42.htm

43rd Alabama Infantry and Gracie's Alabama Brigade
http://www.geocities.com/Pentagon/Barracks/3313/index.html

The History of the 47th Alabama Volunteer Infantry Regiment in the American Civil War
http://www.geocities.com/Heartland/Ridge/9202/

ARKANSAS

3rd Arkansas Infantry Regiment
http://www.rebelyell.com/

History of the 11th/17th Arkansas Mntd. Inf.
http://www.geocities.com/Pentagon/1117/1117inf.html

CONNECTICUT

The 2nd Connecticut Volunteer Regiment
http://members.aol.com/fecook/cw/2ndct.htm

Roster of the 16th Connecticut Regiment, Volunteer Infantry
http://members.aol.com/Sholmes54/rost16ct.html

The 17th Connecticut Volunteer Infantry
http://home.att.net/~DogSgt/Seventeenth.html

The 18th Connecticut Volunteer Regiment
http://members.aol.com/fecook/cw/18thct.htm

History of the 27th Connecticut Infantry

http://home.earthlink.net/~obbie/27inf.htm

FLORIDA

1st Florida Volunteer Infantry Unit History

http://extlab1.entnem.ufl.edu/olustee/1st_FL_History.html

GEORGIA

1st Georgia Infantry (USA)

http://www.izzy.net/~michaelg/n-ga1.htm

Co. "G", 3rd Regiment Georgia Volunteer Infantry

http://www.forttejon.org/ga3/

4th Georgia Calvary Home Page

http://member.aol.com/tomcle3/4th-cav.html

The 5th Georgia Cavalry Regiment Home Page

http://www.pollette.com/5thcavalry/index.htm

8th Georgia Infantry Webpage

http://home.earthlink.net/~larsrbl/8thGeorgiaInfantry.html

CO. "A," 8th GA. Battalion Vols., Gist's Brigade, Army of Tennessee, Recruited from Bartow and Gordon Counties, Sept., 1861

http://www.hardlink.com/~rlk/roster.html

Historical Sketch of Company G, 8th Georgia, CSA

http://www.mindspring.com/~jtfleming/CoG_1.htm

9th Georgia Infantry CSA, 1861–65

http://members.aol.com/Gainf9reg/index2.html

15th Georgia Infantry Regiment

http://home.mho.net/wfparrish/15thGA.html

24th Georgia Infantry C.S.A.

http://www.geocities.com/Heartland/6820/

34th Georgia Regiment

http://members.aol.com/confed1864/34thGaindex.html

65th Regiment Georgia Volunteer Infantry, Army of Tennessee, C.S.A.

http://www.izzy.net/~michaelg/65ga-vi.htm

The Georgia State Line

http://members.carol.net/~rickysahn/GSL/gslmain.htm

ILLINOIS

7th Illinois Mounted Infantry, Men of Company "H," 1861 to 1865, Lincoln, Logan Co, Illinois

http://members.tripod.com/~rjsnyder/Seventh.htm

History of the 30th Illinois Veteran Volunteer Regiment of Infantry

http://pw1.netcom.com/~derson/mcdonald.html

The 37th Illinois Infantry, Company B.

http://www.cswnet.com/~gdavenpo/

History of 93rd Infantry (Adjutant General's Report)

http://www.ioweb.com/civilwar/companyg.htm

100th Illinois Infantry

http://www.outfitters.com/illinois/history/civil/cw100.html

Illinois Greyhounds

http://www.ketzle.com/diary/

INDIANA

The 7th Indiana Cavalry, 119th Regiment

http://viaduct.custom.net/dterrell/7thhome.htm

10th Regiment Indiana Volunteer Infantry

http://members.xoom.com/_XOOM/elagabalus/tenth.html

History of the 12th Indiana Cavalry

http://www.geocities.com/Heartland/Hills/4957/12thcav.html

49th Indiana Volunteer Infantry, 'Company F'

http://www.kiva.net/~bjohnson/49th.html

Indiana in the Civil War

http://www.mach500.net/liggetkw/incw/cw.htm

I O W A

5th Iowa Volunteer Cavalry

http://www.geocities.com/Athens/Forum/1533/5iowacav.html

K A N S A S

2nd Kansas Volunteer Cavalry

http://home.kscable.com/balocca/cavalry.html

Museum of the Kansas National Guard: Historic Units

http://skyways.lib.ks.us/kansas/museums/kng/kngunits.html

K E N T U C K Y

The 1st Kentucky Brigade, CSA: The "Orphan Brigade"

http://www.rootsweb.com/~orphanhm/index.html

1st Kentucky Independent Battery

http://www.wwd.net/steen/battery.htm

The 6th Kentucky Volunteer Infantry Regiment U.S., Web Site

http://www.geocities.com/jreinhart_us/

The 7th Kentucky Inc.
http://www.7thky-us.thecamp.com/

9th Kentucky Volunteer Cavalry, Union
http://www.rootsweb.com/~jadmire/kyhenry/9thky.htm

11th Kentucky ("Chenault's") Calvary, CSA
http://www.geocities.com/BourbonStreet/Delta/3843/

14th Kentucky Volunteer Infantry (USA), 1861–1865
http://www.geocities.com/Pentagon/Quarters/1365/

16th Kentucky Volunteer Infantry
http://www.mt.net/~mtsysdev/16thkyinf.htm

The 39th Kentucky Mounted Infantry Webpage
http://www.geocities.com/Heartland/Ridge/7616/

53rd Kentucky Mounted Infantry
http://www.geocities.com/Heartland/5170/53rdkent.htm

54th Regiment Kentucky Infantry, Union
http://www.rootsweb.com/~jadmire/kyhenry/54.htm

The 65th Kentucky Enrolled Militia
http://www.geocities.com/Heartland/Plains/8629/65thindx.htm

LOUISIANA

See also The Experience of the U.S. Colored Troops

1st Louisiana Cavalry Regiment, Confederate States Army
http://members.tripod.com/%7Etcc230/lacavreg.htm

**The Washington Artillery of New Orleans—5th Company and
The 6th Massachusetts Light Artillery**
http://www.geocities.com/Heartland/Woods/3501/

10th La. Vol. Infantry: "Lee's Foreign Legion"
http://users.interlinks.net/rebel/10th/10th.htm

The 14th Louisiana Regimental History
http://www.fred.net/stevent/14LA/14la.html

Henry Gray's 28th Infantry Regiment
http://members.tripod.com/~pipeslines/

MAINE

Civil War Service of the 9th Maine Infantry
http://members.aol.com/heavsusan/ninthmaine.html

Civil War Page at the Maine State Archives
http://www.state.me.us/sos/arc/archives/military/civilwar/civilwar.htm

MARYLAND

Battalion History of 1st Maryland Cavalry Battalion, CSA
http://www.cybcon.com/~warren/MD1_hist.html

The 2nd Maryland Infantry, U.S., 1861–1865
http://home.att.net/%7Esecondmdus/2md.html

MASSACHUSETTS

See also The Experience of the U. S. Colored Troops

Massachusetts Volunteer Cavalry 1st Regiment
http://members.aol.com/Shortyhack/1stmass.html

"Gordon's Regulars": The 2nd Massachusetts Infantry in the Civil War
http://www.geocities.com/Pentagon/2126/

The Washington Artillery of New Orleans—5th Company and The 6th Massachusetts Light Artillery
http://www.geocities.com/Heartland/Woods/3501/

Sleeper's Battery: The 10th Battery, Massachusetts Light Artillery, 1862–1865

http://www2.control.com/~emoore/tmba.html

16th Massachusetts Volunteer Infantry: "Iron Sixteenth"

http://members.aol.com/inf16mavol/16thmass.html

The Harvard Regiment: 20th Regiment of Massachusetts Volunteer Infantry, 1861–1865

http://www.people.Virginia.EDU/~mmd5f/

22nd Massachusetts Volunteer Infantry: A Civil War Unit

http://www.geocities.com/~22mass/

History of the Original 22nd

http://www.geocities.com/Pentagon/3622/history.html

28th Massachusetts Volunteer Infantry

http://www.28thmass.org/

53rd Massachusetts Volunteer Infantry

http://www.intac.com/~blenderm/53rd_Mass_f/53rd_Mass.html

MICHIGAN

3rd Battery, 1st Michigan Light Artillery, 1861–1865

http://www.cwartillery.org/3rdbattery/civwar.html

2nd Michigan Volunteer Infantry: Company "A"

http://www.geocities.com/Pentagon/Quarters/8558/

Old 3rd Michigan Infantry

http://www.oldthirdmichigan.org/

24th Michigan Infantry Regimental Website, 1862–1865

http://www.geocities.com/CapeCanaveral/Lab/1419/

Michigan in the Civil War, 1861–1865

http://hometown.aol.com/dlharvey/

MISSISSIPPI

History of the 8th Mississippi Infantry Regiment, Confederate States of America

http://www.datasync.com/~davidg59/8th_miss.html

15th Mississippi Infantry Regiment, CSA

http://www.bluecheetah.com/15thmiss/index.htm

The 19th Mississippi Infantry Regiment in the Civil War

http://members.aol.com/bfurr1/19thmiss.htm

33rd Mississippi Infantry Regiment

http://home.att.net/~captnerdo/33rd.htm

MISSOURI

The 23rd Missouri Volunteer Infantry

http://members.aol.com:/rgooch6760/23rdMoVol.html

NEW JERSEY

Homepage of the 3rd Regiment, New Jersey Volunteer Infantry

http://www.geocities.com/Athens/Delphi/1316/thirdjersey.html

8th New Jersey Volunteer Infantry

http://www.8thnj.com

14th Regiment New Jersey Volunteers, Company K: 'The Monocacy Regiment"

http://www.rci.rutgers.edu/~eweber/14thnjvols.htm

N E W   Y O R K

See also The Experience of the U.S. Colored Troops

An SR Books
BEST CIVIL WAR SITE
Selection

5th New York Volunteer Infantry: Duryée's Zouaves

http://www.zouave.org/

5th New York Duryée Zouaves

http://www.geocities.com/Athens/Acropolis/8281/

NY 8th Home Page

http://www.geocities.com/Pentagon/Quarters/1380/

56th New York Volunteer Infantry: The "Tenth Legion"

http://www.webrovcronline.com/56thnyvi/default.htm

64th Regiment New York State Volunteer Infantry, Also Known as "Cattaraugus Regiment"

http://www.vanvlack.net/64thRegiment.htm

"The Fighting 69th": 69th New York State Volunteers, Company A, First Regiment, Irish Brigade, "Faugh a Ballagh"

http://www.69thnysv.org/

"The Saratoga Regiment": 77th New York Volunteer Foot Regiment

http://www.gunsites.com/77th/indexo.html

79th Highlander New York Volunteers

http://www.gunsites.com/79th/indexo.html

112th New York Infantry: The Chautauqua Regiment

http://home.earthlink.net/~cwashburn/112th_ny.html

History and Times of the 124th New York Volunteers: The Orange Blossoms

http://www.geocities.com/~cump/orange.html

128th NYS Volunteer Infantry: "Old Steady"

http://members.aol.com/DTKTT/128th.html

The 134th New York Volunteer Infantry Home Page

http://members.aol.com/gconkman/

The 149th New York State Volunteer Infantry Home Page

http://www.149th-NYSV.org/

The 157th New York Volunteer Infantry

http://members.aol.com/NY157TH/civilwar.html

The 162nd New York Volunteer Infantry: 3rd Regiment, Metropolitan Guard

http://members.aol.com/DAP4477575/index.html

New York Volunteers 188th Regiment

http://home.swbell.net/jcanders/index.html

NORTH CAROLINA

See also The Experience of the U.S. Colored Troops

1st North Carolina Regiment of Cavalry: Stuart's Tarheels

http://firstnccav.home.mindspring.com/

North Carolina Civil War Home Page

http://members.aol.com/jweaver303/nc/nccwhp.htm

OHIO

History of Battle L, 1st Ohio Light Artillery

http://www.geocities.com/Heartland/5060/civilwar.htm

2nd Ohio Volunteer Infantry, April, 1861 to October, 1864

http://members.aol.com/afs2ovi/2nd/2ndpage.htm

3rd Ohio Volunteer Cavalry

http://home.earthlink.net/~df3ovc/

Ohio Volunteer Infantry 4th Regiment: Three Months and Three Year Sevice

http://members.aol.com/Shortyhack/Ohio4.html

16th Ohio Volunteer Infantry, 1861–1864

http://www.mkwe.com/home.htm

22nd Ohio Volunteer Infantry

http://www.bright.net/~lrrp/22nd.html

36th Ohio Volunteer Infantry

http://www.angelfire.com/oh/36OVI/

The 41st OVI Unit History

http://members.tripod.com/~dmcclory/history/

48th Ohio Veteran Volunteer Infantry

http://www.48ovvi.org/

Ohio Volunteer Infantry 51st Regiment

http://members.aol.com/Shortyhack/ohio51.html

73rd Ohio Volunteer Infantry

http://www.geocities.com/Pentagon/Base/5724/index.html

The 126th Ohio Volunteer Infantry: Letters, Accounts, Oral Histories

http://www.iwaynet.net/~lsci/

Ohio Volunteer Infantry 142nd Regiment (100 Day Service)

http://members.aol.com/Shortyhack/142ohio.html

PENNSYLVANIA

An SR Books
BEST CIVIL WAR SITE
Selection

77th Pennsylvania Volunteers: On the March

http://jefferson.village.virginia.edu/vshadow2/HIUS403/77pa/main.html

The Gallant 78th Pennsylvania Volunteer Infantry
http://members.tripod.com/~ProlificPains/service.htm

93rd Pennsylvania Infantry
http://www.angelfire.com/pa/Stump44/index.html

113th Regiment, 12th Pennsylvania Cavalry
http://www.angelfire.com/pa/Stump44/twelfth.html

"Collis' Zouaves": 114th Pennsylvania Volunteer Infantry, Co. A
http://www.concentric.net/~sthutch/114th.html

138th Pennsylvania Volunteer Infantry
http://www.faitnet.com/138th/

148th Regiment Pennsylvania Volunteers
http://www.geocities.com/~k3bs/148menu.html

RHODE ISLAND

Brown's Battery B, 1st Regiment Rhode Island Light Artillery
http://www.geocities.com/BourbonStreet/3604/

SOUTH CAROLINA

13th Regiment of South Carolina Volunteers of the Confederate States of America
http://hometown.aol.com/adj61/page3.htm

The 14th South Carolina Regiment: Gregg's/McGowan's Brigade Army of Northern Virginia
http://members.carol.net/%7Erickysahn/SC14/sc14main.htm

The 16th South Carolina C.S.A.
http://www.geocities.com/BourbonStreet/Square/3873/franklina.html

18th Infantry, Co. G, Mountain Guards, York County, South Carolina Volunteers

http://freepages.genealogy.rootsweb.com/~york/18thSCV/G.htm

Company B of the 22nd Regiment of South Carolina Volunteers

http://hometown.aol.com/adj61/page5.htm

John T. Kanapaux's Battery, Lafayette's Light Artillery, South Carolina Volunteers

http://freepages.genealogy.rootsweb.com/~york/Kanapaux/index.html

---

TENNESSEE

2nd Tennessee Infantry Regiment U.S.A.

http://home.cinci.rr.com/secondtennessee/

7th Tennessee Cavalry—Company D

http://pages.prodigy.net/rebel7tn/

Company C, 8th Tennessee Infantry Regiment, CSA

http://home.att.net/~dmelear/hist_sgb1.htm

9th Tennessee Cavalry

http://tennessee-scv.org/Camp1513/9th.htm

20th (Russell's) Tennessee Cavalry

http://home.olemiss.edu/~cmprice/cav.html

44th Tennessee Infantry

http://www.geocities.com/BourbonStreet/4455/

Alison's Cavalry

http://tennessee-scv.org/Camp1513/allison.htm

Bankhead/Scott's Battery TN Light Artillery; C.S.A

http://personal.bna.bellsouth.net/bna/r/d/rdbaker/main.htm

Huwald's Battery: Tennessee Mountain Howitzers

http://tennessee-scv.org/Camp1513/huwald.htm

The Tennessee Civil War Home Page

http://members.aol.com/jweaver303/tn/tncwhp.htm

T E X A S

6th Texas Infantry

http://www.geocities.com/Vienna/Studio/7746/

Terry's Texas Rangers Website (8th Texas Volunteer Cavalry)

http://www.infomagic.com/~thgroves/ttr.html

Official Historic Website of the 10th Texas Infantry

http://members.aol.com/SMckay1234/

U . S .   C O L O R E D   T R O O P S

See The Experience of the U.S. Colored Troops

V I R G I N I A

18th Virginia Cavalry

http://www.angelfire.com/pa2/Stump45/

24th Virginia Infantry

http://www.geocities.com/Heartland/Ranch/2320/index.html

33rd Regiment Virginia Volunteer Infantry, Company A, Potomac Guard

http://members.aol.com/Vir33rdreg/index.html

42nd Virginia Infantry Regiment, 1861–1865, Company I, Campbell Guards

http://users.erols.com/va42nd/61-65.html

Russell County, Virginia 1860–1865

http://rhobard.com/russell/

The Virginia Civil War Home Page

http://members.aol.com/jweaver300/grayson/vacwhp.htm

WEST VIRGINIA

West Virginia Military Research

http://www.rootsweb.net/~wvgenweb/military/index.html

WISCONSIN

2nd Wisconsin Volunteer Infantry Association Inc.

http://www.secondwi.com/

15th Wisconsin Volunteer Infantry: The Scandinavian Regiment

http://www.15thwisconsin.net/

The 26th Wisconsin Infantry Volunteers

http://www.agro.agri.umn.edu/~lemedg/wis26/26pgmain.htm

28th Regiment Wisconsin Volunteer Infantry, 1862–1865

http://www.execpc.com/~kap/wisc28.html

A Capsule History of the 33rd Wisconsin Volunteer Infantry

http://www.amtma.com/33hist.html

Wisconsin Civil War Regimental Histories

http://badger.state.wi.us/agencies/dva/museum/cwregts/reglist.html

OTHER UNIT HISTORIES

3rd U.S. Infantry, Company B & G

http://www.geocities.com/Pentagon/4217/index.html

Archer's Brigade: "Victory or Death"

http://www.fred.net/stevent/home.html

Battle Flags of the Confederacy

http://home.txcr.net/~flags/

A Brief History of Bradford's Battery Confederate Guards Artillery of Pontotoc County, Miss

http://www.inmind.com/people/bhoy/bradford/history.htm

Harvey's Scouts

http://www.rootsweb.com/~msmadiso/harveyscouts/index.htm

Index of Civil War Naval Forces, Confederate and Union Ships

http://www.tarleton.edu/~kjones/navy.html

The Iron Brigade of the West

http://carroll1.cc.edu/civilwar/ib.html

IGURE CREDITS

Chapter 1—Battles and Campaigns

FIGURE 1.1 A number one carriage, carrying a 6-pounder (from The Civil War Artillery Page)

http://www.cwartillery.org/carriaga.gif

Reproduced by permission of Charles J. Ten Brink, Webmaster, the Civil War Artillery Sites.

FIGURE 1.2 *Chevaux-de-frise* on Marietta Street, Atlanta, Georgia—photographic wagons and darkroom beyond (from Selected Civil War Photographs in the American Memory Collection)

http://lcweb2.loc.gov/pnp/cwp/4a39000/4a39700/4a39775r.jpg

Original is located in the Prints and Photographs Division, Library of Congress, Washington, DC.

FIGURE 1.3 Cannons atop Lookout Mountain (from Chattanooga: A Road Trip Through Time)

http://www.mediaalchemy.com/civilwar/images/fsl001.jpg

Reproduced by permission of Dave Buckhout and T. C. Moore, site coproducers.

FIGURE 1.4 Casualties at the Battle of Fredericksburg (from Battle of Fredericksburg)

http://members.aol.com/lmjarl/civwar/cas.html

Reproduced by permission of John A. R. Longstreet.

FIGURE 1.5 Cannons at the Gettysburg Battlefield (from Military History Online—Battle of Gettysburg)

http://militaryhistoryonline.com/gettysburg/photos/p15015.jpg

Reproduced by permission of R. Scott Dann.

FIGURE 1.6 New Market veterans (from The Battle of New Market, Virginia, May 15, 1864)

http://www.vmi.edu/~arcimage/867grp3.jpg

Reproduced by permission of Preston Library, Virginia Military Institute, Lexington, Virginia.

FIGURE 1.7   The crater (from The Siege of Petersburg)

http://members.aol.com/siege1864/crater2.jpg

From Robert Underwood Johnson and Clarence Clough Buel, eds., Battles and Leaders of the Civil War: Being for the most part contributions by Union and Confederate officers: Based upon "The Century War series," *4 vols. (New York: Century Co., 1887–88), 4:561. Image created by Alfred Waud.*

Chapter 2—Political and Military Leaders

FIGURE 2.1   Cover image from the *War Times Journal* Civil War series (from the *War Times Journal* Civil War Series: Longstreet, Sherman, Hood, and Gordon)

http://www.wtj.com/archives/sherman/

Reproduced by permission of James Burbeck, site owner.

FIGURE 2.2   Cadets at Stonewall Jackson's grave, c. 1868 (from Stonewall Jackson Resources at the Virginia Military Institute Archives)

http://www.vmi.edu/~arcimage/cadetgrv.jpg

Reproduced by permission of Preston Library, Virginia Military Institute, Lexington, Virginia.

FIGURE 2.3   Portrait of Abraham Lincoln (from the Abraham Lincoln Research Site)

http://members.aol.com/RVSNorton/miller.jpg

Reproduced by permission of the artist, Richard R. Miller.

FIGURE 2.4   Lincoln, the rail splitter (from Lincoln/Net: The Abraham Lincoln Digitization Project)

http://lincoln.lib.niu.edu/railspl1.jpg

Reproduced by permission of the Abraham Lincoln Historical Digitization Project, Northern Illinois University, Dekalb, Illinois, and the Chicago Historical Society, Chicago, Illinois.

FIGURE 2.5   Meade at Gettysburg, painted by Daniel R. Knight (from The Meade Archive)

http://adams.patriot.net/~jcampi/society.gif

Reproduced by permission of the Union League of Philadelphia.

Chapter 3—Life of the Soldier

FIGURE 3.1   Soldier's prayer book of Sylvester Carr, 143rd New York Volunteer Infantry (from Camp Life: Civil War Collections from Gettysburg National Military Park)

http://www.cr.nps.gov/csd/gettex/prayer.jpg

Reproduced by permission of the National Park Service, Gettysburg National Military Park, Gettysburg, Pennsylvania.

FIGURE 3.2   Page one of letter from Alex Cressler to Henry A. Bitner, May 17, 1861 (from the Electronic Text Center: Subject: American Civil War)

http://etext.lib.virginia.edu/images/modeng/public/BitCre1a.jpg

Reproduced courtesy of the Virginia Center for Digital History, University of Virginia, Charlottesville, Virginia.

Chapter 4—Naval Operations

FIGURE 4.1   Cross-section of the CSS *Neuse* (from the CSS *Neuse* State Historic Site)

http://www.ah.dcr.state.nc.us/sections/hs/neuse/cros-sec.jpg

Reproduced by permission of the North Carolina Division of Archives and History, Raleigh, North Carolina. Image drawn by Mark A. Moore.

FIGURE 4.2   Feathering sidewheel of the Confederate blockade runner *Denbigh* (from The *Denbigh* Project)

http://nautarch.tamu.edu/projects/images/wheel4.jpg

Reproduced by permission of the Institute of Nautical Archeology, College Station, Texas.

FIGURE 4.3   Diagram of the *H. L. Hunley* (from The Official Site of the *H. L. Hunley*)

http://www.hunley.org/amidship.jpg

Reproduced by permission of Friends of the Hunley, Charleston, South Carolina.

FIGURE 4.4   The USS *Argosy* (from The U.S. Navy in the Civil War: Western Rivers)

http://www.webnation.com/~spectrum/usn-cw/argosy.gif

Original is located in the American Memory Collection, Library of Congress, Washington, DC. Reproduced by permission of Gary Matthews, site designer.

Chapter 5—The Experience of the U.S. Colored Troops

FIGURE 5.1   Obituary from the *Cleveland Gazette*, April 20, 1918 (from The African American Experience in Ohio, 1850–1920)

http://dbs.ohiohistory.org/africanam/page1.cfm?ItemID=7024

Reproduced by permission of the Ohio Historical Society, Columbus, Ohio.

FIGURE 5.2   Regimental flag of the 6th USCT (from The African American Odyssey: A Quest for Full Citizenship)

http://lcweb.loc.gov/exhibits/odyssey/archive/04/0407001r.jpg

Original is located in the Rare Book and Special Collections Division, Library of Congress, Washington, DC.

FIGURE 5.3   USCT recruiting poster (from The Fight for Equal Rights: Black Soldiers in the Civil War)

http://www.nara.gov/education/teaching/usct/broadsid.gif

Original is located in the Textual Reference Unit, National Archives and Records Administration, Washington, DC.

FIGURE 5.4   Image from the home page of The Valley of the Shadow (from The Valley of the Shadow: Two Communities in the American Civil War)

http://valley.vcdh.virginia.edu/choosepart.html

Reproduced by permission of the Virginia Center for Digital History, University of Virginia, Charlottesville, Virginia.

Chapter 6—Slavery and Emancipation

FIGURE 6.1   Title page from *The Confessions of Nat Turner* (from The African American Odyssey: A Quest for Full Citizenship)

http://lcweb.loc.gov/exhibits/odyssey/archive/01/010800ar.jpg

Original is located in the Rare Book and Special Collections Division, Library of Congress, Washington, DC.

FIGURE 6.2   Title page from Harriet Jacobs's *Incidents in the Life of a Slave Girl* (from Documenting the American South: North American Slave Narratives)

http://metalab.unc.edu/docsouth/jacobs/jacobstp.gif

Reproduced by permission of the University of North Carolina, Chapel Hill, North Carolina.

Chapter 7—Women in the Civil War

FIGURE 7.1   Rose O'Neal Greenhow, spy for the Confederacy (from Civil War Women: On-line Archival Collections)

http://scriptorium.lib.duke.edu/collections/greenhow/rose-sml.gif

Image taken from Rose Greenhow, My Imprisonment and the First Year of Abolition Rule at Washington *(London: Richard Bentley, 1863). Reproduced by permission of the Rare Book, Manuscript, and Special Collections Library, Duke University, Durham, North Carolina.*

FIGURE 7.2   "General Stuart's New Aid," from *Harper's Weekly*, April 4, 1863 (from Hearts at Home: Southern Women in the Civil War)

http://www.lib.virginia.edu/exhibits/hearts/images/4hwkly63.jpg

The original image is part of the Edward R. Stettinius Papers (MSS 2723), Special Collections Department, University of Virginia Library, Charlottesville, Virginia.

FIGURE 7.3   U.S. Sanitary Commission seal (from the United States Sanitary Commission)

http://www.netwalk.com/~jpr/logo.gif

Reproduced by permission of Jan P. Romanovich.

Chapter 8—Civil War Regiments

FIGURE 8.1   Reunion of the 5th New York Zouaves (from the 5th New York Volunteer Infantry: Duryée's Zouaves)

http://www.zouave.org/gallery/duryees/images/5ths.jpg

Reproduced by permission of Brian C. Pohanka.

FIGURE 8.2 Searchable compiled military service database (from the 77th Pennsylvania Volunteers: On the March)

http://jefferson.village.virginia.edu/vshadow2/frdossier.html

Reproduced by permission of the Virginia Center for Digital History, University of Virginia, Charlottesville, Virginia.

FIGURE 8.3 Image from The 26th Wisconsin—the official web site of the 26th Wisconsin Infantry Volunteers.

http://www.agro.agri.umn.edu/~lemedg/wis26/26thfron.jpg

Reproduced by permission of Russell Scott; image created by Russell Scott.

ABOUT THE AUTHORS

WILLIAM G. THOMAS teaches history at the University of Virginia where he is director of the Virginia Center for Digital History, Charlottesville, Virginia. He is the author of *Lawyering for the Railroad: Business, Law, and Power in the New South* (1999) and is currently working on a book on the history of Virginia in the Civil War.

ALICE E. CARTER is a project manager for *The New York Times* on the web. She is the former associate director of the Virginia Center for Digital History at the University of Virginia, Charlottesville, Virginia.

ABOUT THE CD

The accompanying CD version of *The Civil War on the Web*, **CivilWar.pdf**, can be viewed with Adobe Acrobat Reader 4.0.

Acrobat Reader 4.0 for Macintosh and PC users is provided on this CD and can be installed simply by clicking on the appropriate icon and following the instructions.

The **WELCOME.txt** file (also provided as **WELCOME.pdf**) contains information on the interactive features of the CD version of the book and some notes on using Acrobat Reader.

The **ReadMe.pdf** file contains additional installation and troubleshooting instructions for Acrobat Reader. Acrobat Reader is provided free of charge by Adobe and can also be downloaded from their web site at http://www.adobe.com/products/acrobat/read-step2.html.